T0305156

China's Economy in the Post-WTO
Environment

ADVANCES IN CHINESE ECONOMIC STUDIES

Series Editor: Yanrui Wu, *Professor in Economics, University of Western Australia, Australia*

The Chinese economy has been transformed dramatically in recent years. With its rapid economic growth and accession to the World Trade Organization, China is emerging as an economic superpower. China's development experience provides valuable lessons to many countries in transition.

Advances in Chinese Economic Studies aims, as a series, to publish the best work on the Chinese economy by economists and other researchers throughout the world. It is intended to serve a wide readership including academics, students, business economists and other practitioners.

Titles in the series include:

China's Economy in the Post-WTO Environment

Stock Markets, FDI and Challenges of Sustainability

Edited by

Lilai Xu

RMIT University, Australia

ADVANCES IN CHINESE ECONOMIC STUDIES

Edward Elgar

Cheltenham, UK • Northampton, MA, USA

Published by
Edward Elgar Publishing Limited
The Lypiatts
15 Lansdown Road
Cheltenham
Glos GL50 2JA
UK

Edward Elgar Publishing, Inc.
William Pratt House
9 Dewey Court
Northampton
Massachusetts 01060
USA

A catalogue record for this book
is available from the British Library

Library of Congress Control Number: 2011925755

ISBN 978 1 84980 934 4

Typeset by Servis Filmsetting Ltd, Stockport, Cheshire
Printed and bound by MPG Books Group, UK

Contents

Contributors

Siamak Ardekani, University of Texas at Arlington, Texas, USA.

Chunlai Chen, Australian National University, Canberra, Australia.

Heng Chen, Fortune SGAM Fund Management Co., Shanghai, China.

Xuebin Chen, Fudan University, Shanghai, China.

Peter Drysdale, Australian National University, Canberra, Australia.

Geoffrey R. Durden, La Trobe University, Melbourne, Australia.

Nicole El-Haber, La Trobe University, Melbourne, Australia.

Jianling Li, University of Texas at Arlington, Texas, USA.

Stephen Mattingly, University of Texas at Arlington, Texas, USA.

K.B. Oh, La Trobe University, Melbourne, Australia.

Changfeng Pan, Shenzhen Zhiyong Investment Co. Ltd, Shenzhen, China.

Ligang Song, Australian National University, Canberra, Australia.

Sizhong Sun, James Cook University, Townsville, Australia.

Wei-Ming Tian, China Agricultural University, Beijing, China.

Jianmei Wang, Beijing Information, Science and Technology University, Beijing, China.

Yanrui Wu, University of Western Australia, Perth, Australia.

Lilai Xu, RMIT University, Melbourne, Australia.

Ying Xu, Australian National University, Canberra, Australia.

James Xiaohe Zhang, University of Newcastle, Newcastle, Australia.

Youwen Zhang, Shanghai Academy of Social Sciences, Shanghai, China.

Yi Zheng, Southwestern University of Finance and Economics, Chengdu, China.

Zhang-Yue Zhou, James Cook University, Townsville, Australia.

Huaiqing Zhu, Xihua University, Chengdu, China.

Foreword

Colin White

It is my pleasure to write this foreword to an important book. A few words stressing the nature of that importance are in order.

The global economy is coming full circle. The brief period of European dominance, which has stretched from the mid-seventeenth century to the present, is coming to an end. Led by China, Asia is reasserting its prime position in the global economy, and at its core is China. After more than 30 years of rapid growth, following the laying of the foundations of modern economic development during the Maoist era and the initiation of significant reform of the Maoist system in 1978, China entered the World Trade Organization (WTO) in 2001, marking in a symbolic way the arrival of China on the international stage as a major player. Many predictions are made extrapolating recent economic success in China into the future and predicting even greater success, the emergence of an economy which will rival the USA in size and strength. The validity of such predictions is often questioned, but they continue to be made.

The method of achievement in China is as striking as the achievement itself. To Western eyes the model of economic development pursued in China has been highly idiosyncratic. It truly represented a departure from the European model, if such an animal existed in the first place. Entry into the WTO put the seal on the accommodation of a market system to the existing highly centralized planning system, itself much influenced by the Stalinist model in the old Soviet Union. Entry also reinforced the validity of reform and of the reintroduction of important aspects of a market system, notably the opening up of the Chinese economy to international influences and interactions.

Both the achievement itself and the method of achievement demand attention. When I was a student back in the 1960s there was a pessimism about the prospects of the global spread of modern economic development. There was clearly a European miracle, but in the background the anomaly of the early development of Japan, often ignored. At that time the Asian economic miracle was in its early stages, but largely unnoticed. Initially it involved relatively small economies, notably the four Asian tigers. It took the emergence of China to dispel the pessimism and to raise dramatically the question of how an Asian miracle was being achieved.

Over the years the Association for Chinese Economic Studies Australia (ACESA) has done sterling work in encouraging analysis of the Chinese experience. This book comprises a set of chapters by leading specialists on the Chinese economy, which were delivered in 2009 in Melbourne at a conference on China in the post-WTO environment. The Association has itself greatly encouraged studies which are very important to Australia, given the increasing importance of the economic relationship between the two countries. But they have wider significance. There is no doubt that continuing economic growth in China has partly shielded Australia from the global financial crisis. However the studies have a greater relevance and highlight the role of Australia in Chinese studies in general. It is natural that there should be a particular interest in China, and fitting that Australian specialists should be working so well in this area.

The chapters in this book explore the implications of both the extension of the markets mechanism into key parts of the Chinese economy and also the partial integration of China into the global economy. The main focus of the chapters in this book is on the role and nature of the financial system and its ability to transform Chinese enterprise and household behaviour and the sources of investment finance, notably in the context of the inter-action of China with the outside world and a two-way flow of investment finance. Different perspectives are adopted in viewing China's success. Some see the incompleteness of market reform as a problem, others are more willing to accept a pragmatic blending of the operation of the free market and government intervention in generating a successful economy.

All the chapters highlight the issue of sustainability – this is the theme which links the chapters. Can the story of economic success in China continue or is the rate of economic growth destined to slow down? Is Chinese economic growth simply a reflection of increased inputs of labour and capital or is there more to it, an increase in productivity arising from technological and organizational innovation which is therefore more likely to continue even when the increase in inputs moderates? As one chapter shows, there are enormous problems in measuring and accounting for an increase in productivity. It is not easy to answer most of the relevant questions.

China has repeatedly defied the doomsayers through its continuing success. The incompleteness of economic reform has repeatedly been identified as the factor most likely to hinder future economic growth. Proponents of the market can find much fault with the Chinese experience: they continue to do so. Will the success continue? In different ways the authors of the chapters in this book try to answer the questions posed in the previous paragraph, or simply to provide an explanation of why China confounds the market proponents.

Sustainability is particularly important to Australia, but it is relevant in a wider context since it offers the prospect of other developing countries succeeding on the basis of similarly idiosyncratic policies and strategies. We live in a period of much greater optimism that the problem of economic development and world poverty will be solved. China is the source of much of that hope. Sustainability has many meanings and not the least of those is the sustainability of economic growth in the largest country in the world. It is interesting to note that in a world where all countries were developed economically there would be no population problem since fertility rates decline as income rises and a stable or contracting global population would relieve the problem of global warming.

Preface

Lilai Xu

Since its accession to the World Trade Organization (WTO) in 2001, China has grown at a rate approximately 7 percent faster than have Western countries. If this trend continues into the new decade, the Chinese economy may become the largest in the world some time between 2020 and 2030.

Clearly, however, we cannot be certain that this pattern of growth evident in the early 2000s will continue into the 2010s. Those of us who study the Chinese economy are fully aware of the problems faced by China. Indeed, there is an influential school of thought that insists on the unsustainability of China's economic system. Mindful of the opportunities and challenges faced by China, the Association for Chinese Economic Studies Australia (ACESA) organized an international conference on 'China in the post-WTO environment', held in Melbourne, Australia on 15–17 July 2009. The conference brought together scholars and experts from universities, research institutions and government bodies to discuss the key issues, the progress and the policy challenges in relation to the Chinese economy.

This book consists of 12 chapters drawn from a total of 40 research papers presented at the ACESA conference. Each of the selected chapters has been subject to anonymous peer review by two academics from the relevant research field. These chapters provide valuable background information on the Chinese economy and offer insights into the many critical issues confronting China in the post-WTO environment.

Part I 'Stock market and financial services' consists of three chapters. In Chapter 1, Yi Zheng and Heng Chen explore the theoretical and practical implications of whether a leading power or a close neighbor is more important to China's stock market. Huaiqing Zhu and Changfeng Pan follow in Chapter 2 with a discussion of the constraints on China's stock market and the behavior of market players. In Chapter 3, K.B. Oh, Xuebin Chen, Jianmei Wang, Geoffrey R. Durden and Nicole El Haber present an examination of recent growth and development in the Chinese financial services market and a commentary on likely future trends.

Part II 'China's FDI and FDI in China' consists of four chapters. Chapter 4 by Lilai Xu offers a close analysis of the structure, determinants and effects of China's outward foreign direct investment (FDI) against the backdrop of the 'Go Global' strategy. In Chapter 5, Chunlai Chen explores the contributing factors of the FDI relations between China and its main source economies. Ying Xu in Chapter 6 proposes a model and presents the statistical findings regarding foreign strategic investment in Chinese commercial banks. In Chapter 7, Sizhong Sun, Ligang Song and Peter Drysdale discuss FDI spillover in relation to the dimension that remains little examined in the literature: the role played by geographical proximity between domestic firms and foreign-invested firms in the occurrence and magnitude of spillovers.

Part III 'Price determinants and policy challenges' presents two studies. Wei-ming Tian and Zhang-Yue Zhou in Chapter 8 discuss potential policy measures to be undertaken by the Chinese government to handle future erratic price movements in the world grain market. Chapter 9 presents a study by James Xiaohe Zhang in which he tackles two different views on the Remnibi (RMB) exchange rate by simulating several policy scenarios on a simple multi-country macro-econometric model.

Part IV 'Distortion and economic sustainability' is comprised of three chapters. Chapter 10 presents a discussion by Youwen Zhang of policy-imposed distortion in China's economic development. In Chapter 11, using transportation in large cities as a case study, Jianling Li, Siamak Ardekani and Stephen Mattingly explore urban sustainability and propose the development of a planning tool to assess policy impacts. In the concluding Chapter 12, Yanrui Wu examines whether capital has been utilized efficiently in China and if capital under-utilization exists, what the causes are. To explore these questions, he proposes a stochastic frontier approach to investigate the efficiency of capital using panel data of China's regional economies. The determinants of regional efficiency variation are also investigated.

PART I

Stock market and financial services

1. Who is more important – a leading power or a close neighbor?

Yi Zheng and Heng Chen

INTRODUCTION

The phenomenon of globalization has been gaining momentum in recent years and its rise looks to be irreversible, despite objections from some quarters. Globalization is a direct result of increasing interaction among the world economies, both developing and developed. In this context of increasingly substantial capital flows across national borders, integration among world stock markets has important practical significance for investors, as greater financial integration implies reduced opportunities for international portfolio diversification. Integration among world stock markets is also an important issue for financial policy makers since co-movement between markets can result in contagious effects whereby investors factor price changes in other markets into their trading decisions in an effort to form a complete information set, meaning that shocks in one market may be transmitted to other markets. Such contagion effects have been exacerbated by certain major events which have affected world stock markets in recent decades, such as the 1987 stock market crash, the Asian financial crisis (1997–98) and the global financial crisis of 2008. Correspondingly, individual countries' monetary and fiscal schemes are being designed to tackle possible external infections.

Among the international markets, China's stock market – in line with its fast-growing economy – has become a rising star that has caught investors' eyes. Initiated in the early 1990s, China's stock market has a relatively short history; therefore, the interactions and relations between China's market and other world markets have not yet been extensively investigated. However, despite its short history, China's stock market has made rapid progress during the past two decades. As of 30 June 2009, China's stock market value totaled US$2.9 trillion, and its market capitalization went beyond 70 percent of GDP with the number of listed companies above 1500. China's rising stock market echoes developments in the country's fast-growing economy and growing interaction with the rest of the world.

After China joined the World Trade Organization (WTO) in 2001, a great number of restrictions previously imposed on Chinese financial markets were lifted. Within three to five years, China's financial market will be completely open to foreign investors. International investment funds are thus preparing to fully grasp the lucrative opportunities offered by China's market. Therefore, at the present time it is particularly worthwhile to assess the integration of China's stock market with the world's market. The resulting inferences could yield valuable insights for both investors and policy makers.

An important determinant of interdependence between national stock markets is economic integration in the form of trade and investment flows. The dividend discount model suggests that a company's current share price represents the present value of future cash flows, which depends on the earnings growth of the company. Earnings growth depends on the macroeconomic conditions of both the domestic market and countries with which a country trades and sources its investment flows. Interdependence in stock markets may also reflect the geographical proximity between markets that have close economic ties, which are expected to exhibit high levels of market linkages because of the presence of similar investor groups and cross-listed companies. A motivation for this study is to increase understanding of these determinants, as it focuses on examining the interdependence between China's stock market and other world markets. Specifically, we examine the relations between China's stock market and world markets represented by the United States (US) and Hong Kong markets. We attempt to identify the relations between China and these two markets for the following reasons. On the one hand, the US market is the leading and most influential market in the world, and the US is the largest trade partner and biggest foreign direct investment source for China. On the other hand, the Hong Kong market maintains the most intimate connection with China economically, politically and geographically. Hence, conclusions regarding the interactions of China's stock market with these two markets may reveal the topology of China's market in the world, as well as showing the importance of geographical distance in explaining movements between markets, and the influence of the world's superpower and its close neighbor on the evolution of China's stock market. Inferences developed from this study may also be valuable to international portfolios covering these markets.

Previous research on the long- and short-run dynamic relations among stock markets has mostly adopted the vector correction model (VECM) pioneered by Engle and Granger (1987). The key aspect of VECM is that the cointegration residual or error, which is supposed to be I(0) process exerts a corrective effect on the long-run dynamics of an underlying series.

Specifically, when cointegrated, variables deviate from the long-run relation, and the immediately previous period cointegration error acts as a force that pulls the drifting variable back toward an equilibrium. This adjustment mechanism is based on the key assumption that the cointegration error is of a stationary I(0) process. However, the cointegration error between economic and financial series has been found to exhibit a long memory feature, which is consistent with neither a stationary I(0) nor a non-stationary I(1) process. This special stochastic process is termed the I(d) process, with d being a fractional real number (Baillie, 1996). When the cointegration error follows the I(d) process, which was found to be the case in this study, the long history of lagged cointegration errors also has a correction effect on the dynamics of cointegrated variables. In light of this, our study extends VECM into fractionally integrated VECM (FIVECM) to account for the long memory in the cointegration error series, which may otherwise bias relevant inferences. FIVECM has been applied to optimizing dynamic hedging ratios in derivatives markets, as in the work of Lien and Tse (1999), while it only appears rarely in studies on cointegration in stock markets. This approach will be further elaborated in the methodology section.

The remainder of this chapter is organized as follows: the next section reviews the major relevant studies in the literature; the third section describes the data and methodology employed in this study; the fourth section discusses the empirical results and their implications; and the conclusion is presented in the final section

LITERATURE REVIEW

The basic tenet of portfolio theory is that international investors should diversify assets across countries provided that returns to stocks across countries are less than perfectly correlated. A requirement for investors to diversify their risk and enhance their return opportunities through international diversification is that stock markets exhibit independent price behaviors. If stock markets are integrated, assets associated with a similar level of risk and/or liquidity will generate similar returns regardless of the location of the country in which the investment is made, therefore minimizing the potential profit for investors.

Whether or not stock markets are cointegrated carries important implications for portfolio diversification. The cointegration of markets implies that there is a common force, such as arbitrage activity, which brings these stock markets together in the long run, meaning that testing for cointegration is a test of the level of arbitrage activity in the long run. In theory, if stock markets are not cointegrated, there is no capacity for arbitrage activity to bring the markets together in the long run. If this is the case, investors can potentially obtain long-run gains through international portfolio diversification (see Masih and Masih, 1997, 1999). On the other hand, if stock markets are cointegrated the potential for making above-normal profits through international diversification is limited in the long run. Any above-normal profits will be arbitraged away in the long run, and, in the absence of barriers or potential barriers generating country risk and exchange rate premiums, one would expect similar yields for financial assets of similar risk and liquidity, irrespective of country or location (Von Furstenberg and Jeon, 1989).

The seminal studies of market interdependence and portfolio diversification are those of Grubel (1968), Levy and Sarnat (1970), Ripley (1973), Lessard (1974), Panto et al. (1976) and Hilliard (1979). Most of these studies used correlation analysis to examine short-run linkages between markets. Since the beginning of the 1990s, several researchers, of which Kasa (1992) was one of the first, have used cointegration methods to examine whether there are long-run benefits of international equity diversification. These studies have investigated integration between developed markets, integration between emerging markets and integration between one or more developed markets and emerging markets.

Several studies have verified the existence of co-movement between the US market and other markets in the world, such as research conducted by Eun and Shim (1989), using Vector Autoregressive Analysis (VAR) analysis, which found evidence of co-movement between the US stock market and other world stock markets. Cheung and Ng (1992) investigated the dynamics of stock market returns in the US, Japanese and Asia-Pacific stock markets, and found that the US market was a dominant global force from 1977 through to 1988. However, not all research has verified the existence of cointegration among international stock markets. Using Bayesian methods, Koop (1994) concluded that there are no common stochastic trends in stock prices across the selected countries in her study. Lee and Kim (1994) examined the October 1987 US stock market crash, and identified that national stock markets became more integrated after the crash. Similarly, using a VAR and impulse response function analysis, Jeon and Von Furstenberg (1990) revealed a stronger co-movement among international stock indices after the 1987 crash.

There is a significant volume of literature on integration between Asia-Pacific markets or integration between major world stock markets and Asia-Pacific markets. Ng (2002) and Daly (2003) have examined market linkages between Southeast Asian stock markets, and several studies have explored whether the Japanese and/or US market is cointegrated with the Asia-Pacific markets (Cheung and Mak, 1992; Chung and Liu,

1994; Ghosh et al., 1998; Janakiramanan and Lamba, 1998; Pan et al., 1999; Sheng and Tu, 2000; Fernandez-Serrano and Sosvilla-Rivero, 2001; Johnson and Soenen, 2002).

Most of the studies that have tested for long-run relationships between markets have typically used the method of cointegration pioneered by Engle and Granger (1987) and Johansen (1988a). Fernandez-Serrano and Sosvilla-Rivero (2001, 2003) examined stock market integration between the Japanese market and Asia-Pacific markets, and between the US market and Latin American markets, respectively, using the Johansen (1988a) and Gregory and Hansen (1996) methods, and found more evidence of cointegration after allowing for a structural shift in the cointegration vector. Siklos and Ng (2001) considered whether stock markets in the Asia-Pacific region are integrated with each other, and with the US and Japanese markets, using the Gregory and Hansen (1996) approach, and identified that the 1987 stock market crash and 1991 Gulf War were both turning points in shifts in the degree of integration.

As previously mentioned, due to its short history, the interactions and relations between China's market and other world markets have not been extensively investigated. One exception is the research of Huang et al. (2000), who have examined whether there is a long-run relationship between the stock markets of the USA, Japan and the South China Growth Triangle, using Gregory and Hansen's (1996) method. They found that among the markets under study the only markets that were cointegrated are those of Shanghai and Shenzhen.

DATA AND METHODOLOGY

Data Description

This study employs weekly data for the period January 1998 through to May 2009, which provided 729 observations. The stock price indices are the Shanghai All Shares Index (SHH_t) for China,[1] the Hangseng Index (HS_t) for Hong Kong and the S&P 500 (SP_t) for the USA. All data are downloaded from Datastream. To avoid the 'day-of-the-week effect', which suggests that the stock market is more volatile on Mondays and Fridays, we use the Wednesday indices. The sample covers the entire history of the Chinese stock market up to the commencement of this study.

The normalized indices (with a starting value for each index of 100) are shown in Figure 1.1. Figure 1.1 suggests that the Shanghai All Shares Index is more volatile than the other two indices. This is also confirmed by summary statistics of the data, which are shown in Table 1.1

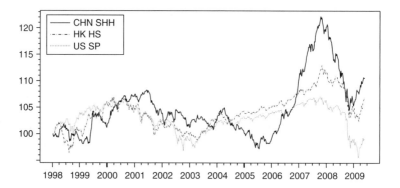

Figure 1.1   Stock indices of China, USA and Hong Kong

Table 1.1   Descriptive statistics of data

Statistics	SHH_t	SP_t	HS_t
Min.	6.928	6.569	8.833
Mean	7.475	7.076	9.537
Max.	8.705	10.353	7.354
Std Dev.	0.389	0.165	0.296
Skewness	1.303	−0.582	0.371
Kurtosis	1.244	−0.318	−0.224

Note: SHH_t is the log of the weekly Shanghai All Shares index, HS_t the log of the weekly Hangsen index and SP_t is the log of the weekly S&P 500 index, the kurtosis here computed with S-PLUS is excess kurtosis.

The standard deviation for the Shanghai All Shares Index is 0.389, which is higher than those of the S&P 500 and Hangseng indices, showing the higher variability in China's stock market. The most striking feature of the S&P 500 index is its continuous growth from early 2003 through to mid-2007, when it reached a peak and then fell following the subprime crisis that later triggered the global financial crisis. Compared with the S&P 500, the Shanghai and Hangseng indices exhibit more large short-lived up-and-downs within the study period.

Methodology

To examine the existence of a cointegration relationship between stock price indices, we employ a Granger two-step procedure. In the first step, we fit the following dynamic ordinary least squares (DOLS) model to the pairs of stock price indices:

$$y_{1t} = \alpha + \beta y_{2t} + \sum_{j=-p}^{p} \omega'_j \Delta y_{2t-j} + \eta_t \tag{1.1}$$

Here, y_{1t}, y_{2t} are pairs of stock indices involving SHH_t, HS_t and SP_t. Regression (1.1) is preferred to ordinary least squares, because the estimate $\hat{\beta}$ here is shown by Stock and Watson (1993) to be super-consistent[2] as well as asymptotically efficient. The estimated cointegration residual ($\hat{z}_t$) can then be constructed as follows:

$$\hat{z}_t = y_{1t} - \hat{\beta} y_{2t} \tag{1.2}$$

The usual definition of cointegration posits that some linear combination of a set of I(1) variables turns out to be a stationary I(0) process.[3] Thus, testing the stationarity of the linear combination of I(1) variables or cointegration residuals is a major statistical approach employed in Engle and Granger's two-step procedures to establish cointegration relations. However, as first noted in the early 1980s, the characteristics of auto-dependence in cointegration residuals are found to comply with neither a I(1) nor a I(0) process, as traditional unit root tests yield ambiguous conclusions regarding the stationarity of the residuals. This vagueness resulting from the statistical tests has spurred some researchers to question and improve the power of stationarity and non-stationarity tests. Baillie (1996) states that the dichotomy between I(1) and I(0) may be too restrictive, and some researchers have turned their attention to the halfway between I(1) and I(0) process, that is, the I(d) process, with d being a fractional real number which leads to the name 'fractionally integrated process'. In econometrics, the focus is on the I(d), $0.5 < d < 0.5$, which is stationary and invertible, and is represented as follows:

$$(1 - B)^d Y_t = a_t$$

$$(1 - B)^d = \sum_{k=0}^{\infty} \frac{\Gamma(d + 1)}{\Gamma(k + 1)\Gamma(d - k + 1)} (-1)^k B^k \tag{1.3}$$

where $\Gamma(.)$ is Gamma function,[4] and a_t is a covariance stationary process with a zero mean. When $d < 0.5$, the process is weakly stationary and has a long memory in the sense that its auto-dependence is more persistent than that of a stationary process. Conversely, as $-0.5 < d$, the process is invertible, and its autocorrelation is negative and decays slowly to zero, presenting intermediate memory as discussed by Baillie (1996). Specifically, for $-0.5 < d < 0.5$, at large lags, the autocorrelation function of the process is shown to be:

$$\rho_k \approx c^* k^{2d-1} \tag{1.4}$$

Therefore, the autocorrelation of the fractionally integrated process decays at a hyperbolic rate, which is lower than the exponential rate as in the case of a stationary process. When the cointegration residual $\hat{z}_t$ is fractionally integrated, the underlying series are said to be fractionally cointegrated.

The long memory process was first investigated in relation to hydrology by Hurst (1951), who proposed a statistic of rescaled range (R/S) to test for long memory in time series. Since Hurst's research, a few methods have been proposed to estimate the fractional difference parameter d based on either time domain or frequency domain, and research along these lines is ongoing (see, for example, Shimotsu and Phillips, 2005). This chapter employs a fractionally integrated Auto-Regressive and Moving Average Model (ARMA) (ARFIMA) model to estimate d with approximate maximum likelihood estimation (MLE),[5] as the ARFIMA model is more flexible in capturing both long memory and short-run dynamics in time series.

Therefore, in the second step we apply an R/S test to the $\hat{z}_t$ series to test for possible long memory. If the cointegration residual follows a long memory I(d)($-0.5 < d < 0.5$)[6] process, y_{1t}, y_{2t} are fractionally cointegrated and we proceed to fit an autoregressive fractionally integrated moving average (ARFIMA) model to each residual series to estimate the fractional difference parameter d:

$$\Phi(B)(1-B)^d \hat{z}_t = \Psi(B)a_t \tag{1.5}$$

Here, $\Psi(B)$ and $\Phi(B)$ represent moving average (MA) and autoregressive (AR) polynomials, respectively; and B is a backward shift operator and $\{a_t\}$ is an *i.i.d.* noise series, which will be interpreted as the equilibrium error in the vector error correction model below. Engle and Granger (1987) assert that, once a long-run relationship among the variables is established, a VECM is an appropriate method to model both the long-run and short-run dynamics among the cointegrated variables. We expand the VECM into a FIVECM by accounting for fractional integration in the $\hat{z}_t$ series using the ARFIMA model as set out in equation (1.5). Following Granger (1986), the bivariate FIVECM can be depicted in the following form:

$$\Delta y_{1t} = c_1 + \alpha_1[(1 - B)^d - (1 - B)]\hat{z}_t + \sum_{i=1}^{m}\phi_{11}^i\Delta y_{1t-i} + \sum_{i=1}^{m}\phi_{12}^i\Delta y_{2t-i} + \varepsilon_{1t}$$

$$\Delta y_{2t} = c_2 + \alpha_2[(1 - B)^d - (1 - B)]\hat{z}_t + \sum_{i=1}^{m}\phi_{21}^i\Delta y_{1t-i} + \sum_{i=1}^{m}\phi_{22}^i\Delta y_{2t-i} + \varepsilon_{2t} \tag{1.6}$$

Here, $\Delta y_t = (\Delta y_{1t}, \Delta y_{2t})'$ is the differenced series vector or return vector of $(\Delta SHH_t, \Delta SP_t)'$ or $(\Delta SHH_t, \Delta HS_t)'$. $\hat{z}_{t-1}$ is estimated by equation (1.2) with an estimate of $\hat{\beta}$ from regression (1.1) fitted to respective pairs of stock index vectors. Note that we employ the VAR (m) structure for the VECM model; in particular, $m = 1$ in this study and $\varepsilon_t = (\varepsilon_{1t}, \varepsilon_{2t})'$ is the error vector. The coefficients $\alpha = (\alpha_1, \alpha_2)'$ capture the reaction of the series when they deviate from the long-run equilibrium, while the magnitudes of the $\alpha_i's$ represent the speed of the adjustment. The lagged terms in equation (1.4) account for the autoregressive structure of the Δy_t series, and at the same time reflect the return transmissions between different stock markets.

As the long memory process exhibits a slower decay of autocorrelation than in the covariance stationary process, accounting for it is crucial to accurately delineate the dynamics of the underlying series, especially in terms of forecasting. In the context of cointegration, as the fractionally integrated series $\hat{z}_t$ have an infinite autoregressive representation (1.3), the FIVECM model (1.6) shows that the dynamics of $\Delta y_t = (\Delta y_{1t}, \Delta y_{2t})'$ are affected by all of the past values of $\hat{z}_{t-i}$, $i \geq 1$, not just $\hat{z}_{t-1}$ as in the VECM model. This structure implies that, in principle, the cointegration errors between two bound series have a long-run contribution to the adjustment of the series toward equilibrium, although the impact of earlier errors may be negligible in terms of magnitude. Compared with the one-time adjustment shown by the VECM model, this gradual adjustment mechanism in FIVECM to long-run cointegration relations is more realistic, especially in modeling high frequency data like daily or weekly data. This gradual adjustment suggests the value of the VECM model in capturing long-run as well as short-run interactions among involved series. Therefore, when the cointegration error series possesses a long memory feature, conventional VECM is misspecified, as it only allows $\hat{z}_{t-1}$ to exert a correction function in the system.

Because it is often observed that the conditional volatilities of financial return series exhibit time-varying characteristics, we employ a multivariate Generalized Autoregressive Conditional Heteroskedasticity (GARCH) (MGARCH) model to capture the heteroskedasticity in the second moment of the series. In other words, we model the conditional mean and conditional variance of the return series simultaneously.[7] By jointly estimating the FIVECM-Baba-Engle-Kraft-Kroner (BEKK) model, the coefficient estimates are more efficient and the relationships among the return series are delineated far more accurately, as Bauwens et al. (2006) have shown.

The time-varying correlation coefficient between two return series can be obtained from the conditional variances and covariances after the model is estimated. The stationarity condition for the volatility series in a BEKK (1, 1) model is that the eigenvalues of the matrix $A_1 \otimes A_1 + B_1 \otimes B_1$ are all less than unity in modulus, where $\otimes$ stands for the Kronecker product of matrices.[8]

EMPIRICAL ANALYSIS

Cointegration Setup

Before modeling cointegration, it is necessary to examine the non-stationarity properties of the stock price indices. To test for non-stationarity we applied the Augmented Dickey Fuller (ADF) and Phillips-Perron (PP) unit root tests to the logarithmic values of SHH_t, HS_t and SP_t. The results are presented in Table 1.2.

Both tests revealed that all of the indices are found to be integrated of order one.[9] This finding is consistent with the results of previous studies which have applied unit root tests to examine the random walk properties of stock price indices in developed markets (see, for example, Narayan and Smyth, 2005a, 2006).

Next, we test for long-run relationships between pairs of stock price indices $(SHH_t, SP_t)'$ and $(SHH_t, HS_t)'$ by fitting the DOLS model in

Table 1.2   Unit root tests for index series

Test	ADF		PP	
Index	*t*-statistic	*p*-value	*t*-statistic	*p*-value
SHH_t	−3.377	0.9198	−4.633	0.8456
SP_t	−1.744	0.4085	−1.781	0.3899
HS_t	−1.969	0.6166	−2.164	0.5081

Note: The ADF tests applied on SHH_t and HS_t are with constant, trend and lag length 1; the ADF test on SP_t is with constant and lag length is 1. The lag length selection for ADF tests is done by the data-dependent procedure of Ng and Perron (1995). The corresponding PP tests have the same structure without lag terms, using Bartlett window with bandwidth 6.

Table 1.3   DOLS model estimates, dependent variable is 'SHH$_t$'

Coef	Ind.var.	SP_t		HS_t	
		estimate	*p*-value	estimate	*p*-value
α		0.6846	0.2849	−2.0020	0.000***
$\hat{\beta}_2$		0.9593	0.000***	0.9937	0.000***
$\hat{\omega}_{-2}$		−1.3290	0.0196**	−2.2519	0.0247**
$\hat{\omega}_{-1}$		−1.3561	0.0168**	−2.1282	0.0337**
$\hat{\omega}_0$		−1.6552	0.0036***	−2.4078	0.0164**
$\hat{\omega}_1$		−0.6862	0.2244	0.5229	0.6012
$\hat{\omega}_2$		−0.5698	0.3130	0.7335	0.4636

Note: **Significant at 5 percent level, *** significant at 1 percent level.

equation (1.1) with a lag length of $p = 2$. The estimated model coefficients are presented in Table 1.3. The results suggest that all of the estimated $\hat{\beta}$ for the two regression models are highly significant.

In order to confirm the existence of a long-run relationship between the series in each pair, we test the stationarity of the cointegration residuals. We construct the $\hat{z}_t$ series following equation (1.2) for each pair of series using the estimated cointegration coefficient $\hat{\beta}$ from the corresponding DOLS model. These constructed cointegration residual series are denoted as z_{sp}^{shh} and z_{hs}^{shh}, respectively (where the superscript stands for the dependent variable and the subscript for the independent variable). To informally examine the auto-dependence in the cointegration residual series, we graph the sample autocorrelation function of both z_{sp}^{shh} and z_{hs}^{shh} series, as shown in Figures 1.2 and 1.3.

The pattern of decay of the sample autocorrelation coefficients in both Figures 1.2 and 1.3 does not resemble that of either the I(1) or I(0) process. It decays faster than the autocorrelation of the I(1) process and exhibits the feature of a stationary process, but its autocorrelation shows a signifi-cant level of persistence and cyclic fluctuations. This pattern is typical of a long memory process as documented by Baillie and Bollerslev (1994) using exchange rate data. Next, to formally test for possible long-range dependence, the R/S test for long memory is applied to these two residual series. The results, which are presented in Table 1.4, confirm that both of the two residual series are fractionally integrated processes manifesting a long memory property.

Therefore, we proceed to fit an ARFIMA model equation (1.5) to each of the residual series to estimate the fractional difference parameter in the cointegration residuals. The results are shown in Table 1.5; the estimates

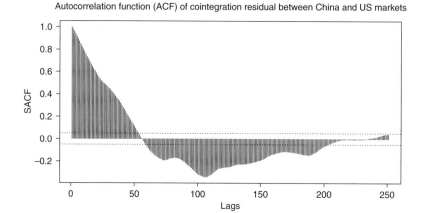

Note: The two dashed lines denote the 95 percent confidence interval of the sample autocorrelation function (SACF).

Figure 1.2   Sample autocorrelation of cointegration residual series between China and the USA

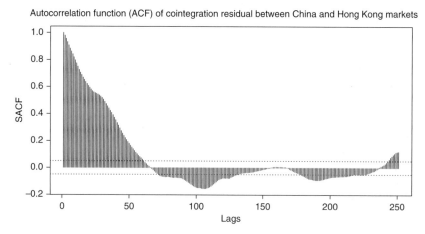

Note: The two dashed lines denote the 95 percent confidence interval of the sample autocorrelation function (SACF).

Figure 1.3   Sample autocorrelation of cointegration residual series between China and Hong Kong

Table 1.4   Stationarity and long memory tests on cointegration residuals

Test	Range over standard deviation (R/S) test	
Residuals	test statistic	*p*-value
z_{hs}^{shh}	2.7647	<0.01
z_{sp}^{shh}	3.104	<0.01

Note: The residual series are constructed using equation (1.2) in the text based on the corresponding DOLS model in Table 1.3. The bandwidth used in the R/S test is the integral part of $4(N/100)^{1/4}$, N is sample size. The null hypothesis in the R/S test is 'No long-term dependence'.

Table 1.5   ARFIMA fit results

Estimates	z_{hs}^{shh}		z_{sp}^{shh}	
Parameters	value	*p*-value	value	*p*-value
d	0.0847	0.0170**	0.0775	0.0168**
AR(1)	0.9665	0.0000***	0.978	0.0000***

Note: The series z_{hs}^{shh}, z_{sp}^{shh} are constructed with equation (1.2). The superscript stands for dependent variable, while the subscript denotes the independent variable. The choice of AR lags is based on an examination of the ACF and partial autocorrelation function (PACF). **Significant at 5 percent level, *** Significant at 1 percent level.

of d confirm that the two cointegration residual series are fractionally integrated.

The resulting $\{a_t\}$ series from ARFIMA model equation (1.5) are tested as either a I(0) or a stationary process.[10] Therefore, the above results confirm that both pairs of stock indices, namely $(SHH_t, SP_t)'$ and $(SHH_t, HS_t)'$, are fractionally cointegrated.

Empirical Results for the Chinese and US Markets

Now that the cointegration relations are established, we proceed to fit a FIVECM model augmented by an MGARCH model. Specifically, we fit a FIVECM-BEKK (1, 1) model to the two pairs of differenced index series in logs – the pair of Shanghai All Shares Index and the S&P 500, and the pair of Shanghai All Shares Index and the Hangseng Index – and the differenced series are actually the return series of the respective markets. The variable sequences in the fitting FIVECM are $(\Delta SHH_t, \Delta SP_t)'$ and $(\Delta SHH_t, \Delta HS_t)'$

Table 1.6   Estimated coefficients for FIVECM-BEKK (1, 1) fitted on $(\Delta SHH_t, \Delta SP_t)'$

Parameters	Estimate	Standard error	t value	$Pr(>|t|)$
C(1)	0.0006	0.0012	0.5318	0.5950
C(2)	0.0010	0.0009	1.1117	0.2667
AR(1; 1, 1)	1.3566	0.5104	2.6580	0.0008***
AR(1; 2, 1)	0.4766	0.3518	1.3545	0.1761
AR(1; 1, 2)	−1.1648	0.5100	−2.2838	0.0227**
AR(1; 2, 2)	−0.5968	0.3456	−1.7267	0.0848
α_1	−1.3188	0.5208	−2.5323	0.0011***
α_2	−0.5275	0.3530	−1.4943	0.1356
A(1, 1)	0.0068	0.0018	3.7191	0.0000***
A(2, 1)	0.0024	0.0014	1.7540	0.0799**
A(2, 2)	0.0001	0.0599	0.0011	0.9991
ARCH(1; 1, 1)	0.2496	0.0474	5.2639	0.0000***
ARCH(1; 2, 1)	−0.0043	0.0133	−0.3263	0.3721
ARCH(1; 1, 2)	0.0366	0.0671	0.5449	0.5860
ARCH(1; 2, 2)	0.2734	0.0439	6.2276	0.0000***
GARCH(1; 1, 1)	0.9481	0.0199	47.5456	0.0000***
GARCH(1; 2, 1)	0.0005	0.0052	0.1034	0.4589
GARCH(1; 1, 2)	−0.0025	0.0217	−0.1163	0.9074
GARCH(1; 2, 2)	0.9592	0.0138	69.190	0.0000***

Note: The estimated model is FIVECM-BEKK (1, 1) (equation systems (1.6) + (1.8)); the dependent variable is ΔSHH_t the error structure is bivariate t-distribution, the estimated degrees of freedom are 6.965 with standard error 1.026. The use of an ARFIMA (1, d, 0) model reduces the actual sample size to 729. **Significant at 5 percent level, *** significant at 1 percent level.

in both the conditional mean and conditional variance equations, where ΔSHH_t is a dependent variable in both models. An AR (1) structure is employed in the FIVECM equations, and multivariate student-t distribution is assumed for the error series of both FIVECM-BEKK (1, 1) models. The fitted model estimates for $(\Delta SHH_t, \Delta SP_t)'$ are listed in Table 1.6.

In order to interpret the results, we first focus on the conditional mean equation. C(i), i =1, 2 are the constant terms in the conditional mean equation, AR(i, j, k), i =1, j =1, 2, k =1, 2 stand for the AR term coefficients, and α_i, i =1, 2 represent the adjustment speed parameter in the FIVECM model equation (1.6). The estimates of AR coefficients show that both return series present serial dependence, which is verified by significant AR(1; 2, 2); in particular, the ΔSP_t series shows mean reversion as AR(1; 2, 2) is negative. It is noteworthy that the AR(1; 1, 2) is significant,

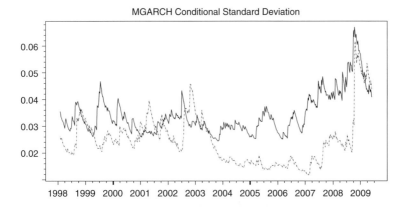

Figure 1.4   Conditional standard deviations for ΔSHH_t *and* ΔSP_t

which means that there is return transmission between the stock markets of China and the USA – in other words, the US market Granger-causes China's market. The sign of the first adjustment speed parameter estimate is correct, conforming to cointegration theory. The negative value of α_1 implies that the Shanghai All Shares Index, SHH_t, returns to a long-run equilibrium after initially deviating from it. However, the US stock index SP_t appears not to be bound by the cointegration relation between the two markets, or the adjustment scheme is only unilateral.

For the conditional variance equation, A(i, j) denotes the elements of the constant matrix A_0; and for ARCH(1; i, j) and GARCH(1; i, j) the elements of the ARCH and GARCH coefficient matrices are A_1 and B_1, respectively. It is easy to observe that all of the diagonal elements of the coefficient matrices are highly significant, while all of the off-diagonal elements are not significant according to conventional significance levels. The fitted MARCH model, BEKK (1, 1), acts just as the diagonal multivariate volatility model. This result indicates that GARCH (including ARCH) effects are substantial in the return vector series $(\Delta SHH_t, \Delta SP_t)'$, which is consistent with common conclusions about return series. In addition, according to the non-zero values of A(1, 1), the unconditional variances of both return series are not zero, as shown in Figure 1.4, which depicts the fitted conditional standard deviation of two return series. This suggests that China's stock market is far more volatile than the US market.

The estimated results indicate no volatility spillover or shock transmission between the Chinese and US stock markets. Although there is a long-run cointegrating relationship between the two markets, information on one market does not immediately influence the other. This could be due to institutional distinctions, because one is the leading mature market, while

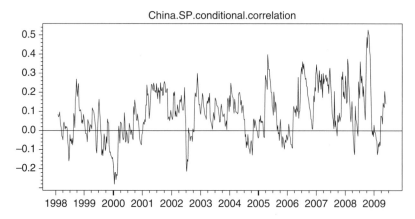

Figure 1.5   Conditional correlation between return series ΔSHH_t *and* ΔSP_t

the other is a new market born of a highly centralized economy. Although certain fundamental differences mean that these two markets still act on their own information, the links between them have surely been strengthened by the increasing integration between the two economies. The growing interaction between the Chinese and US stock markets can be verified by the evolution of the fitted conditional correlation coefficients, as shown in Figure 1.5.

There is no obvious long-lasting trend in the conditional correlation over time; however, it seems that the correlation between the two market return series has moved slightly upwards since 2000, albeit interrupted in late 2002 when there was a collapse on China's market. At this time, the Chinese government attempted to convert a huge volume of non-tradeable shares (most of which were state-owned shares) into tradeable shares,[11] which induced panic and a crash in the market.

Finally, the eigenvalues of $\hat{A}_1 \otimes \hat{A}_1 + \hat{B}_1 \otimes \hat{B}_1$ ($\hat{A}_1$ and $\hat{B}_1$ are estimated as ARCH and GARCH coefficient matrices, respectively) are 0.997, 0.984, 0.981, 0.972; thus, all are less than unity. Therefore, the conditional volatilities of the two stock return series are stationary. The model adequacy diagnostics are listed in Table 1.7. Specifically, a Ljung-Box test of white noise is applied to both the standardized residuals and squared standardized residuals to test for possible remaining serial correlation in the first and second moments of residuals. The number of lags employed in both Ljung-Box tests is 12; thus, the test statistics follow a Chi-square distribution with a value of 12 as the degree of freedom. All of the tests are applied to the two individual residual series separately.

Table 1.7   Model diagnostic statistics for ΔSHH_t *and* ΔSP_t

Test Series	Normality test (Jarque-Bera)		White noise test (Ljung-Box)		GARCH effect test (Ljung-Box)	
	statistic	*p*-value	statistic	*p*-value	statistic	*p*-value
ΔSHH_t	22563	0.0000***	9.8954	0.1291	29.110	0.5118
ΔSP_t	1029	0.0000***	5.0439	0.5382	26.5266	0.6480

Note: The Jarque-Bera statistic asymptotically follows Chi-squared distribution with degree of freedom 2. The other Normality test, Shapiro-Wilk's test, was also employed, the conclusion is essentially the same. These results corroborate the assumption of student-*t* for the error terms which is based on the Normality test of the original series. *** Significant at 1 percent level.

The test statistics show that the fitted model is adequate, and successful for capturing the dynamics in the first and second moments of the index return series.

Empirical Results for the Chinese and Hong Kong Markets

Table 1.8 lists the coefficient estimates for the FIVECM-BEKK (1, 1) fitted on the other pair of return series, that is, $(\Delta SHH_t, \Delta HS_t)'$, representing the Chinese and Hong Kong markets.

Overall, the results presented in Table 1.8 show a stronger relationship between the Chinese and Hong Kong markets than between the Chinese and US markets, a result that is unsurprising since the former two economies are closely related and interdependent. For the AR terms, the significance of AR (1; 1, 1) indicates there is serial correlation with China's stock market while the opposite is true for Hong Kong's stock market (AR (1; 2, 2) which is insignificant. The significant AR (1; 1, 2) indicates that there is return transmission from Hong Kong to China's market. This could be due to the exemplary role Hong Kong plays for the stock market on the mainland, as the former colony has long been a reference for China in establishing and building its own stock market. Next, the highly significant α_1 with the right sign dictates that China's stock index is also restricted by the long-run equilibrium between it and the Hong Kong market. Again, the adjustment to the cointegration relation is unilateral, as the Hong Kong market appears not to respond to disequilibrium between the two markets.

Finally, the estimates for the conditional variance equation show an interesting interaction between the volatility of the two markets. In particular, the significant GARCH (1; 2, 1) and ARCH (1; 2, 1) suggest

Table 1.8   Estimated coefficients for FIVECM-BEKK (1, 1) fitted on
(ΔSHH$_t$, ΔHS$_t$)′

Parameters	Value	Standard error	*t* value	Pr(>|*t*|)
C(1)	0.0006	0.0001	0.5295	0.5966
C(2)	0.0018	0.0013	1.3873	0.1659
AR(1; 1, 1)	0.9468	0.2593	3.6506	0.000***
AR(1; 2, 1)	−0.0352	0.2581	−0.1367	0.8913
AR(1; 1, 2)	−0.8387	0.2683	−3.1255	0.0018***
AR(1; 2, 2)	−0.0095	0.2637	−0.0359	0.9713
α_1	−0.9248	0.2674	−3.4582	0.0000***
α_2	−0.0331	0.2617	−0.1263	0.8995
A(1, 1)	0.0077	0.0018	4.0790	0.0000***
A(2, 1)	0.0019	0.0021	0.8992	0.3689
A(2, 2)	0.0000	0.1503	0.0003	0.9997
ARCH(1; 1, 1)	0.2683	0.0510	5.2569	0.0000***
ARCH(1; 2, 1)	0.1033	0.0523	1.9729	0.0489**
ARCH(1; 1, 2)	−0.0296	0.0438	−0.6754	0.4997
ARCH(1; 2, 2)	0.2192	0.0549	3.9899	0.0000***
GARCH(1; 1, 1)	0.9318	0.0257	36.1752	0.0000***
GARCH(1; 2, 1)	0.0138	0.0069	2.0222	0.0217**
GARCH(1; 1, 2)	0.0137	0.0127	1.0748	0.2829
GARCH(1; 2, 2)	0.9773	0.0148	65.709	0.0000***

Note: The estimated model is FIVECM-BEKK (1, 1) (equation systems (1.6) + (1.8)); the dependent variable is Δ*SHH$_t$*; the error structure is bivariate *t*-distribution, the estimated degrees of freedom are 7.029 with standard error 1.142. The use of an ARFIMA (1, *d*, 0) model reduces the actual sample size to 729. **Significant at 5 percent level, *** significant at 1 percent level.

that the volatility spillover moves from China's market to the Hong Kong market. Further, the information transmission is unidirectional as the other two off-diagonal coefficients are not statistically different from zero. This information flow may reflect the fact that the economy of Hong Kong relies heavily on the mainland and a substantial part of foreign direct investment (FDI) in the mainland comes from Hong Kong. Thus, information about macroeconomic conditions and policies as well as micro-market structures on the mainland would exert a very significant influence on the Hong Kong stock market. In addition, many large state-owned inland companies listed on the Hong Kong exchange (some of which are cross-listed in both markets) may also contribute to the passing of market shocks from the mainland to Hong Kong. In this sense, China's stock market can be said to lead the Hong Kong market in information absorption. Moreover, the significant diagonal elements

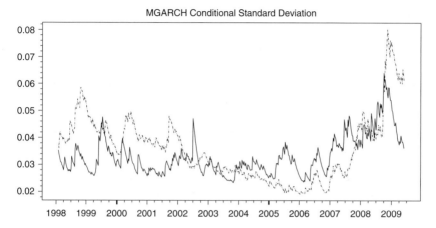

Figure 1.6   Conditional standard deviations for ΔSHH$_t$ *and* ΔHS$_t$

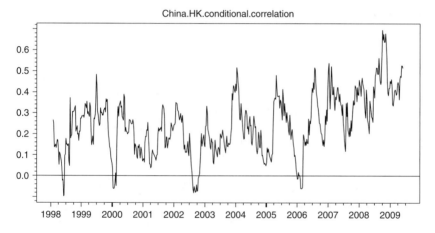

Figure 1.7   Conditional correlation between return series ΔSHH$_t$ *and*
ΔHS$_t$

of the ARCH and GARCH matrices confirm the property of conditional heteroskedasticity of the two return series. The fitted conditional standard deviations of the two series are shown in Figure 1.6, which also affirms the higher variability of mainland China's market compared to the Hong Kong market.

Figure 1.7 represents the dynamics of the contemporaneous correlation between the two index return series, Δ*SHH$_t$* and Δ*HS$_t$*. The fitted conditional correlation between the two return series was quite volatile before

Table 1.9   Model diagnostic statistics for ΔSHH_t *and* ΔHS_t

Test	Normality test (Jarque-Bera)		White noise test (Ljung-Box)		GARCH effect test (Ljung-Box)	
Series	statistic	*p*-value	statistic	*p*-value	statistic	*p*-value
ΔSHH_t	1098	0.0000***	44.278	0.0450	30.214	0.4547
ΔHS_t	49.73	0.0000***	30.460	0.4422	22.4701	0.8364

Note: The Jarque-Bera statistic asymptotically follows Chi-squared distribution with degree of freedom 2. The other Normality test, Shapiro-Wilk's test, was also employed, the conclusion is essentially the same. These results corroborate the assumption of student-t for the error terms which is based on the Normality test of the original series. *** Significant at 1 percent level.

mid-2001, while after that point in time it became less volatile and gradually settled firmly in the positive range, with only a few interruptions – a typical instance of which occurred in late 2002 when China's stock market collapsed. This pattern coincides with the increasing institutional and economic links between the two sides followed the return of Hong Kong's sovereignty to China.

Comparing Figure 1.7 with Figure 1.5, it is evident that the positive range of conditional correlation between the Chinese and Hong Kong markets is larger than that between the Chinese and US markets. Indeed, the median of the former contemporaneous correlation is 0.087, whereas that of the latter is −0.032. The model diagnostics shown in Table 1.9 reveal the adequacy of the FIVECM-BEKK (1, 1) model fitted on ΔSHH_t and ΔHS_t.

Further, the eigenvalues of $\hat{A}_1 \otimes \hat{A}_1 + \hat{B}_1 \otimes \hat{B}_1$ are 0.996, 0.977, 0.977, 0.970, all of which are less than unity. Therefore, the fitted conditional volatilities of the Chinese and Hong Kong stock return series are again stationary.

CONCLUSION

This chapter employed the FIVECM model to investigate the cointegration relations between the Chinese and USA stock markets, and between the Chinese and Hong Kong stock markets. Applying the Engle-Granger two-step procedure to estimating and constructing the cointegration vector, this chapter set up FIVECM in the general VAR framework, which reveals long-run equilibrium, short-run dynamic movement, as well as the lead-lag relations between the index return series. Further, by augmenting the FIVECM model using an MGARCH model, the dynamic dependencies in the second conditional moments of index return series are brought into the picture.

The empirical results confirm our conjecture that there are fractional cointegration relations or long-run equilibrium between the Chinese and US stock markets, and between the Chinese and Hong Kong stock markets. However, according to the estimates, only China's market appears to be bound by the cointegration relations; the other two markets do not make adjustments in response to deviations from the equilibrium. The US and Hong Kong markets are also found to lead China's market in the first conditional moments – that is, return transmissions run from both the US and Hong Kong markets to China's market. This finding is as expected, as the USA and Hong Kong are more developed and mature markets, and investors on China's stock market are likely to follow what their counterparts have done in the other two markets. However, a volatility spillover effect is shown by the estimates to flow from China's market to the Hong Kong market; thus, there is information transmission from the mainland to Hong Kong's market. This may well be due to the heavy dependence of the economy of Hong Kong on mainland China, and the increasing number of cross-listed companies on both markets.

The evolutions of the two fitted conditional correlation series reveal that China's stock market has been experiencing stronger and more stable ties with both the US and Hong Kong markets in recent years. Further, judging from the magnitude of the dynamic correlation coefficients, China's market seems to be more closely tied to the Hong Kong than the US market, as China's stock market is more positively correlated with its close neighboring market than with that of the world's leading superpower. This finding potentially provides important implications for international portfolio managers investing in these three markets.

In conclusion, although China's stock market has a long-run cointegration relation with the world's market represented by the US and Hong Kong markets, the short-run interactions, namely return and volatility transmissions, between China's market and the other markets are not ample. We believe that the ongoing liberalization and deregulation in China's financial market may increase the integration of its stock market into the world's market. In terms of future research, this study only exploits the stock market indices and their differenced series; incorporating other relevant exogenous variables into the model may shed additional light on the results.

NOTES

1. The two stock exchanges in China issue respective indices. The Shanghai All Shares Index (SHH) is more commonly quoted as representing China's stock market, because more large (especially state-owned) companies are listed on the Shanghai Stock Exchange (SHSE), the market capitalization of Shenzhen Stock Exchange (SZSE) is about half that of SHSE, and daily trading volumes also have approximately the same relative magnitudes.
2. This means that the estimate $\hat{\beta}$ converges to the true value β at a faster rate than the usual ordinary least squares (OLS) estimate.
3. This is actually one particular cointegration called C (1, 1), as defined by Granger (1986). The general concept of cointegration is that if $I(d)$ random vector y_t has some linear combination $\alpha' y_t$ which is $I(b)$ process, $0 < b \leq d$, then the component series of y_t are said to be cointegrated, denoted as $C(d,b)$.
4. The complete Gamma function has the form: $\Gamma(x) = \int_0^\infty t^{x-1} e^{-t} dt$.
5. The Approximate MLE is based on the procedure proposed by Haslett and Raftery (1989), which essentially approximates infinite autoregressive coefficients in the ARFIMA model by asymptotic values; the log-likelihood function for estimation is actually concentrated one.
6. While I(d) for $-0.5 < d$ is sometimes said to have short memory, its autocorrelation function also decays at a slower rate than a stationary process.
7. For multivariate GARCH modeling, see Appendix.
8. For detailed covariance stationarity conditions for general BEKK model, see Proposition 2.7 of Engle and Kroner (1995).
9. We then test the null hypothesis $H_0 : I(2)$ versus the alternative hypothesis that $H_1 : I(1)$, but the results reject $I(2)$.
10. The applied tests are again ADF and PP tests, yet the results are not reported here due to limitations of space.
11. Non-tradeable shares, which are of the form of state shares and legal entity shares alike, account for about two thirds of the total shares issued on China's domestic exchanges.

REFERENCES

Baillie, R.T. (1996), 'Long memory processes and fractional integration in econometrics', *Journal of Econometrics*, **73**, 5–59.

Baillie, R.T. and T. Bollerslev (1994), 'Cointegration, fractional cointegration and exchange rate dynamics', *Journal of Finance*, **49**(2), 737–45.

Bauwens, L., S. Laurent and J. Rombouts (2006), 'Multivariate GARCH models: a survey', *Journal of Applied Econometrics*, **21**(1), 79–109.

Cheung, Y.L. and S.C. Mak (1992), 'The international transmission of stock market fluctuation between the developed markets and the Asian-Pacific markets', *Applied Financial Economics*, **2**, 43–7.

Cheung, Y.W. and L.K. Ng (1992), 'Stock price dynamics and firm size: an empirical investigation', *Journal of Finance*, **47**, 1985–97.

Chung, P.J. and D.J. Liu (1994), 'Common stochastic trends in Pacific Rim stock markets', *Quarterly Review of Economics and Finance*, **34**, 241–59.

Daly, K.J. (2003), 'Southeast Asian stock market linkages: evidence from pre- and post-October 1997', *ASEAN Economic Bulletin*, **20**, 73–85.

Engle, R. and C.W.J. Granger (1987), 'Cointegration and error correction: representation, estimation and testing', *Econometrica*, **55**, 251–76.

Engle, R.F. and F.K. Kroner (1995), 'Multivariate simultaneous generalized ARCH', *Econometric Theory*, **11**, 122–50.

Eun, C.S. and S. Shim (1989), 'International transmission of stock market movements', *Journal of Financial and Quantitative Analysis*, **24**, 41–56.

Fernandez-Serrano, J.L. and S. Sosvilla-Rivero (2001), 'Modeling evolving long-run relationships: the linkages between stock markets in Asia', *Japan and the World Economy*, **13**, 145–60.

Fernandez-Serrano, J.L. and S. Sosvilla-Rivero (2003), 'Modeling the linkages between US and Latin American stock markets', *Applied Economics*, **35**, 1423–34.

Ghosh, A., R. Saidi and K. Johnson (1998), 'What moves the Asia-Pacific stock market: US or Japan?' *Financial Review*, **34**, 159–70.

Granger, C.W.J. (1986), 'Developments in the study of cointegrated economic variables', *Oxford Bulletin of Economics and Statistics*, **48**, 213–28.

Gregory, A.W. and B.E. Hansen (1996), 'Residual-based tests for cointegration in models with regime shifts', *Journal of Econometrics*, **70**, 99–126.

Grubel, H.G. (1968), 'Internationally diversified portfolios: welfare gains and capital flows', *American Economic Review*, **58**, 1299–314.

Haslett, J. and A.E. Raftery (1989), 'Space-time modeling with long-memory dependence: assessing Ireland's wind power resource', *Journal of Royal Statistical Society Series C*, **38**, 1–21.

Hilliard, J. (1979), 'The relationship between equity indices on world exchanges', *Journal of Finance*, **34**, 103–14.

Huang, B.N., C.W. Yang and J.W.S. Hu (2000), 'Causality and cointegration of stock markets among the United States, Japan and the South China Growth Triangle', *International Review of Financial Analysis*, **9**, 281–97.

Hurst, H.E. (1951), 'Long-term storage capacity of reservoirs', *Transactions of the American Society of Civil Engineers*, **116**, 770–99.

Janakiramanan, S. and A.S. Lamba (1998), 'An empirical examination of linkages between Pacific-Basin stock markets', *Journal of International Financial Markets, Institutions and Money*, **8**, 155–73.

Jeon, B.N. and G.M. Von Furstenberg (1990),'Growing international comovement in stock price indexes', *Quarterly Review of Economics and Business*, **30**(3), 15–30.

Johansen, S. (1988a), 'The mathematical structure of error correction models', *Contemporary Mathemetics*, **8**, 359–86.

Johnson, R. and L. Soenen (2002), 'Asian economic integration and stock market comovement', *Journal of Financial Research*, **25**, 141–57.

Kasa, K. (1992), 'Common stochastic trends in international stock markets', *Journal of Monetary Economics*, **29**, 95–124.

Koop, G.(1994), 'An objective Bayesian analysis of common stochastic trends in international stock prices and exchange rates', *Journal of Empirical Finance*, **1**, 343–64.

Lee, S.B. and K.J. Kim (1994), 'Does the October 1987 crash strengthen the co-movement in stock price indexes?', *Quarterly Review of Economics and Business*, **3**, 89–102.

Lessard, D.R. (1974), 'World, national and industry factors in equity returns', *Journal of Finance*, **29**, 379–91.

Levy, H. and M. Sarnat (1970), 'International diversification of investment portfolios', *American Economic Review*, **60**, 668–75.

Lien, D. and Y. Tse (1999), 'Fractional cointegration and futures hedging', *Journal of Futures Markets*, **19**, 457–74.

Masih, A.M.M. and R. Masih (1997), 'Dynamic linkages and the propagation mechanism driving major international stock markets: an analysis of the pre-and-post-crash eras', *Quarterly Review of Economics and Finance*, **37**, 859–88.

Masih, A.M.M. and R. Masih (1999), 'Are Asian stock market fluctuations due mainly to intra-regional contagion effects? Evidence based on Asian emerging stock markets', *Pacific Basin Finance Journal*, **7**, 251–82.

Narayan, P.K. and R. Smyth (2005a), 'Are OECD stock prices characterized by a random walk? Evidence from sequential trend break and panel data models', *Applied Financial Economics*, **15**, 547–56.

Narayan, P.K. and R. Smyth (2006), 'Random walk versus multiple trend breaks in stock prices: evidence from fifteen European markets', *Applied Financial Economics Letters*, **2**(1), 1–7.

Ng, T.H. (2002), 'Stock market linkages in Southeast Asia', *Asian Economic Journal*, **16**, 353–77.

Ng, S. and P. Perron (1995), 'Unit root tests in ARMA models with data-dependent methods for the selection of the truncation lag', *Journal of the American Statistical Association*, **90**, 268–81;

Pan, M.S., Y.A. Liu and H.J. Roth (1999), 'Common stochastic trends and volatility in Asian-Pacific equity markets', *Global Finance Journal*, **10**, 161–72.

Panto, D.B., V.P. Lessig and M. Joy (1976), 'Comovement of international equity markets: a taxonomic approach', *Journal of Financial and Quantitative Analysis*, **11**, 415–32.

Ripley, D.M.(1973), 'Systematic elements in the linkage of national stock market indices', *Review of Economics and Statistics*, **55**, 356–61.

Sheng, H.C. and A.H. Tu (2000), 'A study of cointegration and variance decomposition among national equity indices before and during the period of the Asian financial crisis', *Journal of Multinational Financial Management*, **10**, 345–65.

Shimotsu. K. and P.C.B. Phillips (2005), 'Exact local whittle estimation of fractional integration', *Annals of Statistics*, **33**(4), 1890–933.

Siklos, P.L. and P. Ng (2001), 'Integration among Asia-Pacific and international stock markets: common stochastic trends and regime shifts', *Pacific Economic Review*, **6**, 89–110.

Stock, J.H. and M.W. Watson (1993). 'A simple estimator of cointegrating vectors in higher order integrated systems', *Econometrica*, **61**, 783–820.

Von Furstenberg, G.M. and B.N. Jeon (1989), 'International stock price movements: links and messages', *Brookings Papers on Economic Activity*, **1**, 125–79.

APPENDIX

To estimate the second moment, let

$$H_t \equiv \operatorname{cov}_{t-1}(\varepsilon_t) \equiv \begin{pmatrix} \sigma_t^{11} & \sigma_t^{12} \\ \sigma_t^{21} & \sigma_t^{22} \end{pmatrix}$$

denote the variance-covariance matrix of ε_t conditioning on past information. The most flexible MGARCH model is the BEKK model, proposed by Engle and Kroner (1995) in the following form*:

$$H_t = A_0 A_0' + \sum_{i=1}^{p} A_i (\varepsilon_{t-i}\varepsilon_{t-i}') A_i' + \sum_{j=1}^{q} B_j H_{t-j} B_j' \qquad (1.7)$$

Here, A_0 is a lower triangular matrix, $A_i's$ and $B_j's$ are unrestricted coefficient matrices and H_t is symmetric and positive semi-definite. In general, allowing p = 1 and q = 1 suffices for modeling volatility in financial time series. With this formulation, the dynamics of H_t are fully displayed in that the dynamics of the conditional variance as well as the conditional covariance are modeled directly, thereby allowing for volatility spillovers across series to be observed. The volatility spillover effect is indicated by the off-diagonal entries of coefficient matrices A_1 and B_1. This can be clearly seen from the expansion of BEKK (1,1) into individual dynamic equations:

$$\sigma_t^{11} = (A_0^{11})^2 + [A_1^{11}\varepsilon_{1t-1} + A_1^{12}\varepsilon_{2t-1}]^2 + [(B_1^{11})^2\sigma_{t-1}^{11} + 2B_1^{12}B_1^{11}\sigma_{t-1}^{12}$$

$$+ (B_1^{12})^2\sigma_{t-1}^{22}]$$

$$\sigma_t^{22} = (A_0^{21})^2 + (A_0^{22})^2 + [A_1^{21}\varepsilon_{1t-1} + A_1^{22}\varepsilon_{2t-1}]^2 + [(B_1^{21})^2\sigma_{t-1}^{11}$$

$$+ 2B_1^{21}B_1^{22}\sigma_{t-1}^{21} + (B_1^{22})^2\sigma_{t-1}^{22}]$$

$$\sigma_t^{12} = A_0^{11}A_0^{21} + A_1^{11}A_1^{21}\varepsilon_{1t-1}^2 + (A_1^{11}A_1^{22} + A_1^{12}A_1^{21})\varepsilon_{1t-1}\varepsilon_{2t-1}$$

$$+ A_1^{12}A_1^{22}\varepsilon_{2t-1}^2 + B_1^{11}B_1^{21}\sigma_{t-1}^{11} + (B_1^{12}B_1^{21} + B_1^{11}B_1^{22})\sigma_{t-1}^{12} + B_1^{12}B_1^{22}\sigma_{t-1}^{22}$$

$$(1.8)$$

The above equation system is more complicated than a univariate GARCH model because of the interactions among the two conditional variances and residuals. In the case of student-*t* distribution, which is assumed for the error vector of (1.6) in this chapter, the log likelihood of the bivariate FIVECM-MGARCH ((1.6)+(1.8)) model is:

$$\log L(\theta, v \mid Y) = T^*G(v) - \frac{1}{2}\sum_{t=1}^{T}|H_t| - \frac{v+2}{2}\sum_{t=1}^{T}\ln[1 + (v-2)^{-1}\varepsilon'_t H_t^{-1}\varepsilon_t]$$

$$G(v) = \ln(\Gamma(v+2)/2) - \ln(\pi(v-2)) - \ln(\Gamma(v/2))$$

(1.9)

where θ denotes the parameter vector (in both mean and variance equations) to be estimated; $\varepsilon_t = (\varepsilon_{1t}, \varepsilon_{2t})'$ is the error vector from (1.6); $H_t \equiv \text{cov}_{t-1}(\varepsilon_t)$ is the conditional variance-covariance matrix of error vector; T is sample size; $\Gamma(.)$ is Gamma function; and v is the degree of freedom of the bivariate student-t distribution which will be estimated along with the other parameters. The parameters in the conditional mean and variance equations enter the likelihood function through ε_t and H_t, respectively. Since the conditional variance matrix H_t can be recursively evaluated according to equation (1.7) or (1.8), the log likelihood function equation (1.9) can be calculated without extreme complexity. The log likelihood function is then maximized to obtain the estimates of the parameters, conditioning on the starting value of conditional variance; the popular optimization algorithm BHHH is employed in maximizing the likelihood.

NOTE

* The complete form of BEKK as outlined by Engle and Kroner (1995) accommodates more generality (interested readers are referred to the original paper); the model (1.7) here is essentially the BEKK $(1, p, q)$ shown in their paper.

2. Condition constraints and player behavior in China's stock market

Huaiqing Zhu and Changfeng Pan

INTRODUCTION

China has undergone a process of reform of its non-tradeable shares, but stock market observers are still puzzled by the deviation of the share price from broader macroeconomic trends. Financial economics assumes that the stock market is a barometer of national economic performance. From a long-term perspective, trends in share prices reflect trends in a country's economy. When an economy moves through the four stages of an economic cycle – recession, recovery, growth and decline – the stock market will simultaneously experience a similar cycle. The reason why the performance of the stock market is parallel to the performance of the national economy is largely due to the fact that a stronger economy reflected by listed companies' greater profitability, households' higher income and investors' positive expectation will usually push up the stock market, and vice versa. In China, however, a very unique phenomenon has been witnessed of severe deviation of stock prices from the macro economy (Pan, 2006). Focusing on the evidence captured in the first half of the 2000s, this chapter discusses the condition constraints placed on the stock market and market players' behavior under such constraints. The chapter seeks to provide insights into the situation in China, and suggests that, if those constraints cannot be removed and if there are no significant changes in the behavior of players, the Chinese stock market (a government policy-oriented market) is most likely to remain much the same in the foreseeable future.

CONDITION CONSTRAINTS IN CHINA'S STOCK MARKET

Numerous research papers published in China have examined the role of stock market player behavior in this rapidly emerging stock market. The best way to understand such behavior is to investigate the endogenous constraints placed on the market (Li and Zhu, 2004). Under circumstances of economic transition, the institutional transition setting and the underlying ethics of China's stock market have led to particular constraints on the institutional and structural transition of the stock market. In the context of such constraints, the behavior of market players will have very different characteristics from that seen in a mature market (Wang, 2004).

The background of the state-owned asset management system has had a profound effect on the institutional and structural transition of China's stock market. Its constraints, in essence, involve the restrictions imposed on property rights (Cheng, 2002), which effectively determine the nature of the Chinese stock market system and impose restrictions on the market in a range of ways, which are detailed below.

Administrative Regulations Under the Institutional and Structural Transition Constraints

The logical starting point of China's stock market transition rests with the financial control implemented as a response to financial stress. These new government financial controls involved the reform of state-owned enterprises (SOEs), and were aimed at solving the financial difficulties of SOEs. The rapid development of the stock market is owing to its 'commitment' to perform the function assigned to it. The non-tradeable share reform, which came at a later stage after one or two unsuccessful attempts to reduce state holdings in listed companies, was also determined by the state-owned asset management system, reflecting the weakening of traditional socialist ideology in China and efforts to establish a modern enterprise system in SOEs. Under these conditions, and in order to ensure the conformity of the stock market with progressive economic reform of China, the government will implement comprehensive control and intervention in the selection of listed companies, the size of financing, initial public offering (IPO) prices, the overall market size and even the fluctuation of market prices.

Shareholding Structure and Marketability of Listed Companies

In order to maintain an economic system that is dominated by public ownership, it is necessary to make full use of the market financing function, and to ensure that listed enterprises remain state owned. The government has made the following provisions regarding the core of the shareholding structure by making use of its status as provider of the compulsory system: (1) in respect to the shareholding structure of SOEs, the government specified the holding position of state-owned shares and legal-person shares, and formed the basic shareholding structure of listed companies – that it be dominated by state-owned shares and legal-person shares; (2) in order to maintain the state-holding nature of state-owned shares and legal-person shares, the government restricted the circulation of state-owned shares and legal-person shares in the market. In the mid-2000s, all legal-person shares became tradeable, but the amount of holdings allowed for large shareholders remained subject to restrictions.

Government-dominated Corporate Governance Structure

In the vast majority of the listed companies in China, the government retains a majority stake. To maintain its interest, the government selects who will be appointed as chairman of the board of directors, chief executive officer (CEO) and other senior executives of a company. This government-dominated corporate governance structure will lead to certain consequences, as outlined in the following. First is a failure to conduct fair assessments of business performance. Since the market is unable to price the non-tradeable state-owned shares and legal-person shares, the listed companies cannot be fairly priced. Second, the standard used by the state to evaluate the management of state-owned assets is focused on whether the value of these assets is appreciated. The simplest logical measurement employed, therefore, is the earning per state-owned share. Third, a series of policies and measures were introduced to increase this earning per state-owned share, such as the high IPO price, high-price rights issue, high-price new issue and high retained earning ratio. Although they are suspected of damaging the interests of minority individual tradeable-share holders, these policies and measures have been welcomed by large shareholders, who are well protected by stock exchange rules (Hu and Long, 2010).

Prudent Regulations on Market Access, Floatation and Share Prices

It is important to note that the Chinese government views the stock market as crucial to the country's economic development because it has provided an alternative to bank finance and a mechanism that is capable of facilitating reform in the public sector of the Chinese economic system. In order to ensure the full effect of this function, with regard to the institutional provision the government has implemented a number of discriminatory policies, namely: (a) encouraging the financing of SOEs by listing and restricting the listing of private enterprises; (b) restricting the funds of state-owned listed companies, banks and SOEs to access the stock market; and (c) imposing tight controls over the licenses granted to financial institutions. The government has also implemented quota control systems on the total market size and the size of each floatation. The IPO price is also determined by the government rather than by fair competition in the market. Frequent government intervention has meant that China's stock market is known as a 'policy-oriented market' (Zuo, 2006; He, 2009; Song, et al., 2009).

However, since China's World Trade Organization (WTO) entry in 2001, globalization has penetrated into every area of the Chinese economy. The process of globalization has produced, and will continue to produce, significant impacts on China's stock market in the three ways outlined below.

Primary function of the stock market

When China initiated its enterprise reform in the mid-1980s, the banking sector replaced the government fiscal sector as the main source of long-term funds. However, the banking sector, which had to improve its asset-liability management, had a very small margin to meet increasing capital demand from SOEs. China, therefore, gave higher priority to the supply of long-term funds for SOEs through the stock market. The stock market also relieved state banks' non-performing loans burden and diversified the credit risks involved. Nevertheless, the post-WTO environment and accelerated economic globalization in the 2000s and the 2010s will inevitably alter the resource allocation pattern within China's stock market. Establishing the sole function of the stock market as fundraising for SOEs violates the primary nature and function of a free market, instead working on the basis of segmentation and direct government control (Fan, 2008; Gao and Li, 2009).

Moving towards an efficient market

The course of globalization is a process of comprehensive evolution from an emerging stock market towards an integrated, efficient and more mature market structure. The core of this process rests with the envisaged market pricing function through free competition over all aspects of stock offering and trading.

Moving from a segmented market to an integrated market

A global market must be an open market. The interaction with the world's mature markets calls for an end to market entry restrictions and the opening of the market to all potential players. The development of the market can only evolve from segmentation to integration, from closing to opening. New market players and new stakeholders introduced by the market opening will bring a comprehensive change in the market structure – from a structure of listed companies, and structure of investors, to market pricing mechanisms, market valuation methods, and then to the innovation of risk management tools with which both systematic and non-systematic risk may be effectively hedged through the market rather than through government intervention. In short, the marketization of the Chinese stock market requires that the excessive reliance on compulsory administrative provisions be abandoned (Zuo, 2006).

GOVERNMENT BEHAVIOR AND THE DEVIATION OF STOCK PRICE FROM THE MACRO ECONOMY

Condition constraints determine player behavior while players' behavior determines the market. In the Chinese stock market, the behavior of the government under the given constraints inevitably leads to the phenomenon of the deviation of stock price from the macro economy. Figure 2.1 and Figure 2.2 show how the stock indexes in China deviated from macro economic performance over the period 2001–05.

Public Ownership Dominance and its Consequences

In the process of restructuring SOEs into listed companies, to maintain the dominant position of public ownership the government must retain a

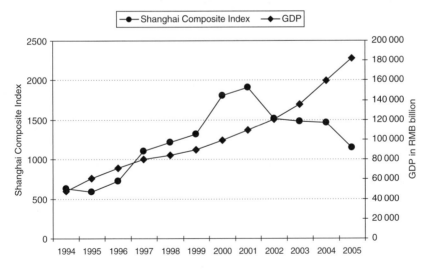

Source: Calculated based on Shanghai Stock Exchange database.

Figure 2.1 Shanghai Composite Index versus GDP

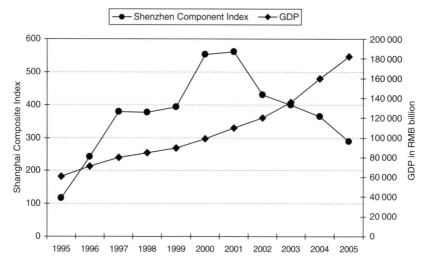

Source: Calculated based on Shenzhen Stock Exchange database.

Figure 2.2   Shenzhen Component Index versus GDP

majority stake in the newly listed companies' equity structure. The trade-ability of shares was thus restricted through the system, based on which, as discussed in the second section, equity was divided into two categories: tradeable and non-tradeable shares.

The most direct consequences of this division included that: (1) due to the fact that the market could not reasonably price listed companies over two thirds of the equity of listed companies was non-tradeable; (2) government-oriented corporate governance, non-transparent manage-ment, insider trading and manipulation of stock prices became common-place among listed companies; (3) the interests of minority shareholders were damaged; and (4) almost all listed companies were in favor of a low dividend payout ratio, so investors had to turn to the market for short-term capital gain.

Segmentation of Financial Sectors and Its Consequences

As mentioned above, China's stock market was created to alleviate the financial stress and difficulties faced by SOEs, and to provide a channel through which households could directly support economic and enter-prise reforms, rather than via an intermediary such as a bank. It was a deliberate decision of the government to establish a segmented financial system, whereby all of the financial sectors were kept separate and funds from commercial banks were kept away from the stock market.[1] The system of institutional segmentation has enabled the government to directly intervene in stock prices. For example, in 2002 some well-informed institutional investors used funds raised from the repo market to purchase large quantities of shares. A government investigation was launched, and a penalty was imposed, but the market plunged. The government's intervention to cool down the overheated expansion increased the government's burden in maintaining the unilateral and steady rise of stock price indicators. Once the stock price dropped dramatically and the IPO encountered difficulties, the government had to create and implement a series of favorable policies, or 'save-the-market policies' as the Chinese media referred to them. Table 2.1 presents data on two such actions carried out in 2001–05, compared to a total of three in 1994–2000 and only one between 2006 and 2009. Figure 2.3 depicts stock exchange index trends before and after the government released its save-the-market policies.

Why did China's stock market experience a long-term unilateral slump from 2001 to 2005? On the surface, this may be because the government revived and extended reforms to transform non-tradeable shares into tradeable ones, or because it introduced a new rule and plan to reduce state holdings in listed companies, which led to the excess of supply over demand, resulting in the share price plunging. The real reason for the slump, however, is the system of segmented banking and securities sectors. The absence of access to credit in the stock market means the offering of new shares equates to an absolute increase in share supply; if a corresponding increase in demand is not foreseeable, investors will inevitably expect a share price drop, and the share price will experience a further downturn in a bearish market. In 2001, the consensus was reached that all non-tradeable shares should be tradeable in the stock market. In terms of the size of the stock market, this means the quantity of tradeable shares would at least double. On the one hand, the banking and securities sectors are separate and funds from commercial banks are kept away from the stock market. On the other hand, under such circumstances, the share price will drop. If the expectation of a share price drop persists, the whole market will drop continuously. The underlying fundamental cause of the deviation in the price trend in the stock market and the macro economy from 2001 to 2005 is the absence of services such as margin borrowing, which enables an investor to take out a loan from a bank to buy stock, and of a financial system in which the banking, insurance, trust and securities sectors are integrated rather than separate.

*Table 2.1   Government policies introduced to save the market
             (1994–2008)*

Date	Background	Policy content	Market reaction
30 July 1994	The bear market continued for one and a half years.	'Four No' measures: (1) 5.5 billion new shares shall not be offered; (2) no income tax will be levied on share transaction; (3) state-held shares will not be traded; (4) listed companies shall not make new allotment arbitrarily.	SSE Composite Index raised 33.2 percent on that day, and increased from 325 to 1052 in the next 33 business days.
18 May 1995	SSE Composite Index dropped from 1052.94 (13 September 1994) to 582.39 (17 May 1995).	State Council's Notice on the Suspension of T-bonds Futures was announced.	SSE Composite Index peaked to 897 and increased by 54 percent within three days.
19 May 1999	SSE Composite Index slumped from 1510 to 1059 from 12 May 1997 to 18 May 1999.	Insurance funds were allowed to trade shares. The central bank announced the seventh round decrease in interest rates.	SSE Composite Index raised by 4.64 percent on that day, and grew by 64 percent in the next 30 business days.
23 June 2002	In 2001, the stock market continued to go down due to the expected government sell-off of state-owned shares.	The government canceled the plan to reduce state holdings in listed companies.	SSE Composite Index increased by 9 percent on the next day.
2 February 2004	The stock market was shocked by fears of SARS.	A nine-point guideline announced on opening-up and stable development of the capital market.	SSE Composite Index stepped up to 1783 on 7 April 2004.
18 September 2008	Global financial crisis; reduction of institutional investors' holdings of formerly non-tradeable shares; SSE Composite Index dropped by 68.5 percent over one year.	Stamp duty on share trading slashed; SOEs encouraged to increase their holdings of other companies' shares.	SSE Composite Index surged by 9.46 percent with a growth rate that peaked to 10.7 percent in the next four days.

Source: Securities Times Database (http:// www.stcn.com) – various editions.

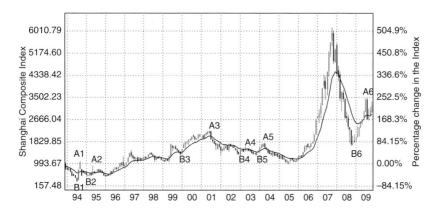

Note: B Before the policy release; A after the policy release.

Source: Calculated based on Shanghai Stock Exchange database.

Figure 2.3 *Market response to government save-the-market policies (1994–2009)*

Supervisory Authorities' Behavior and its Consequences

The function of the stock market is set by the central government in China, as are the constraints placed on the supervisory system in the stock market. This determines the behavior of supervisory authorities, who must fulfill the financing tasks assigned to them by the state. Subject to the constraints, China Securities Supervisory Commission (CSSC) as one of the most important players in the stock market can only make the choices outlined below in respect to its behavior.

Supervision priority

The CSSC's first priority is to ensure the success of IPOs and to raise funds for SOEs. The focus of supervision is to safeguard the financing function of the stock market. In the absence of a sell short mechanism, to ensure the smooth offering of new shares, the CSSC must maintain the unilateral stock price hike and promulgate temporary provisions and policies as required to control the share price. The consequence of excessive supply of some unnecessary provisions is artificial share price fluctuation. Under such circumstances, some tasks assumed to be the responsibility of the supervisory authorities may be neglected or ignored, such as the protection of investor interests, ensuring the compliance of companies' liabilities and commitment on capital investment as specified in listing announcements, and investigations into insider trading and market manipulation.

Supervision mode

Listing an enterprise is a behavior related to a company's contract. Once a company is listed, all relevant information about that company, including its governance structure, use of capital, progress of operation, asset and liability structure, performance and material changes in the company's business environment, must be disclosed. This is necessary for contracts to be performed. Active supervision of the contract performance of listed companies is important to protect the interests of investors. The CSSC has adopted a passive approach to the supervision of contract performance, in contrast to the very active supervision and regulation of the listing quota, size and price, which should be determined by the market rather than by the supervisory authorities. This focus on the financing aspect rather than the compliance of listed companies' organizational behavior will inevitably lead to a deviation from the purpose that supervision and regulation are supposed to serve.

Offside regulatory behavior

The deviation of the role of supervision by supervisory directors is reflected in offside regulatory behavior: supervisory authorities detour from what they should and could do well, instead doing what should be done by the market and what they do not perform well. First, they ignore the self-development rules of the market, controlling the size of finance by distributing the listing quota through administrative instruction. Second, they decide on the IPO price through an administrative examination and approval system. Third, they intervene or seek to intervene in the stock price index through administrative measures. Fourth, they pay very little attention to the corporate governance of listed companies. Finally, they neglect the need to protect the rights and interests of tradeable-share holders. The success of channeling funds to SOEs has been at the expense of individual investors (Zhang, et al., 2008).

The impact of this supervisory behavior on share price fluctuation is obvious: the entanglement of offside supervision and the government's direct regulation of the stock market makes the IPO price deviate from the fundamentals of listed companies. The 'one-way' market leads to an absence of the sell short mechanism. As a result, the offering of new shares can only progress with a continuous stock price hike boosted by buying long. Under these circumstances, the price in China's stock market has been seriously distorted. The long-term and significant overpricing of listed companies has become common. This has a negative impact on the development of the stock market, which is reflected in a number of ways, as discussed below.

Distortion of resource allocation function

Under the administrative pricing system, if the offering price of a stock is impractically high, its market value will be much higher than its intrinsic value or the company's real value. Even worse, because the government holds a majority position in a company's equity, when that company's performance is unsatisfactory management will not be ticked off because a government-dominated company will not undergo hostile acquisition through a secondary market, as occurs in overseas stock markets. On the contrary, this situation will ironically encourage the new share offering and refinancing of enterprises. The financing function of the stock market for SOEs will be further emphasized.

Increase in short-term speculation

Overestimated stock prices will result in exuberant short-term speculation and a highly volatile market, and can easily trigger a financial crisis. Given the segmentation of the banking and securities sectors in China, the large amount of money needed to maintain a high stock price in the secondary market comes from financial institutions including commercial banks through illegal channels. Therefore, the base to maintain the high stock price structure is fragile. Moreover, in relation to the overly high stock price, it is almost impossible to obtain a steady long-term return (by holding stocks for a long period of time) that is higher than the interest paid on long-term bank deposits. Therefore, the capital in the market has to aim at short-term speculation and capital gains.

Dilution of price discovery function

The administratively overestimated stock price makes the stock market lose its price discovery function. In mature markets, the stock price is obtained through a full bid, while the overestimated stock price in China's stock market due to administrative pricing results in a chaotic price system, and the market has basically lost its function of stock price discovery.

Supervisory offside behavior has led China's stock market to become an inefficient market. In such a market, both the IPO price and the trading price have been overestimated for a long period of time. Since China's WTO entry in 2001, China's stock market has been increasingly integrated with the world markets. In this context, the unilateral stock price drop from 2001 to 2005 can be seen not only as an inevitable trend of globalization, leading China's stock market to adopt more market-oriented valuation standards, but also as the corollary of the restoration of investment concept and the assortment of pricing mechanisms. In other words, the deviation of the share price from the macroeconomic developments of the period is to be expected and welcomed.

LISTED COMPANY BEHAVIOR AND STOCK PRICE FLUCTUATION

Compared with other criteria, the price criterion is the only known criterion that will not lead to (or only rarely leads to) economic waste in the traditional sense (Barzel, 1974). In China's stock market, a place for allocating capital, it is the government that decides who should be listed and how much should be allotted. Under this non-price criterion, the behavior undertaken by enterprises to obtain a listing permission and their behavior after the listing are unique, and have a particular impact on stock price fluctuation.

Seek Public Listings

Under the administrative examination and approval system, a company's listing position is granted without much consideration of its fundamentals. The behavior of enterprises seeking to be listed includes the following: (1) companies spend a significant amount of money on lobbying relevant government departments at various levels, which breeds a high level of trading between money and rights; (2) under the administrative IPO pricing system, to achieve a higher IPO price and raise more funds, companies manipulate false revenue and net profit, and become listed through collusion with local government, and legal and accounting firms, resulting in the situation where 'bad money drives out good money'; and (3) companies wait in a queue to obtain an IPO qualification to be rationed. Figure 2.4 illustrates the downturn pattern of the IPO on the poorly performing stock market in the first half of the 2000s, a period when the country's economic growth remained strong.

'Tunneling' of Listed Companies

The shareholding structure of listed companies affects their governance structure in terms of the make-up of ownership and ownership concentration. Excessive concentration of ownership can trigger the problem of majority shareholders damaging the interests of minority shareholders. The formation of a more balanced distribution of shares has a positive impact on a company's governance, while too little decentralization of ownership results in higher agency costs for shareholders. Shareholders usually prefer free riding, yet this weakens the influence of monitoring the management of the company and creates a situation in which shareholders' wealth is not maximized. As for ownership more generally, the inclusion of shareholders with a range of interests is important to improving corporate governance.

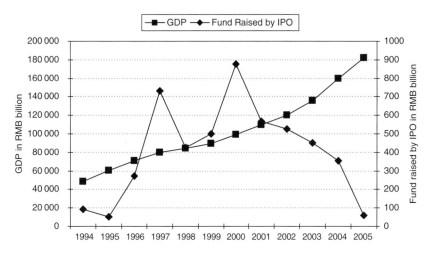

Source: Securities Times Database (http://www.stcn.com) – various editions.

Figure 2.4 Fund raised by IPO versus GDP

Before China commenced its reform to transform non-tradeable shares into tradeable shares in August 2005, 70 percent of listed companies were state-holding companies, and 70 percent of the total equity of listed companies was non-tradeable. This resulted in a number of problems for China's listed companies, as described in the following. First, an over-concentration of state ownership and the unrestricted behavior of majority shareholders have thwarted the protection of the interests of shareholders of tradeable shares. Second, single ownership, and the consequent absolute control of the business, by holders of non-tradeable shares led to excessive credit guarantees, and an excessive use of funds by majority shareholders. Third, as state-owned shares were non-tradeable, it was impossible to determine the company's market value, which is ordinarily a major indicator of business performance. Instead, the state could only take net assets as a measure for assessment. This situation has paved the way for tunneling, an illegal business practice in which a majority shareholder or high-level company insider directs company assets or future business to themselves for personal gain. Actions such as excessive executive compensation, dilutive share measures, asset sales and personal loan guarantees can all be considered forms of tunneling. The common thread is the loss to minority shareholders, whose ownership is lessened or otherwise devalued through inappropriate actions that harm the overall value of the company.

According to official statistics,[2] the 'tunneling effect', deriving from absolute domination of non-tradeable shares in listed companies, is reflected in a number of ways. First, the irregular huge capital occupation by majority shareholders directly frustrates the normal production and operation of listed companies. Up until the end of 2002, 676 listed companies in China had provided RMB96.7 billion to controlling shareholders and their subsidiaries. In 2003, capital occupation by majority shareholders was found in 623 companies, and amounted to a total of RMB57.7 billion. Up to the end of 2004, the amount of capital occupied dropped to RMB50.9 billion. To 30 June 2005, there were still 131 companies whose controlling shareholders occupied more than RMB20 million of the aforesaid listed companies – the amount occupied was RMB48 billion in total. Until the end of 2005, although the RMB14.4 billion of 164 listed companies that had been occupied had been settled, RMB36.5 billion of 234 listed companies was still occupied by majority shareholders. Second, the shareholding structure of Chinese listed companies is such that the controlling shareholders and shareholders of tradeable shares have no common interest base. In order to realize their own interests, controlling shareholders have made use of listed companies to offer irregular and malicious guarantees. The 301 listed companies in 2005 are exemplary: 157, or up to 52.16 percent, were involved in providing guarantees, totaling RMB28.479 billion; the total guarantees of the top 20 companies with the highest guarantee amounted to RMB14.589 billion; 13 companies had a total guarantee equal to above 50 percent of their net assets as of 31 December 2005; and the guarantee of ST Ming Feng, ST Ya Hua and China Union Holdings accounted for over 100 percent of their net assets.

Third, majority shareholders encroached the interests of listed companies through a tremendous quantity of related transactions. According to the statistics developed by the Securities Times, among the 719 listed companies in Shanghai and Shenzhen Stock Exchanges in China in 2000, 93.2 percent disclosed related transactions of different types, while this figure was 95 percent and 97 percent in 2004 and 2005, respectively. Majority shareholders often replaced good assets of listed companies with their own inferior assets; related transactions enabled listed companies to transfer profits to controlling shareholders through the acquisition of raw materials or the sale of products.

Share Price Fluctuation

The share price of listed companies is ultimately determined by their profitability. The overestimated stock price of companies that get listed by forging profits will ultimately regress to be aligned with the fundamentals of the company.

Upon the combination of non-tradeable and tradeable shares and the unification of listed companies' equities, the value of a company will be reflected in its market value. The phenomenon whereby the interests of majority shareholders are irrelevant to the tradeable stock price will be eliminated, as will the differentiation between the rights of shareholders of tradeable and non-tradeable shares. When shareholders find out their common interest – the maximization of market value determined by the stock price – the tunneling behavior of management seeking to transfer interests to majority shareholders will be likely to end. However, the rational pricing of listed companies requires that the overestimation of share prices be reduced to a reasonable level. In 2001–02, the expectations in response to the non-tradeable share reform, and the resultant full circulation of company shares, is just one of the factors that led to the 2001–05 unilateral price drop in China's stock market, and the market's deviation from macroeconomic fundamentals. Given such expectations, ensuring that the same shares enjoy equal rights and the unification of shareholders' interests will inevitably require the rational regression of the tradeable stock price that was overestimated.

INVESTOR BEHAVIOR AND STOCK PRICE FLUCTUATION

The behavior of investors in China's stock market, under certain constraints and conditions, also shows its own particularity (Feng et al., 2004), which is summarized below.

Absence of Selling Short

In the stock market, the products usually available include ordinary shares, investment funds and stock index futures. Investors can purchase a share and hold it for dividend to be paid by the listed company or/and sell it at a higher price at some future time for capital gain. If the share price is anticipated to drop, investors can sell short by selling futures contracts today and buying back the share from the physical market on the settlement date to execute the contracts. Alternatively, they close out the futures position by buying the same number of futures contracts at a point in time prior to the settlement date, to gain from the net difference of today's price and the price at the future time.

Given the absence of selling short in China's stock market, the 'rational' behavior of investors is to find an underestimated share, buy at a low price (the process known as value discovery) and then sell at a higher price

(Cai and Zhang, 2008). A lack of alternative investment instruments in the stock market has, on the one hand, compelled investors to buy and hold shares passively, and then, if they are able to, pour a huge amount of money into the market to create new demand for the same share and drive the price up so that they will ultimately gain as a market maker. However, a lack of risk management instruments has, on the other hand, made it almost impossible for investors to hedge their exposed risk if the market crashes without warning.

Value Discovery and free Riding

The information required for investment decision-making in the stock market falls into four categories. The first is that of micro fundamentals, including ratios and other measures of financial characteristics and performance. Those companies with the most favorable combination of indicators would then be selected. The second is macro fundamentals, such as the inflation rate, household disposable income and export (Sun, 2009). These fundamentals reflect the overall economic climate and how developments in the overall economy would impact companies and sectors. The top-down approach, based on the analysis of the macro fundamentals, should be used to determine those sectors most likely to be favored and those sectors likely to be harmed (Zhai et al., 2010). Investors can combine the top-down approach with the bottom-up approach based on the analysis of micro fundamentals to select the most robust companies within the favored sectors. Similarly, when selling shares of companies in the less favored sectors, the first shares to be sold should be those from the least robust companies in that sector (Hu, 2007). The third category involves market prices, including individual share prices, the stock market index, and index futures prices, and their trading volumes. When the market is above what the fundamentals would support, an alternative approach to adopt is technical analysis. This approach seeks to explain and forecast share price movements on the basis of their past behavior. The final category is government industry policy and local development plans that might favor a particular sector or company in the foreseeable future.

As far as the costs of information searching are concerned, individual investors in China have always been at a disadvantage. Moreover, institutional investors can take advantage of seminars, forums and other functions where they have the opportunity to obtain new knowledge and insider information. This has enabled institutional investors to undertake the role of initiator of value discovery and make full use of individual investors' free-riding behavior to obtain huge profits through market

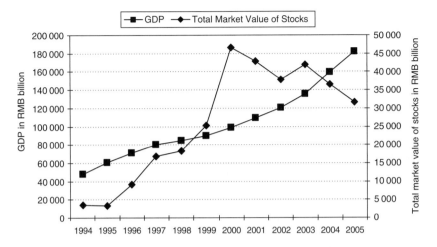

Source: Calculated based on Shanghai Stock Exchange database.

Figure 2.5   Total share market value versus GDP

making and market manipulation. Even worse, many institutional investors have been engaged in producing false profits news and false financial decision-making news by colluding with listed companies to maximize their interests.

Deviation of Share Prices from Economic Dynamism in 2001–05

Because of investors' long position in the market without any other financial instruments available for hedging purposes, once the stock market crashes, although investors usually prefer to limit their trading, their only choice is to sell the shares they hold. Given the predominance of individual investors and their speculative and short-term orientation, people sell shares when prices drop; and when they sell their shares, prices drop further. When people successively sell shares, only institutional investors holding a large proportion of tradeable shares remain in the market. When the so-called value discovery can no longer attract individual investors, institutional investors then have to sell shares, driving the market into a real panic, by which time institutional investors will have turned out to be the real losers (Jiang and Yang, 2009). To some extent, this explains why the stock market price deviated to a large extent from macroeconomic dynamism of 2003–05, as shown in Figure 2.5. Table 2.2 provides major indicators of the stock market over the period 2001–05, compared with those of the previous five years.

Table 2.2   Major indicators of China's stock market 1990–2005

	GDP (billion yuan)	Number of listed companies	Net income of listed companies (billion yuan)	Total market capitali- zation (billion yuan)	Total market capitali- zation/ GDP (%)	Market value of tradeable shares (billion yuan)	Market value of tradeable shares/ GDP (%)	Total share trading account (million)
1990	1859.8	8	1.1	1.2	0.07	0.3	0.02	n.a.
1991	2166.3	12	3.3	10.0	0.46	4.9	0.23	n.a.
1992	2665.2	50	6.9	93.8	3.52	25.3	0.95	n.a.
1993	3533.4	165	21.7	327.5	9.27	75.2	2.13	8.3
1994	4819.8	273	37.9	348.9	7.24	87.4	1.81	11.1
1995	6079.4	299	45.1	333.7	5.49	86.5	1.42	12.9
1996	7117.7	487	54.4	910.5	12.79	266.2	3.74	24.2
1997	7897.3	694	70.4	1678.5	21.25	496.6	6.29	34.8
1998	8440.2	798	67.1	1838.5	21.78	542.9	6.43	42.6
1999	8967.7	896	86.4	2529.4	28.21	790.1	8.81	48.1
2000	9921.5	1039	111.8	4660.0	46.97	1582.5	15.95	61.5
2001	10965.5	1118	92.5	4285.1	39.08	1415.6	12.91	69.7
2002	12033.3	1189	96.1	3789.3	31.49	1232.8	10.25	72.0
2003	13582.3	1256	132.2	4188.7	30.84	1303.9	9.60	73.4
2004	15987.8	1356	185.4	3645.5	22.80	1157.5	7.24	75.9
2005	18232.1	1371	186.2	3173.7	17.41	1446.8	7.94	77.1

Source: Securities Times Database (http:// www.stcn.com) – various editions.

CONCLUSION

The analysis conducted in this chapter reveals that in 2001–05 the Chinese stock market failed to reflect the dynamism of the country's economy, which at that time was expanding at an annual rate of 8–10 percent. If the share prices serve as a summary statistic of listed company performance, guiding capital to the most productive, best-managed enterprises, why do they not play this critical market signaling role in China? Possible expla- nations might be that: (1) the two exchanges allowed only SOEs to list their shares while the most dynamic sectors – private and foreign-funded companies – were deliberately excluded; (2) the government retained a majority stake in most listed companies and two thirds of the shares were not tradeable; (3) the interference of the government in the operation of many listed companies degraded the efficiency of decision-making; and (4) financial sector segmentation depressed the demand for shares, while the supply was accelerated in the context of new IPOs and the expected mass sell-off of non-tradeable shares.

Theoretically, had the constraints on China's stock market been gradually removed, the market would ultimately have become a barometer of the national economy. In a rapidly changing economic and financial environment such as that of China, the stock market should not be confined to achieving the goal set for SOEs almost 20 years ago. While there are reasons to expect the stock market to play an important role in China's integration into the global economy, including a move towards full convertibility of the RMB, there is still no sign that any primary functions will be assigned in this regard in the near future.

With accelerated financial innovation, the launch of margin trading and short selling of securities in March 2010 can be seen as an effort on the part of the authorities to enhance the marketability of IPOs and the liquidity of the secondary market. Moreover, the launch of index futures in April 2010 is envisaged to enable investment funds to hedge systematic risk as well as appealing to individual investors, risk-averse investors in particular. On the other hand, the establishment of the CinNext high-tech market in October 2009, a Nasdaq-style second board, will pave the way for more venture capitalists to invest in high-tech start-ups. It should be noted, however, that the condition constraints specified in the second section of this chapter remain unchanged, direct credit control is still a monetary policy tool in the post-WTO environment, and China on the whole is still undergoing a process of transition from a planned economy to a market economy. In such a context, new financial instruments like margin trading and futures on the stock index can only play a limited role in an emerging stock market.

By fostering a stock market that is mainly accessible to large SOEs, the Chinese government has effectively stimulated household holdings of financial assets and channeled the funds towards productive uses. Nevertheless, the success of China's stock market in facilitating SOE reform (and banking sector reform) has been at the expense of individual investors. Costs to individual investors, including stamp duty and commissions, may account for 30–40 percent of the total net income of all listed companies, making investment costs in China the highest in the world (ChinaStakes, 2008).

It should also be noted that a strong stock market requires strong property rights, a strong supervisory regime, strong corporate governance, strong financial institutions, objective and independent financial information, analysis and research, and a meaningful disclosure regime – each of which strengthens development in other sectors of the economy. China still has a lot to do over time to make the stock market more advanced and sophisticated, which will then put it in a better position to abide by international standards of performance.

NOTES

1. This has basically put an end to the credit facilities in China's stock market. In other words, there was no such service as margin borrowing, which enables an investor to take out a loan to buy more stock or borrow against the shares they already own. There was also no stock lending, where the owner of shares can lend them out for a fee to the borrower, who is free to use them in any way they like although the shares remain owned by the lender, who can recall them from loan at any time.
2. See Securities Times Database (http://www.stcn.com) – various editions.

REFERENCES

Barzel, Y. (1974), 'A theory of rationing by waiting', *Journal of Law & Economics*, **17**(1), 73–95.

Cai, Y. and X. Zhang (2008), 'China's economic growth and development of stock market', *Finance and Economy* (in Chinese), **10**, 34–6.

Cheng, S. (2002), *China's Stock Market: Diagnosis and Therapy* (in Chinese), Beijing: Economic Science Press.

ChinaStakes (2008), 'China's A-share market gloom and doom as non-tradables loom', Chinastake.com, available at http://www.chinastakes.com/2008/4/chinas-a-share-market-gloom-and-doom-as-non-tradables-loom.html (accessed 7 September 2009).

Fan, D. (2008), 'China's stock market and economic growth during transitional period', *Commercial Time* (in Chinese), **23**, 71–2.

Feng, Y., Q. Wang and J. Gou (2004), 'Rationality and investors' behavior under constraints', *Finance Research* (in Chinese), **9**, 57–64.

Gao, C. and Y. Li (2009), 'The correlation between China's macro economy and stock market', *Economic Research Report* (in Chinese), **1**, 86–7.

He, J. (2009), 'The development of China's IPO pricing mechanism and policy suggestion', *Journal of Hubei University of Economics (Humanities and Social Sciences)* (in Chinese), **12**, 39–41.

Hu, L. (2007), 'Game analysis on medium and small investors on stock market', *Science & Technology Innovation Monthly* (in Chinese), **20**(8), 59–60.

Hu, R. and F. Long (2010), 'New characteristics of policy oriented stock market in China', *Theory and Practice of Finance and Economics* (in Chinese), **3**, 48–52.

Jiang, S. and M. Yang (2009), 'The influence of institutional investors upon the stability of China's stock market', *Economic Research Report* (in Chinese), **1**, 93–4.

Li, G. and H. Zhu (2004), 'Investors' behavior under risk, rationality or semi-rationality', *Finance and Economics* (in Chinese), **5**, 48–51.

Pan, C. (2006), *China's Stock Market: Regulation, Structure and Price Fluctuation* (in Chinese), Chengdu: Chinese Finance Research Institute of Southwest University of Finance and Economics.

Song, Y., W. Wang and Y. Yao (2009), 'Game analysis on stock market failure and government behavior', *Jilin University Journal of Social Sciences* (in Chinese), **49**(5), 102–9.

Sun, W. (2009), 'Overconfidence of China's stock investors', *China Economy and Trade Herald* (in Chinese), **7**, 43–4.

Wang, Q. (2004), *Empirical Research on Overconfidence of Investors in Chinese Stock Market* (in Chinese), Chengdu: Chinese Finance Research Institute of Southwest University of Finance and Economics.

Zhai, W., J. He, H. Zhou and J. Cai (2010), 'Trading preference of Chinese investors and its impact on stock volatility', *Chinese Review of Financial Studies* (in Chinese), **3**, 53–64.

Zhang, D., L. Liu and P. Li (2008), 'Exploitation of minority shareholders in listed companies', *Investment and Securities* (in Chinese), **1**, 70–74.

Zuo, X. (2006), 'Reforms required for stock issuing', *Security Times* (in Chinese), 6 April.

3. China's changing demographics and their influence on financial markets

K.B. Oh, Xuebin Chen, Jianmei Wang, Geoffrey R. Durden and Nicole El-Haber

INTRODUCTION

This chapter reports the findings of a study into the recent growth and development of the Chinese financial services market. More specifically, it explores and analyses the relationship between recent demographic changes, pertaining to household income, savings patterns, economic growth and wealth creation, and demand for personal and household financial services.

The Chinese economy has experienced a remarkable transformation since the implementation of its 'open door' policy in 1978. Since 2003, China's economy has grown at an average annual growth of 10.3 percent per annum. The nominal gross domestic product (GDP) was US$4.8 trillion in 2009, making it the world's second largest economy after the USA. However, China's per capita nominal GDP in 2009 ranked number 98 in the world at US$3678.

China is currently experiencing a high level of inflation driven by high economic growth fueled mainly by the higher prices of food. The consumer price index (CPI), a main gauge of inflation, rose to 3.1 percent year on year in May 2010, exceeding the government target of 3 percent. CPI rise is becoming demand and cost driven rather than demand driven as earlier. The price pressures stem from excess liquidity because of the lag impact of 6–12 months from the four trillion yuan (US$585 billion) stimulus package in 2009 in response to the global economic slowdown, which prompted a record surge in loans of 9.5 trillion yuan (US$1.5 trillion). In addition, the recent rise in international commodity prices is also driving up the costs of production.

The Chinese government no longer focuses solely on GDP growth, but prefers growth with a more socio-economic balance. This implies that future growth will have more deliberate structural impetus for better redistribution of wealth. Equally, the transformation of the financial services market has been shaped by the quite dramatic changes that have taken place in the structure of Chinese society over this same period, including demography, its associated profile of personal and household income and savings, and pattern of wealth creation. Empirical evidence suggests financial system developments goes through bank, market and securitized phases (Rybczynski, 1997), while during the bank phase, all financial transactions are through banks, securities markets progressively develop in both the market phase and securitized phase. China's financial system is gradually moving to a market phase allowing households and individuals greater investment options from bank savings.

Goldsmith (1969), Shaw (1973), Kindleberger (1978) and Minsky (1982) have studied and supported the correlation between financial markets and real economic activity in the process of economic growth. Along with its impressive economic growth, China is undergoing unprecedented changes in its demographics from an aging population and increased longevity, dependency ratios, higher disposable income, urban migration, educational attainment, employment status and mobility. These demographic forces are creating a new paradigm in Chinese financial markets through their influence on capital accumulation, saving behavior, labor supply, asset prices and returns (Poterba, 1998), and personal and household demand for different types of financial assets. Modigliani and Brumberg (1954) and Wells and Grubar (1966) highlight the direction and magnitude of these effects based on the life cycle hypothesis that people save more during their productive years and spend their savings during retirement. China's economic prospects remain optimistic, supported by urbanization, market-oriented reform, industrialization and demographic dividend. China is still going through the demographic transition from a predominantly rural agrarian society to an urban society and one where the rural population has a higher fertility and mortality rate. Many western provinces still lag behind those in the eastern seaboard in industrialization, urban development and household income. In time, their per capita income will increase as economic development shifts to these regions.

There is a considerable body of literature describing the relationship between changes in a country's demographic profile and its associated level of macroeconomic activity (McMorrow and Roeger, 2003; Batini et al., 2006). For economic growth to happen, it is necessary to have an efficient system of financial markets that accumulates and channels capital from lenders to borrowers with high return projects. Generally, there is limited research into the impact of demographic changes on financial market structure and financial assets from asset allocation decisions. In

China, one of the world's leading economic powers and the most populous country, there is a lot of interest among business people, policy makers and academics to gain a better understanding of the relationships between demographic changes and financial markets. This chapter provides an insight into these relationships and discusses the implications thereof. We discuss the changing environment affecting financial services markets in China and set the scene for the development of financial markets in light of these environmental developments. We conclude with commentaries on likely future trends in the development of China's financial markets from the impact, implications and policy aspects of demographic changes.

CHINA'S CHANGING DEMOGRAPHY

China's population is aging as the fertility rate declines and longevity increases and these collective forces give rise to slower population growth and an increasing proportion of the elderly in the population. These demographic changes have many important implications for Chinese financial markets. China is the world's largest and most populous country. Its population is over 1.3 billion people (as of July 2009) covering all 31 provinces, autonomous regions and municipalities. China represents a full 20 percent of the world's population of approximately 6.7 billion or one in every five people on the planet.

China's total fertility rate is 1.77[1] per woman in 2008; therefore, each woman gives birth to an average of 1.77 children throughout her life. The necessary total fertility rate for a stable population is 2.10. Even though the fertility rate is relatively lower, China's population has continued to increase, but is somewhat slowed by China's one-child policy introduced in 1979 (Riley, 2004). The population growth rate is 0.50 for 2008. China's population was about 600 million in the 1950s, and grew dramatically to reach over one billion people in the 1980s.

China's population will continue to grow in the next few decades and this is due mainly to lower infant mortality and a lower death rate as a result of better health care. China's population is expected to peak at 1.5 billion by 2040 and it is anticipated that it will decrease after that. With this population profile, China will likely experience lower asset prices and returns to capital in the long run as a result of a variable supply of capital from a rising birth rate and then a falling birth rate, reducing the rate of return relative to that in an economy with a stable birth rate. This characteristic is implied in the overlapping generations model by Abel (2001, 2003), whereby individuals who are born into large cohorts are more likely to experience lower investment returns than those individual born into smaller cohorts.

Table 3.1   Gender ratio in different age groups (2008)

Age groups	Gender ratio	Percentage of total population
≤ 14 years	1.20 male(s)/female(s)	17.32
15–64 years	1.01 male(s)/female(s)	73.13
≥ 65 years	0.94 male(s)/female(s)	9.55
Total population	1.03 male(s)/female(s)	100

Source: National Bureau of Statistics of China (NBSC) (2009).

Males and females represented 50.77 percent and 49.23 percent of the population, respectively, in 2008 (National Bureau of Statistics in China, NBSC). The sex ratio of males to females and the proportion of the total population of different age groups are presented in Table 3.1.

CHINA DEMOGRAPHY: AGE

The higher life expectancy and lower fertility in China in the last four decades have resulted in a dramatic demographic shift in a rapid rate of aging in the population. According to the United Nations, the proportion of the population aged 65 or over will increase from 6.9 percent in 2000 to 15.7 percent in 2030 and 22.7 percent in 2050.

China's rapid population aging has concerned scholars and policy makers due to its potential adverse effects on sustainable economic growth (Peng, 2008). The increasing population of older people is likely to have an adverse effect on the value of financial assets. Working people save for retirement by investing in assets and pushing up their price and selling assets at retirement causing prices to fall as the supply of assets increases in the market.

Declining mortality and fertility are driving demographic changes in the Chinese population age structure. Life expectancy in China has almost doubled since the 1950s. In 2008, the population age was as follows: 204 million (17.32 percent) people were in the age range 0–14 years; 862 million (73.13 percent) were in the age range 15–64; and 112.4 million (9.54 percent) were aged 65 or over (Table 3.1). China's one-child policy will result in a rapid aging of its population over the next few decades, with a simple extrapolation of existing data confirming that 31 percent of the population (432 million people) will be aged 60 or over in 2050 (NBSC). This rapid population aging means there will be fewer young people to

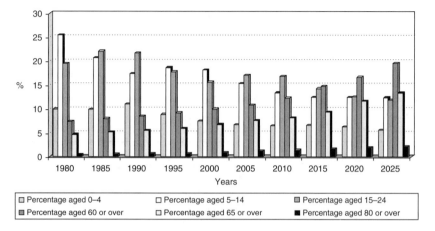

Source: www.esa.un.org (accesed 20 July 2010).

Figure 3.1   Population age profile (1980–2025)

support the growing elderly population (Riley, 2004). China's aging population will lead to an increase in the amount of money invested in long-term financial securities such as managed funds. Some of this managed fund growth will be invested in overseas funds, with further market liberalization, spurred by the aging population demand for higher returning investments of offshore equities and bonds.

At the start of China's recent economic boom in the 1980s, the age structure was largely one characterized by a young and growing population (Feng and Mason, 2005). In contrast, by the middle of the 1990s, the population age structure was comprised of a more mature working age population. Projected to 2025, with assumptions of a further moderate improvement in life expectancy and stable fertility, China's demography will be one with a much older population. Thus, this implies that within a half century, China's age structure would have moved from one characterized by a young growing population to on old and declining one (Figure 3.1).

Today, China's young professionals earn a higher income and are more sophisticated when it comes to managing wealth compared to their predecessors who only had very limited financial services such as cash withdrawals and bank deposits. Since the deregulation of the banking sector in 2006, the range of financial products and services has increased allowing better financial choices to Chinese consumers. This includes sophisticated financial products and services such as credit cards, life assurances, stocks, derivatives, managed funds and bonds instead of merely savings account services.

RURAL AND URBAN REGIONS AND EDUCATION

The migration of people from rural areas to the cities has resulted in mass urbanization and the urban population is likely to exceed the rural population by 2020. The provision of financial services in rural areas in China is left wanting, as the major financial institutions are reluctant to serve rural areas. As a result, the majority of the rural population does not have access to the formal financial system. This lack of access means that rural households rely on informal ways of accessing financial services. Therefore, the microfinance services remain the key to meeting the financial needs of rural household and micro-enterprises. The gradual withdrawal of state-owned commercial banks from rural areas has further magnified the unfulfilled demand for rural micro-credit services. Even with the huge population migration from rural to urban areas, there is still a significant demand for financial services in the rural areas. According to the People's Bank of China (2007), there were 230 million rural households in September 2007, which indicates a significant rural microfinance market.

China's rapid urbanization is causing a strain on urban infrastructures. The balance between urban and rural populations was 42.2 percent and 57.8 percent, respectively (Figure 3.2) in 2008, showing that the urban population had grown by 6.77 percent when compared with the 2000 Census figure. The rate of urbanization is expected to grow at 2.7 percent of the annual rate of change until 2010. Overall, 1.24 billion people were living within family units in 2008, a figure which has remained relatively stable over the last decade. Figure 3.2 presents the rural and urban population trends from 1970 to 2030.

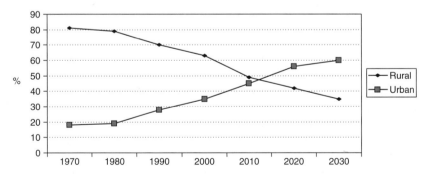

Source: United Nations (2004).

Figure 3.2 Rural versus urban population trends

Education levels have risen steadily over the last ten years with the number of people holding a university degree rising from 45.71 million in 2000 to 67.64 million in 2005, an increase of 48 percent. The numbers holding advanced vocational education diplomas increased from 141.09 million in 2000 to 150.83million in 2005, an increase of 7 percent. This improvement is due in major part to the considerable increases in public expenditure on higher education especially, but also in vocational education and training (Durden and Yang, 2006).

It is important to note that education in China is regionally unbalanced (Parsons and Smelser, 1964) and as education is a key driver in the socio-economic process, this will have different impacts on socio-economic development and may cause further disparities between rural and urban China. The government has been addressing this unbalance with more investments in rural education and Cao (2000) has stated that educational success in both rural and urban China would continue in the future. However, the level of education remains higher for the urban than for the rural population. Furthermore, the education disparity by gender between the rural and urban populations is evident and the rural population has the highest gender difference, where males vastly exceed females when it comes to receiving education (Cao, 2000). The general level of education in China continues to improve, especially with strong economic development in rural areas, and the demand for financial services will rise because of higher financial literacy and income.

CHINA'S HOUSEHOLD INCOME PROFILE

Vittas and Frazer (1982) considered the level of income and wealth as one of the most significant factors influencing the level of financial services consumption. The income gap between rural and urban residents is widening despite rapidly rising rural incomes. This gap in income has been attributed to social inequities in the growing Chinese economy. The average income in Chinese cities as of 2009 was RMB17175 (US$2525) compared with the average income of RMB5153 in rural areas (NBSC, 2010). According to *China Daily*, this is the widest disparity in average income for more than three decades. Furthermore, in 2008 the average annual disposal income for a rural worker was around US$690 while those in the cities earned US$2290 (NBSC)

In 1995, China's urban Gini coefficient[2] was 0.28, rural Gini coefficient was 0.34 and national Gini coefficient was 0.45. In 2005, the urban Gini coefficient rose to 0.37, rural Gini coefficient rose to 0.38 and national Gini coefficient rose to 0.47. With continuing income disparity, the difference

Table 3.2   Urban and rural fixed asset investments (billion yuan)

Year	Urban	Rural
2008	14816.7 (up by 26.1%)	2412.4 (up by 21.5%)
2007	11741.4 (up by 25.8%)	1982.5 (up by 19.2%)
2006	9347.2 (up by 24.5%)	1639.7 (up by 21.3%)
2005	7509.6 (up by 27.2%)	1350.8 (up by 18%)

Source: National Bureau of Statistics of China (2008).

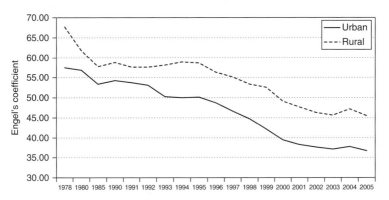

Figure 3.3   Engel's coefficient for rural and urban households

in per capita income between urban and rural areas in 2008 increased by more than three times (NBSC, 2009).

The government has recently accelerated the development of inland rural areas by introducing agricultural reforms and infrastructural investments to reduce this disparity. In 2001, the introduction of the 'two-waiver and one subsidy' policy made education compulsory in rural areas. As a result, government investment in rural areas doubled nationally between 2005 and 2008. Table 3.2 presents the completed investments in fixed assets in urban and rural areas in 2008.

The proportions of disposable income spent on food in both rural and urban households are declining as shown in Figure 3.3. The Engel's coefficients for Chinese rural and urban households in 2008 are 43.7 and 37.9, respectively. This infers that more income is now available for saving and investments.

However, despite the increased investment in rural areas, fixed asset investment in rural areas still lags behind the urban areas. Rural fixed asset investment actually decreased, as a proportion to urban areas, from 27.5 percent in 1990 to 14 percent in 2008 (Table 3.3). This is another reason for

Table 3.3   Proportion of rural and urban investment in fixed assets

	1990	2000	2007	2008
Urban	72.5	79.7	85.5	86.0
Rural	27.5	20.3	14.5	14.0

Source: China Statistical Yearbook (2008).

the reluctance of the big state-owned banks to increase their investments in the rural banking sector.

China's financial services sector is being reformed to boost domestic spending, particularly during and after the recent global financial crisis. One of the measures of this reform was the introduction by the Banking Regulatory Commission, in July 2009, of the 'Measures for Administration of Pilot Consumer Finance Companies' to provide more consumer loans at all levels. China's overall savings rate remains high, but younger and unmarried consumers are spending more. While 'deficit spending' or 'living on credit' is not yet common, consumers are spending more on high-value goods and services, and consumer lending would boost spending growth.

HOUSEHOLD SAVINGS AND INVESTMENT PORTFOLIOS

China's economic growth has brought about a strong growth in household savings. Households in China contribute significantly to national savings. China's saving rate is even higher than the average of other high-saving countries and high saving and not weak investment is responsible for China's large excess saving (Hung and Qian, 2010). The reasons for high savings in China include the one child policy which results in a lower birth rate and one child having to take care of their parents and grandparents in older ages, and the absence of government expenditure on health, education and social security. Over the period 1978–2006 the household savings rate rose from 5 percent of household disposable income to 20 percent, which is greater than the investment rate (Kuijs, 2006). This means that China routinely exports more capital than it imports, which in turn has significant implications for its international trading partners.

China's private consumption as a percentage of GDP has declined in recent years. As the propensity to consume is influenced by the level of

Table 3.4 Household uses of funds (financial transactions – 100 million yuan)

Uses of funds	2006	2007	% change
Currency and deposits	23 808	13 148	−45
Securities	1083	1912	77
Investment funds	1519	3438	126
Deposits in securities trading account	3416	8986	163
Insurance technical reserves	4365	6221	43
Miscellaneous (net)	185	1410	662

Source: National Bureau of Statistics of China (NBSC) (various issues).

income and age structure of the population, the propensity to consume is inversely related to the income level and is lower in the high-income population. The widening income disparity means that more wealth is concentrated in the high-income population with low propensity to consume.

China's demographic composition determines its saving rate as people save to prepare for old age and the saving rate rises with a higher proportion of prime savers. Thus, the high rate of saving in Chinese households reflects the country's rapid economic development, which results in higher employment from the high percentage of working age population.

In comparison with Western developed countries and global indicators, cash and deposits, as shown in Table 3.4, dominate the financial asset portfolios of resident in China. This indicates that the market for financial services is in its early stages of development and that there is considerable potential for further growth and development in the financial services sector, including the introduction of more sophisticated financial instruments. However, between 2006 and 2007 there was a significant shift in the household flow of funds from cash to investment in financial securities (Table 3.4).

Looking more specifically at investments in Table 3.4, securities, investment funds, deposits in securities trading accounts and insurance technical reserves have registered significant increases ranging from 43 percent to 163 percent between 2006 and 2007. At the same time, currency and deposits declined indicating a shift from savings to investments.

China's new wealthy individuals are perceptive investors who value investment strategies that mitigate against market volatility in order to preserve their family's wealth. In this regard, China's wealthy individuals will demand banking services that provide portfolio management.

DISTRIBUTION OF HOUSEHOLD AND PERSONAL WEALTH

Urban household per capita real income in China doubled between 1988 and 2002 (Gao, 2006). China's urban and rural personal financial assets were 35 trillion yuan in 2003 (NBSC). In 2004, one of China's premier merchant banks, Golden Sunflower, reported that 2.3 million people possessed more than 500000 yuan of personal or household financial assets and that in the main these people were senior managers of private sector businesses, located in Beijing, Shanghai, Guangzhou, Wuhan, Chengdu, Xi'an and Shenyang. In 2007, China was reported as having 310000 households with more than US$1 million in liquid assets, with a forecast that this will rise to over 600000 by 2011. The report goes on to state that in terms of the existing pattern of wealth distribution, these households account for only 0.1 percent of the total number of households, yet represent 41.4 percent of the country's total wealth. By comparison, approximately 1.0 percent of American households have ownership of one third of the US national wealth.

Atsmon et al. (2009) suggest that China's wealthy consumers currently account for less than 1 percent of urban Chinese households and are likely to grow at around 16 percent per annum. It is also important to demonstrate the difference between wealthy consumers and the general consumer. Wealthy consumers in China are more receptive to imported goods and are more willing to pay a premium for high-quality products. Atsmon et al. (2009) further state that China's wealthy consumers have different consumption behavior to their foreign peers and less wealthy Chinese consumers.

According to a survey by KPMG (2010, p. 2), 'Chinese luxury consumers maintain reasonable confidence about their economic situation, as well as being comfortable with paying large sums of money, and are even more discerning and sophisticated in the retail choices they make.' This new generation of professionally successful and wealthy individuals are generally young and middle-aged, who have a sophisticated understanding of the economy. They are confident of their own judgment and ability to invest and invest mainly in the real estate market, the domestic stock market and investment funds (China Merchant Bank, 2009).

DEMOGRAPHIC FACTORS INFLUENCING FINANCIAL MARKET EVOLUTION

Demographics shape a society's spending and saving patterns and China's financial services market is rapidly evolving because of demographic changes and the influx of the foreign financial institutions after the banking deregulation in 2006. There are now more financial products and services available to Chinese customers as their demands shift from putting all their money into saving accounts to investing in diverse financial products or services. The factors driving this evolution are demographic changes in population aging structure, urbanization, higher per capita income, better education, distribution of household wealth, lower fertility and mortality, and market competition. The following sections discuss the pervasive demographic factors that impact and implicate the Chinese financial markets and the resulting developments in the financial markets.

Urbanization

China is undergoing the biggest urbanization wave in history and by 2025, it is expected that 65 percent of China's population will be living in cities. Larger cities and those affected by the recent government's shift in economic focus to inland provinces will see more capital accumulation in the local market, which is required to fund infrastructure development, and more financial services to cater for a more educated and higher income labor force in general. As Chinese households become more urbanized and affluent, their financial choice changes as it begins to incorporate special features such as having to plan over long but finite horizons as well as the need to maintain a balanced portfolio consistent with expected asset returns that are consistent with contemporary needs. Therefore, China's changing household asset demands and investment decisions are important in asset pricing as they influence the availability of the types of financial assets or services in the market.

Education and Demographic Dividend

Significant changes have taken place in the demographic structure of Chinese society since the reform process began in 1978. In 2007, both urban and rural residents enjoyed significantly higher disposable incomes, were more highly educated and in possession of significant personal financial assets. China's education system continues to generate a growing number of high net worth individuals such as professionals and self-employed who need a wide range of specialized financial services. China can be said to be still enjoying the first dividend (Bloom et al., 2002) of its demographic transition, where it still has abundant labor for investment in economic development and, other things being equal, per capita income is also growing rapidly. This dividend period started with the introduction of market reform and it has continued for over three decades. China is beginning to experience lower fertility from an aging population, which reduces the growth rate of the labor force. A second dividend is likely from the powerful incentive to accumulate assets because of a bigger concentration of the population in older working age groups and those facing an extended period of retirement. These additional assets will raise national income when they are invested domestically or abroad. Therefore, China's first dividend yields a transitory bonus from high economic growth and the second transforms that bonus into more assets and sustainable development. Over the years, China has acted to capitalize on demographic dividend advantages by implementing appropriate policies to ensure the best outcomes because each demographic dividend is a limited window of opportunity. As China is a large country with a distinct rural and urban population characterized by a east-west divide and income discrepancy, the dividend periods overlap. The western region, which is still largely agrarian and low income, is undergoing the first dividend period as the government invests more in industrialization and the eastern seaboard is entering the second dividend period with an aging labor population and higher income. Therefore, in both urban and rural areas, the government is creating more jobs to capitalize on the 'dividends' of the changed age distribution – if it fails to do this it might have to struggle with the social unrest of millions of unemployed citizens. The current shift away from a very young age distribution to working adults results in greater personal and national savings, especially as those individuals born prior to the one-child policy move into their 40s and their own children are self-supporting.

Per Capita Income and Saving

China's economic reform has brought about spectacular growth; however, GDP per capita in China remains much lower compared with industrialized countries. Therefore, China may still face a potential social security crisis due to the fiscal gap from virtually zero superannuation contributions in the past and a rapidly aging population. The projected demographic transition to an older population means that fewer workers will provide pensions for more retirees and China's public pension system will be adversely impacted upon in the future leading to severe strain on the social security system unless it is thoroughly overhauled. The high degree of uncertainty of investing in financial markets will remain a major factor why people will continue to concentrate on higher household savings to avoid risk.

Aging Population

China's population age structure is experiencing a fundamental change, arising from a rapidly aging population due to declining fertility and mortality rates. China's aging population is expected to increase the capital intensity of the economy resulting in a decline in the rate of return to capital. According to Bohn (2006), in a dynastic model an expected decline in the rate of return discourages generational wealth transfer as parents consume their extra wealth rather than pass it on to their children. This helps to maintain a relatively stable capital-labour ratio in the presence of demographic changes. Bohn (2006) also argues that the dynastic model provides a better 'approximation of future patterns of saving and capital accumulation in developing countries because public pension and other transfer systems in these countries are more rudimentary, and most wealth is concentrated in family-based firms where ownership tends to be inherited and not purchased'. As a developing economy, China's welfare system is basic with inflexible transfer systems because households are burdened by heavy investments in housing and high family-based wealth concentration. Yoo (1994), Brooks (2002) and Geanakoplos et al. (2004) also use overlapping generation models to explore how changing cohort size affects asset returns and conclude that a demographic transition affects capital market returns.

China's changing age distribution influences aggregate saving according to the life-cycle hypothesis. Longer lives imply more funds are needed for the extra time spent in retirement, which contributes to capital accumulation. An aging population also affects labor supply as a decline in fertility reduces the relative size of successive age cohorts, therefore raising the capital-labour ratio. On the other hand, rising longevity encourages longer working lives, lowering the capital-labour ratio. The aggregate effects of China's population aging suggest a long-run rise in the capital-labour ratio and rising wages.

Relative to financial markets in developed economies, the structures of Chinese residents' financial asset portfolios are unsophisticated, comprised in the main of cash and savings. As China's economy continues to grow – and with it consumer affluence – so too will the market for more sophisticated financial assets, including additional non-derivative based instruments, such as insurance products and securities, and derivative based instruments, such as mutual funds, treasury bonds and education funds. Changing population demographics and increased consumerism have also raised the demand for retail-lending products such as credit cards, mortgages and automobile loans.

Life-cycle Hypothesis and Current Account

A useful way of articulating the possible future development of the market for financial services in China is through the lens of the life-cycle model (Fisher, 1939; Modigliani and Brumberg, 1954; Ando and Modigliani, 1963). The theory propounds that the consumption plans of individuals are related to their level of income and income expenditure as they pass from childhood into the world of work and then on into retirement.

The existing literature suggests that as people move from their prime working life toward retirement, their net demand for assets changes with corresponding effects on asset prices. In the early-life phase of the cycle, the relatively young consumers typically have a level of consumption that exceeds their income. This is often the result of their behaviors in respect of building a career, buying a new house or starting a family. In this phase consumers would generally need to borrow, based on their expected future incomes – accepting that the market was sufficiently well developed to allow this. The financial instruments consumed at this stage include house mortgages, personal loans and life insurance products. In mid-life, these expenditures are expected to decrease while income increases. At this point individuals typically repay debt and start to save for retirement by investing in financial instruments such as bonds, equities and superannuation. Upon retirement, income would typically decrease and individuals may start to disinvest by selling off certain of their financial assets as well as drawing on their superannuation funds. This is consistent with Yoo (1994), who found that demand for risky assets, bonds and equities increased with age and decreased on retirement. Additionally, the level of risk aversion may also vary over the life cycle as individuals seek lower risk in later life by investing in lower risk products such as fixed income securities. The maturity or duration of financial assets would also change over the life cycle, with younger individuals preferring to invest in those assets with longer maturities, such as equities and long-term bonds.

According to Wilson and Ahmed (2010) demographics are a major determinant of balance of payments current account trends as countries with a high proportion of 'prime savers', those aged between 35 and 69 years, tend to run current account surpluses, that is, driven by life cycle savings. On the other hand, people up to the age of 35 years invest more than they save. There is a clear distinction in demographic shifts between emerging markets (mostly in surplus) and developed markets (mostly in deficit). Therefore, it is most likely emerging markets, like China, could continue to lend to developed markets and future developments of capital markets in emerging markets may offset demographic pressures for capital flows from the emerging markets to the developed markets. China will likely experience a savings glut in the foreseeable future as its population continues to have a large proportion of prime savers, putting a downward pressure on real interest rates.

CONCLUSION

In the extant context, our research has shown that China's financial services market remains significantly underdeveloped and that the financial services sector is very much in its infancy. Chinese financial markets still lag behind in sophistication compared to those in Western countries; therefore, a high degree of uncertainty is involved in investments in financial markets. In terms of the life-cycle model, this means that in the main the existing set of financial institutions is capable of providing only a relatively modest set of financial services, typically those demanded by early-life consumers. The segments of the population characterized as mid-life and retirement are not well catered for, except to a limited extent by foreign banks, and then only in respect of high net worth clients.

In terms of the performance of the existing financial services sector, our research indicates a very low level of client satisfaction with domestic provider institutions. The reasons for this are manifold but principally relate to the low level of consumer knowledge about the operation of the instruments in question and the equally low level of product knowledge displayed by staff of the respective financial institutions. Banks, particularly, were criticized for the inadequacy of the available infrastructure relating to the provision of automated services, including ATMs, and their inability to offer sound professional advice. We found also that levels of consumer confidence and trust in service providers was extremely low. Overall, it was our view that in respect of their dealings with clients domestic financial institutions were operating from within an essentially production-oriented paradigm and that services were being rationed (demarketed) accordingly. The corollary to this is that the degree of market orientation of these institutions was low, as was the associated level of marketing practice.

There are profound implications for the financial services sector in respect of its future ability to provide a comprehensive and integrated portfolio of financial services across existing market segments. It is recognized that the industry is in its infancy and that capacity building is a protracted and expensive activity. Equally, though, the evidence we have gathered from key domestic industry players leads us to believe that their strategic mindset has still not engaged with the notion of being market oriented and as such little investment is taking place in respect of the operationalization of the concept within those institutions. There is a need to formulate appropriate policies to generate capital in order to fuel growth and China's high savings rates, individual, government and business savings, have been important sources of capital as well as foreign investments.

China's accession to the World Trade Organization (WTO) has allowed foreign firms to enter the domestic market for financial services in recent years and to operate in an independent fashion. It is clear from our research that these institutions are beginning to have a significant impact in the marketplace, especially in Beijing, Shanghai, Guangzhou and Shenyang. More specifically, these firms are importing their own international marketing infrastructure and practices and it is clear that these capabilities are resonating with domestic consumers. However, the level of latent demand for financial services, even with the involvement of foreign financial service providers, is unlikely to lead to a remediation of the problems alluded to above in the short to medium term. One area where both domestic and foreign firms are investing, however, is in the provision of private banking services to the high wealth clusters mentioned previously.

NOTES

1. The World Bank, World Development Indicators: http://data.worldbank.org/data-catalog/world-development-indicators?cid=GPD_WDI (accessed 20 July 2010).
2. The Gini coefficient measures the inequality of wealth/income distribution, a value of 0 expressing total equality and a value of 1 maximal inequality.

REFERENCES

Abel, A.B. (2001), 'Will bequests attenuate the predicted meltdown in stock prices when baby boomers retire?', *Review of Economics and Statistics*, **83**, 589–95.

Abel, A.B. (2003), 'The effects of a baby boom on stock prices and capital accumulation in the presence of social security', *Econometrica*, **71**, 551–78.

Ando, A. and F. Modigliani (1963), 'The "life-cycle" hypothesis of saving: aggregate, implications and tests', *American Economic Review*, **53**(1), 55–84.

Atsmon, Y., J. Ding, V. Dixit, I. Maurice and C. Suessmuth-Dyckerhoff (2009), *The Coming of Age: China's New Class of Wealthy Consumers*, London: McKinsey & Company.

Batini, N., N. Callen and W.J. McKibbin (2006), 'The global impact of demographic change', IMF Working Paper No. WP/06/9.

Bloom, D., D. Canning and J. Sevilla (2002), *The Demographic Dividend: A New Perspective on the Economic Consequences of Population Change*, RAND, MR-1274, Santa Monica, California.

Bohn, H. (2006), 'Optimal private responses to demographic trends: savings, bequests and international mobility', in C. Kent, A. Park and D. Rees (eds), *Demography and Financial Markets* (Conference Proceedings), Sydney: Australian Government and Reserve Bank of Australia, pp. 47–82.

Brooks, R. (2002), 'Asset market effects of the baby-boom and social security reform', *American Economic Review*, **92**, 402–6.

Cao, G.-Y. (2000), *The Future Population of China: Prospects to 2045 by Place of Residence and by Level of Education*, Interim Report IR-00-026, Laxenburg, Austria: International Institute for Applied Systems Analysis.

Chen, A. (2005), 'Urbanization: the Chinese way', *China & World Economy*, **13**(1), 15–31.

China Merchant Bank – Bain & Company (2009),'China's private banking industry: an opportune time', available at http://www.bain.com/bainweb/publications/publications_detail.asp?id=27168&menu_url=publications_results.asp (accessed 18 August 2010).

Durden, G. and G. Yang (2006), 'Higher vocational education in China: a preliminary critical review of developments and issues in Liaoning Province', *Journal of European Industrial Training*, **30**(8), 662–8.

Feng, W. and A. Mason (2005), 'Demographic dividend and prospects for economic development in China', paper prepared for the UN Expert Group Meeting on Social and Economic Implications of Changing Age Structures, Mexico City.

Fisher, I. (1939), 'The double taxation of savings', *American Economic Review*, **29**(1), March, 16–33.

Gao, Q. (2006), 'The social benefit system in urban China: reform and trends from 1988 to 2002', *Journal of East Asian Studies*, **6**(1), 12–14.

Geanakoplos, J., M. Magill and M. Quinzii (2004), 'Demography and the long-run predictability of the stock market', *Brookings Papers on Economic Activity*, **1**, 241–301.

Goldsmith, R.W. (1969), *Financial Structure and Development*, New Haven, CT: Yale University Press.

Hung, J. and R. Qian (2010), 'Why is China's saving rate so high? A comparative study of cross-country panel data', paper presented at Venice Summer Institute, Bay of Venice, Italy, 23–24 July.

Kindleberger, C. (1978), *Manias, Panics and Crashes*, London: Macmillan.

KPMG China (2010), 'Refined strategies: luxury extends its reach across China', Consumer Markets, KPMG China.

Kuijs, L. (2006), 'How will China's savings-investment balance evolve?', *World Bank China Research Paper*, **4**(7), 1–31.

McMorrow, K. and W. Roeger (2003), 'Economic and financial market consequences of ageing populations', European Commission Economic Papers No. 182.

Minsky, H. (1982), 'Can "It" Happen Again?', *Essays on Instability in Finance*, New York: Sharpe.

Modigliani, F. and R. Brumberg (1954), 'Utility analysis and the consumption function: an interpretation of cross-section data', in K.K. Kurihara (ed.), *Post-Keynesian Economics*, New Brunswick, NJ: Rutgers University Press, pp. 388–436.

National Bureau of Statistics in China (NBSC) (various years), http://www.stats.gov.cn.

National Bureau of Statistics in China (NBSC) (2008), *Statistical Communiqué of the People's Republic of China on the 2008 National and Economic Development.*

Parsons, T. and N. Smelser (1964), *Economy and Society – A Study in the Integration of Economic and Social Theory*, 3rd edn, London: Routledge and Kegan Paul.

Peng, X. (2008), 'Demographic shift, population ageing and economic growth in China: a computable general equilibrium analysis', *Pacific Economic Review*, **13**(5), 680–97.

People's Bank of China (2007), *Report of Monetary Policy of the PBOC*, Monetary Analysis Group of the PBOC, 8 November.

Poterba, J.M. (1998), 'Population structure and asset returns: an empirical investigation', NBER Working Paper.

Riley, N.E. (2004), 'China's population: new trends and challenges', *Population Bulletin*, **59**(2), the Population Reference Bureau.

Rybczynski, T.M. (1997), 'A new look at the evolution of the financial system', in J. Revell (ed.), *The Recent Evolution of Financial Systems*, London: Macmillan Press, pp 3–15.

Shaw, E. (1973), *Financial Deepening in Economic Development*, London: Oxford University Press.

United Nations (2004), *World Population Prospects: The 2004 Revision and World Urbanisation Prospects*, New York: United Nations.

Vittas, D. and P. Frazer (1982), *The Retail Banking Revolution*, London: Lafferty.

Wells, W.D. and G. Grubar (1966), 'The life cycle concept in marketing research', *Journal of Marketing Research*, **3**, 355–63.

Wilson, D and S. Ahmed (2010), 'Current accounts and demographics: the road ahead' Global Economics Papers No. 2020, Goldman Sachs Global Economics.

Yoo, P.S. (1994), 'Age dependent portfolio selection', Federal Reserve Bank of St Louis Working Paper No. 94-003A.

PART II

China's FDI and FDI in China

4. Going global: China's outward foreign direct investment

Lilai Xu

INTRODUCTION

The rapid emergence of China as a major player in the global economy has been remarkable, yet has had mixed consequences for the rest of the world. An important element in this economic rise is foreign direct investment (FDI). Following the global financial crisis, FDI outflows from developing countries amounted to US$229 billion in 2009, a fall of 23 percent over 2008, marking the end of a five-year upward trend (UNCTAD, 2010). This contraction, however, was less severe than that which occurred in developed countries. As a result, developing countries have since strengthened their position as emerging sources of FDI.

Starting from virtually no outward foreign direct investment (OFDI) in the 1980s, FDI from China in 2009 reached US$56.5 billion (including investment in the financial sector), standing respectively as the first and fifth largest among developing economies and in the world (see Appendix Figure 4.A1). Yet outflows from China still remain well below its share of FDI inflows, which amounted to US$108 billion in 2009.

Drawing on recent Government of China statistics (2002–09), this chapter takes a closer look at the structure, determinants and effects of FDI from China against the backdrop of the country's 'Go global' strategy. Emphasis is placed on the mode of entry into industrialized economies and the importance of integrating quickly and deeply into local communities. The prospects for China's future FDI outflows are discussed based on its own and Japan's past experience. The remainder of this chapter is structured as follows: the second section surveys the determinants of and motivations for China's OFDI; the third section examines the current status and opportunities of Chinese FDI in developing and transitional economies; the fourth section sketches the major patterns of and potential frictions engendered by Chinese FDI in developed countries; the fifth section puts forward some pertinent observations for Chinese policymakers and transnational company (TNC) executives to consider; and the final section presents the conclusion.

DETERMINANTS AND MOTIVATIONS FOR CHINA'S OFDI

A study by UNCTAD (2010, p. 7) indicates that TNCs from BRIC countries – Brazil, Russia, India and China – initially expanded FDI into their own region, often into economies with which they had close culture links. A large number of them are motivated by strategic considerations rather than by short-term profitability. Supportive government policies, China's 'Go global' policy, for example, successfully encouraged domestic enterprises to invest globally.

The Chinese official statistics supports the above observation that most of the increase in China's OFDI has taken place since 2002 when China officially initiated a 'Go global' strategy to promote its OFDI, but a great leap has been seen only over the past few years (Figure 4.1).

Compared with other major source countries for FDI, Chinese outward investment is highly regulated. In fact, China's central authorities generally discouraged OFDI prior to introduction of the 'Go global' strategy. Chinese enterprises are now allowed to make independent decisions on cross-border mergers and acquisitions (M&As) projects; only investments of over US$30 million require government approval. Technological feasibility of such overseas investment is also at the discretion of the investor (Ma, 2008). OFDI has since received a great boost from government supportive policies.[1]

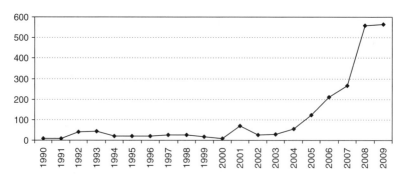

Source: Calculated from NBSC (various years).

Figure 4.1   China's FDI outflows 1990–2009 (in US$ billion)

While a number of policies have been designed to give impetus to companies going global, five key drivers explain China's accelerated OFDI.

First, one of the motivations most reported in both the media and academic writing is China's need to secure natural resources (Schüller and Turner, 2005). China's increasing reliance on foreign hydrocarbon resources has forced the country to look abroad for new oil and gas supplies.[2] By encouraging Chinese companies to buy foreign assets in strategic sectors such as minerals or energy, China is able to absorb some of the uncertainty in relying on foreign providers. For instance, in February 2008 Chinalco teamed up with Alcoa to purchase a 12 percent stake in Rio Tinto for US$14.5 billion, to secure its bauxite and iron ore reserves (Nie and Lu, 2010).

Second, while many of China's exports are from foreign-owned enterprises, large domestic companies also export large volumes. Manufacturers in China became plagued by overcapacity and cut-throat price wars that made domestic markets hypercompetitive. Foreign markets consequently became more attractive because they had higher margins and provided an opportunity for Chinese manufacturers to capture a larger portion of the value chain. They therefore require services such as shipping, insurance, wholesale facilities and after-sales services to support their export transactions. The coastal provinces and municipalities, heavily engaged in international trade, are the main sources of China's OFDI in this respect.

Third, FDI is undertaken in order to access intangible resources and gain new capabilities in a host country. This is particularly true for Chinese TNCs because, as latecomers, they urgently need to engage in FDI to address their competitive disadvantage and improve their global competitiveness. Statistics testify to the fact that Chinese companies are using cross-border M&As as major stepping stones to overseas investment, their targets being foreign companies experiencing difficulties in management but which still possess good core assets – such as technology, brand names and distribution networks (Jiang, 2006). In this way, many Chinese companies have acquired core technological capabilities and brand names that are recognized worldwide. For example, in December 2005 Lenovo acquired IBM's PC division. The deal gave Lenovo the right to continue using the IBM logo on its products for the first five years, and quadrupled Lenovo's PC business, realizing the company's globalization goals (Stratfor Global Intelligence, 2007).

By prompting local companies to invest abroad, China is also raising local businesses' exposure to, and developing their skills in, managing overseas assets. This is all part of the greater plan of nurturing more Chinese global conglomerates in future. In this regard, Hong Kong has been playing an extremely important role as the first stop along the path of internationalization of large Chinese state-owned enterprises (SOEs).

Fourth, SOEs are losing their monopoly position at home and are diversifying internationally. Many of them are seeking to move their labor-intensive operations to cheaper overseas locations (Davies, 2009). This is taking place in parallel to a shift of low-value-added manufacturing from China's coastal regions to its inland provinces as a result of rapidly increasing production costs in coastal cities since the mid-2000s.

Fifth, in addition to the need for Chinese companies to invest, there is an element of recycling dollar revenues (Wheatley, 2009). China has amassed huge foreign reserves (US$2.374 trillion as of December 2009). As pressure from the United States (USA) mounted on China to float its currency upward, the Chinese government responded by acquiring assets overseas (Nie and Lu, 2010). From an economic perspective, speeding up foreign exchange outflows reduces appreciation pressures. The Chinese government will also obtain higher rates of return on its foreign reserves as it takes some of the money mostly invested in US Treasury Bills and moves it into higher-yielding FDI. Additionally, a stronger RMB tends to favor FDI over exports.

The relative strength of these motivations is reflected in the sectorial/ industrial distribution of China's OFDI, published by the NBSC (2010).[3] Figure 4.2 displays the composition of OFDI stock at the end of 2009. Based on Chinese government data, business services account for the largest percentage of China's overseas operation (29.7 percent), followed by finance (18.7 percent), mining (16.5 percent), wholesale and retailing (14.5 percent) and transportation (6.8 percent). Manufacturing remains modest at 5.5 percent, and real estate and construction even lower at 2.2 percent and 1.4 percent, respectively. Business services and mining are the fastest growing sectors, with the respective share of 36.2 percent and 23.6 percent in the OFDI in 2009. Manufacturing OFDI is small (4 percent) but this is not surprising as China still has a comparative advantage in production efficiency, and manufacturing activities therefore tend to be performed domestically rather than offshore. However, manufacturing OFDI is likely to grow faster with the rise of domestic production costs (Davies, 2009).

PATTERNS OF CHINESE FDI IN DEVELOPING AND TRANSITION ECONOMIES

By the end of 2009, China had invested in 13000 projects around the world, across 177 countries. Figure 4.3 shows the number of projects with

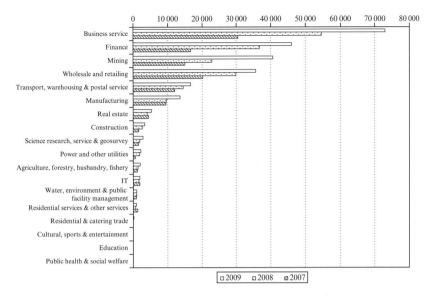

Source: NBSC (2010).

Figure 4.2   China OFDI stocks by industry, 2007–09 (in US$ billion)

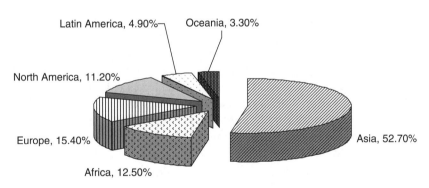

Source: NBSC (2010).

Figure 4.3   Number of OFDI projects with percentage share in destination regions

the percentage share by destination region, while Figure 4.4 depicts the geographical distribution of Chinese FDI outflows in dollar terms in the period 2005–09. For China's OFDI flows by major destination countries in 2009, see Table 4.A1 in the Appendix. Based on these data, Asia is

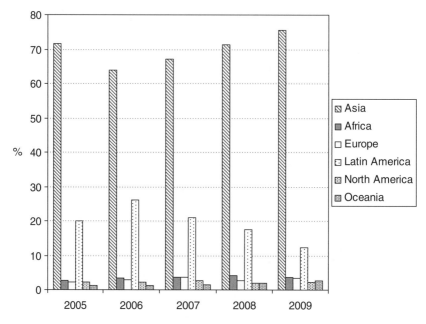

Source: NBSC (2010).

*Figure 4.4   FDI outflows in percentage share by destination region,
                2005–09*

attracting the largest share of Chinese overseas operations, with increasing importance over the years 2007–09. Latin America can also be regarded as a leading destination, but its significance has decreased over time (Gattai, 2009). It is worth noting that a close relationship exists between the sector/industry and geographical distribution of Chinese outward investments in developing and transitional economies.

Asia

The bulk of China's FDI in Asia goes to Hong Kong, which accounted for 63 percent of total Chinese OFDI stock up to the end of 2009 (Table 4.1). As revealed in Figure 4.5, out of US$115.85 billion worth of stock, 28.2 percent was directed to business service, followed by finance (24.2 percent), and then wholesale and retail (18.6 percent). These three industries attracted almost two thirds of mainland China's total FDI in Hong Kong. This reflects Hong Kong's longstanding historical tie with the mainland and (Havrylchyk and Poncet, 2007). For instance, the first

Table 4.1 *Major indicators of China's OFDI by destination in 2009 (in US$ billion)*

	OFDI flows			OFDI stocks	
	Amount	Growth rate over 2008 (%)	Percentage of total outflow (%)	Amount	Percentage of Total Stock (%)
Hong Kong	35.60	–7.9	63.0	164.50	66.9
EU	2.97	535.1	5.3	6.28	2.6
USA	0.91	96.7	1.6	3.34	1.4
Australia	2.44	28.8	4.3	5.86	2.4
Russia	0.35	–11.9	0.6	2.22	0.9
ASEAN	2.70	8.6	4.8	9.58	3.9
Total	44.34	161.6	79.3	133.09	72.3

Source: NBSC (2010).

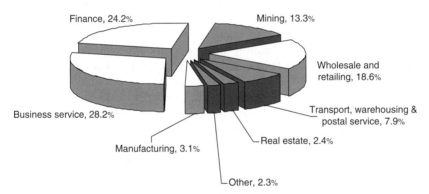

Source: Personal elaborations from NBSC (2010).

Figure 4.5 *Chinese OFDI stock in Hong Kong by industry, 2009*

generation of Chinese TNCs were large SOEs operating in monopolized industries such as banking, shipping, international trading and natural resources. Hong Kong played an important role in training their managers and providing them with international experience to further their internationalization, and Hong Kong remains the major destination for Chinese TNCs to commence their FDI activities in the 2000s (UNCTAD, 2006).

Hong Kong is also a location for 'round-tripping', which refers to domestic investment in China being routed through Hong Kong and back into the mainland to take advantage of preferential policies available only

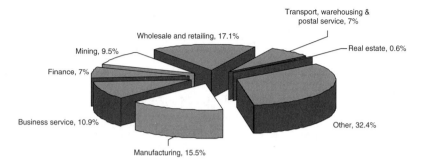

Source: Personal elaborations from NBSC (2010).

Figure 4.6   Chinese OFDI stock in ASEAN by industry, 2009

to foreign investors. This explains why the same high percentage of FDI in China, which was within the range of 45–65 percent in 2002–09, comes from Hong Kong. Since its accession to the World Trade Organization (WTO) in 2001, China has removed many of the preferential terms for FDI. Improvements in the application of national treatment to both domestic and foreign investment are reducing incentives for round-tripping.[4]

China's FDI in the Association of South East Asian Nations (ASEAN) countries, as shown in Figure 4.6, is still intended to secure raw materials and usually involves SOEs. However, the vast majority of these projects are now driven by international and domestic competition. This is reflected in the weight of manufacturing (15.5 percent). Due to the rising costs of production, a new round of industrial restructuring is taking place in China. Some Chinese companies in the textile and automotive industries have been shifting parts of their operations to ASEAN countries. To better serve the OFDI, Chinese banks such as the Industrial and Commercial Bank of China (ICBC) have recently acquired a number of banks in South East Asia.

The relocation of low-end, export-oriented manufacturing activities from China has provided opportunities for latecomers to become involved in TNC production networks. The least developed countries (LDCs) in the region – Cambodia, Laos and Myanmar – have also started to reap the benefits of increased intra-regional FDI. A UNCTAD study indicates that China's FDI has made an increasing contribution to industrial upgrading. While the contribution of Japan as a major driver of industrial upgrading has been declining and the strength of the newly industrialized economies such as Korea and Taiwan has been weakened by the recent crisis, China's role in the region has expanded, with its market share increasing to 13.3

percent in 2009. Regional economic integration has boosted intra-regional investment, which now accounts for around 40 percent of the total FDI stock of the region (UNCTAD, 2010).

Latin America

China's interest in Latin America is a fairly new phenomenon, developing over the past few years. China's primary interest in the region is to gain greater access to oil, copper, iron and other resources, but it may also have a political and diplomatic dimension and may have longer-term implications for US interests.[5] The top recipients of China's FDI are the British Virgin Islands (US$15.06 billion), the Cayman Islands (US$13.58 billion), Brazil (US$0.36 billion), Peru ($0.28 billon), Venezuela (US$0.27 billion), Mexico (US$0.17 billion) and Argentina (US$0.17 billion). China's investment in Latin America is difficult to track. This is partly because the destinations are tax haven economies, such that the funds will likely be redirected elsewhere, quite similar to the round-tripping via Hong Kong discussed above. Indeed, these small, developing island states amounted to 25 percent of world FDI inflows and stocks in 2009 (UNCTAD, 2010).

Africa

While China's OFDI is predominantly South–South, the results show that Africa's share remains quite small, concentrated among only a few countries like Sudan, Nigeria, Algeria and Zambia (Buckley et al., 2007). Most of China's investments in the region are resource-seeking and often involve SOEs such as the China National Offshore Oil Corporation (CNOOC).[6] The greatest numbers of FDI projects, however, are in manufacturing and infrastructure, with private investors playing an increasingly active role (Gu, 2009). The technology used by Chinese investors is likely to be suitable for African countries and contributes to technological upgrading in host countries.[7] FDI from China often also carries benefits for infrastructure. Chinese loans, backed by natural resources extracted through FDI projects involving Chinese investment, are earmarked for infrastructure development (Bräutigam, 2010). Chinese investors are also involved in setting up special economic zones, which are expected to improve infrastructure, technology transfer, employment opportunities, as well as educational and health services (Sohlman, 2009).

Whereas much attention has been focused on the role of Chinese SOEs, there is reason to believe that for the coming years, as more of China's private sector companies begin to play an active role in investments in Africa, there will be more diversified investments in non-extractive countries and sectors (Kiggundu, 2008). It appears that China is trying to ensure that its investment in developing economies, in the bottom of the pyramid in particular, is envisaged to form part of a sustainable and beneficial business model. China has become one of the most significant foreign investors in some sub-Saharan African countries.

Russia

China is Russia's third-largest trade partner, importing mostly energy and timber, while Russia is China's eighth-largest trade partner, importing a wide range of finished goods. Compared to the sizeable trade, the FDI flows between the two countries remain low. The stock of China's FDI in Russia is US$2.22 billion, less than 6 percent of total FDI inflows in Russia. However, the size of the Chinese OFDI in Russia is likely to be underestimated, mainly due to the use of offshore vehicles based in the Cayman Islands, Hong Kong and the British Virgin Islands. The key determinants of Chinese investments include location, market size and the ability to use Russia's natural resources. Investments by Chinese companies are concentrated in Siberia, the Far East, Moscow and St Petersburg, with a prominent role in the natural resources-related sectors including oil, gas and forestry (Krkoska and Korniyenko, 2008).

To sum up, China's OFDI in developing and transitional economies is motivated to internationalize business operations through a variety of 'push' and 'pull' factors. While the distribution of Chinese investments (except for those directed to Hong Kong) shows a concentration in the resource sector, and when measured in value many of the investments are resource-seeking and often involve SOEs, the largest numbers of investment projects undertaken in developing and transitional economies are market-seeking, with Chinese private investors increasingly becoming active players. China's FDI also reflects new features and opportunities with regard to industrial upgrading in Asia. While the USA played a leading role in the 1960s and 1970s, followed by Japan in the 1980s and newly industrialized economies (NIEs) since the 1990s, over the past few years both new sources and recipients of intra-regional FDI flows have emerged. In parallel to growing trade links, China has been relocating production within the region to take advantage of lower costs, thereby enhancing its competitiveness and promoting industrial restructuring at home. This has benefited many ASEAN nations by offering them new access to foreign capital, technology and market links.

EMERGING TRENDS FOR CHINESE FDI IN DEVELOPED COUNTRIES

As previously discussed, while traditional investment patterns based on Dunning's Ownership, Location and Internalization (OLI) paradigm (Dunning, 1993) were explained by resource transfer to a host country, strategic asset-seeking FDI is focused on intangible resources and new capabilities in a host country. This is particularly evident in relation to China's FDI in the European Union (EU) and the USA. Driven by global ambitions and strategic considerations, while European and American TNCs are primarily interested in protecting their intangible resources when expanding abroad, Chinese TNCs try to access those resources, and select entry modes accordingly. They tend to choose the industries for which a given country has a particular strength: they invest in machinery in Germany, in automobiles in the UK and in design in Italy, to capture externalities created by host country intangible asset clusters (UNCTAD, 2004).[8]

In fact, Chinese companies operate mainly by acquiring ailing or financially distressed firms, competitive niche producers, former partners or contractors. Chinese companies contribute financial strength whereas European companies supply know-how; hence, a perfect match results when they decide to partner (Schüller and Turner, 2005). As shown in Figure 4.7, manufacturing accounts for 15.9 percent of China's OFDI stock in the EU, more than triple the mere 5.5 percent of China's manufacturing in its total OFDI, while in the USA the proportion of manufacturing reaches as high as 28.2 percent (Figure 4.8).

China's FDI in South Carolina highlights the characteristics of Chinese investment in the USA. In today's global and mobile economy, the role of

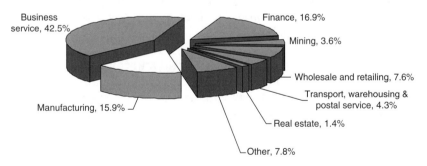

Source: Personal elaborations from NBSC (2010).

Figure 4.7 Chinese OFDI stock in the EU by industry, 2009

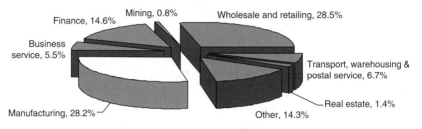

Finance, 14.6%   Mining, 0.8%   Wholesale and retailing, 28.5%

Business service, 5.5%

Transport, warehousing & postal service, 6.7%

Real estate, 1.4%

Manufacturing, 28.2%   Other, 14.3%

Source: Personal elaborations from NBSC (2010).

Figure 4.8   Chinese OFDI stock in the USA by industry, 2009

FDI in South Carolina, as identified by the state government, is expected to provide both direct and indirect jobs, tax revenue, international trade, leadership, corporate citizenship and cultural exchange.[9] South Carolina scored a first with the Haier Group, a leading Chinese appliance manufacturer. Haier America in Camden is the company's first overseas manufacturing plant. It is also the first Chinese company to establish a manufacturing facility in the USA and is still the largest investment by a Chinese company in the USA (as of 2007). By the end of 2008, a total of 1891 jobs had been created by the 11 Chinese investment projects in South Carolina (see Appendix Table 4.A2).

To date, Chinese FDI in both the EU and the USA has had little impact and is disproportionately small considering the high proportion of China's trade with these economies, but this depends on reasons that do not have to hold forever: (1) Chinese investment is a small share of total inward FDI, and most has come only very recently; (2) many acquisitions have not yet succeeded in restoring the health of ailing companies;[10] (3) investment is seldom targeted at the industries where unemployment impacts could be anticipated; and (4) a lack of readiness to compete with global giants on their home territory (Davies, 2009; Gattai, 2009).

Unlike the EU and the USA, the apparent attractiveness of Australia to Chinese investors is based in the richness of that country's basic raw materials, notably liquefied natural gas, coking and steaming coal, iron ore and bauxite. Australia has perhaps the most efficient mining industry in the world. Its openness to foreign investors brings with it the technology, management and market that are essential for fostering a world-class industry.[11] China's investments in Australia are typically driven by ambitious executives and their international investment bankers, and encouraged and coordinated by the Chinese government. In 2009 China became Australia's second-largest source of FDI, from negligible levels

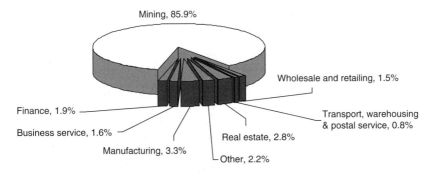

Source: Personal elaborations from NBSC (2010).

Figure 4.9   Chinese OFDI stock in Australia by industry, 2009

only three years prior. About 85.9 percent of the FDI stock was directed to the mining industry (Figure 4.9). According to the annual report of the Foreign Investment Review Board, AU$26.6 billion of Chinese investment was approved in 2008–09, or about 16 percent of total approvals by value. That puts China second only to the USA, which accounted for AU$39.6 billion of approvals (24 percent of the total). Of that Chinese total, virtually all of it – AU$26.3 billion – was in the mineral exploration and development sector. China accounted for 29 percent of total approvals in this sector, well ahead of the second-placed USA (AU$19.8 billion, or 22 percent of approvals) (Thirlwell, 2010).

From the recipient's perspective, the surge of Chinese investment in Australia is viewed as both an opportunity and a threat. While Chinalco's effort in 2008 was seen as an opportunity, Chinalco's interest in investing an additional US$19.5 billion in Rio Tinto in February 2009 was not viewed as favorably. As a result, Rio Tinto unilaterally abandoned its deal with Chinalco in June 2009 (Nie and Lu, 2010).

As a matter of fact, over the past few years the predominance of SOEs in China's OFDI, as exhibited in Figure 4.10, has raised concerns about the motivations for and quality of Chinese equity investment (Davies, 2009). With abundant assets to support them, the China Investment Corporation (CIC), China's sovereign wealth fund, and the State Development and Investment Corporation (SDIC), both directly administered by the Chinese government, are attempting to purchase large-scale assets overseas (Ma, 2008). In the USA, for example, the failed attempt by CNOOC to purchase a small US energy company (Unocal) generated much heat and passion among US legislators and editorialists (Woo and Zhang, 2005). Some senators even appealed to examine every investment, 'no

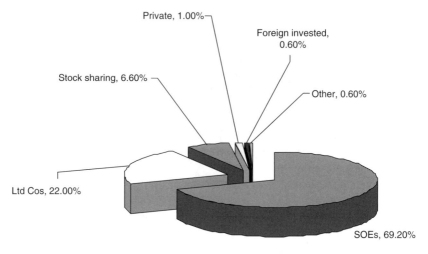

Source: NBSC (2010).

Figure 4.10   China OFDI stock by investors, 2009

matter how small it is', in US enterprises by funds established by foreign governments (Ma, 2008).

In Australia, a survey of people's attitudes towards China's FDI revealed that 40 percent of most investment-focused Australian citizens see Chinese FDI as typically 'under government influence' and therefore a potential threat to the 'national interest'. Another 42 percent think Chinese companies already own too much or that Australia should not sell its assets to 'pay for our debts'. Only 19 percent of Australians believe that China 'is just another trading partner' and that 'a free market enhances prosperity', as well as helps 'keep the peace between nations'. These results should disturb Chinese companies and policymakers alike. Whether true or not, China is perceived as an unfair player in the markets, and Chinese investments as potentially posing a threat to national interest (Ferguson, 2010).

This has generated increasing interest in the national treatment of FDI. Clarification of the attitude and approach to investment by Chinese SOEs and sovereign wealth funds has thus become a priority. Notwithstanding the central importance of the concept of the national interest to the Australian or American approach to FDI, there is no generally agreed definition of national interest. It is not possible to distinguish the concept from related concepts such as public interest, national welfare or community welfare, let alone an agreed definition to applications by foreign investors (ITS Global, 2008).

It is likely that SOEs' involvement in OFDI has been overstated. As China evolves from a centrally planned to a market economy, SOEs need to generate wealth and they are increasingly being driven and reformed to operate according to normal commercial considerations. In this regard, the rapid growth of China has been based on export-oriented manufacturing sectors. From the perspective of downstream users, upstream investments can be seen as no more than improving the security of raw material supply, as well as providing a natural hedge against adverse commodity price movements. It can also be argued that, in a transitional market economy, there may be different notions of the role of government. Even in Japan, an advanced market economy, the government can exercise considerable influence over business. Indeed, close links between the government and business are well documented. The Japanese government takes an active interest in where and how Japanese companies invest. The American and Australian approach to Japanese investment in the past suggests similar aspects of Chinese investment can be managed in the same way (ITS Global, 2009).

OBSERVATIONS FOR CONSIDERATION

It is beyond the scope of this chapter to draw the possible trajectory and form of China's FDI, but China will most likely continue its OFDI at a two-digit growth rate per annum for the foreseeable future, so long as it continues to run large current account surpluses. A gradual appreciation of the yuan will increase the purchasing power of the Chinese currency, making OFDI all the more attractive to Chinese companies (Woo and Zhang, 2005). The following observations are offered for consideration if the 'Go global' strategy is to be implemented with greater success.

Mode of Entry

A preference for M&A over greenfield investment as the dominant mode of FDI lies in part on asymmetric information. The stock market usually provides the mechanism for setting the value of M&A targets,[12] while there is no such mechanism to assess the value of greenfield investment. In the wake of the global financial crisis, after a 16 percent decline in 2008, cross-border acquisitions contracted by 34 percent (65 percent in value) in 2009, as compared to a 15 percent retrenchment in the number of greenfield FDI projects (UNCTAD, 2010).

Cross-border M&As, however, are expected to pick up. In innovation industries, M&As have been used to gain fast and exclusive access to technology. Chinese TNCs are likely to take advantage of lower asset prices to further their foreign expansion through M&As. Recent transactions have highlighted opportunities in the automotive industry in particular. It should be noted, however, that while some countries introduced policy measures to promote foreign investment by improving the general investment policy environment, there was also a tightening of the regulatory framework by adding local content requirements or by introducing new foreign ownership limitations in specific sectors. According to UNCTAD (2010), out of the 102 new national policy measures affecting FDI identified in 2009, 31 were aimed at tighter regulations for FDI. These measures are driven in part by increased concern over the protection of strategic industries, national resources and national security.[13] Australia, for example, has expressed a preference for joint projects with less than 50 percent ownership for greenfields or less than 15 percent for major producers in resource sectors.[14]

How might the Chinese mitigate the forthcoming frictions? The Japanese experience might offer a more optimistic road map for China. In the 1980s, the Japanese used greenfield investment in many industries to avoid or defuse protectionism in the USA. Greenfield investment creates new jobs and tax revenues as opposed to the 'mere' change of ownership entailed in an acquisition (Milhaupt, 2009).[15] Furthermore, from the perspective of TNCs, greenfield investment could be less costly and less risky. It also provides greater flexibility in adjusting the activity at the initial stage of establishment, which enhances the ability to respond promptly to crises.

Where M&As are unavoidable, it is wise for Chinese investors to take horizontal M&A transactions rather than vertical (that is, upstream/downstream) M&A transactions. On the horizontal M&A model, various forms of cooperation other than equity investment should be used. This is aimed at having a secure supply of resources and pricing power on the global market, rather than gaining control over targets, influence over pricing or the ability to appoint directors to the targets (Oisson and Xiong, 2010). It is also essential that any acquisitions include measures to assuage public concern over the transfer of sensitive technology or predatory investment practices.

Integration into Local Communities

So far as TNCs are concerned, 'if you want to be accepted, you must be good local citizens and demonstrate a commitment to the market and society as a whole' (Milhaupt, 2009, p. 38). However, many TNCs have been targeted by civil society and suffered a loss of reputation due to the exposure of their poor labor, environmental or human rights practices. This has led to various initiatives under the banner of good corporate citizenship and the TNC universe calling for a new investment-development paradigm (UNCTAD, 2010).

Regardless of mode of entry, it is important for Chinese TNCs to integrate quickly and deeply into local communities. In this regard, companies should be mindful of the following:

- To avoid even the appearance of employment discrimination or mistreatment of employees (most Chinese TNCs have misguided attempts to employ Chinese human resource policies and practices).
- To adopt best practices of corporate governance and appoint local people as independent directors.
- To lobby through collective organizations rather than on behalf of individual Chinese companies or interests.
- To demonstrate good will at the local level (Japanese companies in the USA established foundations, such as the Toyota USA Foundation, in support of education and care for the disabled).
- Whenever feasible, stakeholders should be included in existing or new forums for discussion and debate to increase information flow and bridge cultural difference.

For the above to happen, several questions deserve attention:[16]

- Will Chinese TNCs have sufficient political leeway to undertake the sort of integration into the American, Australian or European communities and business associations that proved helpful to Japanese companies two decades ago?
- Will Chinese executives have sufficient autonomy to respond to local conditions in Western countries? (They are accustomed to receiving direction and guidance from political authorities in Beijing or elsewhere.)
- Can Chinese companies effectively lobby policymakers in Washington, Canberra or Paris without triggering criticism that the Chinese government is intruding in their political process?
- Will Chinese companies' governance practices in Western countries be significantly better than their domestic practices, or will the problems of poor disclosure, corruption and insider dealing follow Chinese companies going global?
- Will the low or even dangerous quality of some Chinese products fuel negative public reaction to Chinese FDI?

- Will Chinese companies resist the temptation to acquire high-profile or sensitive assets (such as the Rockefeller Center purchase by Mitsubishi Estate Co. in 1989) that might inflame public opinion?

The above questions are impossible to answer at this stage, but Japan's experience suggests that Chinese executives and political leaders would do well to focus on these important questions.

Low-carbon FDI

The global policy debate on tackling climate change is no longer about whether to take action; rather, it is about how much action to take and which actions need to be taken and by whom. According to UNCTAD (2010), US$440 billion of recurring additional global investments per year are required over 2010–15 to limit greenhouse gas emissions to the level needed for a 2 percent target. Low-carbon foreign investment therefore needs to be incorporated into national economic and development strategies. TNCs have an indispensable contribution to make in the shift towards a low-carbon economy.

Low-carbon foreign investment can be defined as either the transfer of technologies, practices and products by TNCs to host countries, or FDI undertaken to acquire or access low-carbon technologies, practices and products. There are two types of low-carbon foreign investment: the introduction of low-carbon processes, and the creation of low-carbon products and services.

Low-carbon FDI had already reached US$90 billion in 2009 in three key industries alone: alternative/renewable electricity generation, recycling and manufacturing of environmental technology products (such as wind turbines, solar panels and bio-fuels). Between 2003 and 2009, as much as 40 percent of low-carbon FDI by value was directed towards developing economies, and about 10 percent of the low-carbon FDI projects was generated by TNCs from developing and transitional economies. Established TNCs are major investors, but new players are emerging, including from the South (UNCTAD, 2010).

In relation to Chinese FDI, the push factors of low-carbon foreign investment such as government policies and public opinion are weighing on decision-making. As most new low-carbon projects are not competitive in the start-up phase, government support such as feed-in tariffs for renewable energy or public procurement is essential. Pull factors are likewise crucial. In addition to general determinants of OFDI, there are certain variations specific to climate change which draw in market-seeking FDI. Similarly, 'cutting-edge green' technologies in particular countries should attract the attention of asset-seeking Chinese TNCs. As with any dynamic technologies, collaboration in research and development by M&A activity may occur in the low-carbon area. Chinese investors may also wish to participate in industry or technology clusters to obtain the sought-after technologies, practices and products.

CONCLUSION

China's OFDI for the period 2002–09 grew at a rate of more than 60 percent per year. The prospect of China becoming a major source of FDI is received with a mixture of enthusiasm and apprehension by many recipient countries. Most economies, including ASEAN countries, would welcome the inflow of long-term equity investment, but there are concerns – especially in developed countries – about the motivations and quality of Chinese capital. While China's OFDI will continue to focus on natural resource-rich regions/countries such as Australia, Africa and Latin America, asset-rich companies (in technology, skilled people, distribution networks) with strong brands in North America and Europe will also continue to be potential FDI targets (Nie and Lu, 2010).

From a long-term perspective, the Japanese experience in the USA and Australia should provide some grounds for optimism around Chinese OFDI in Western countries, although the duration of the process may depend heavily on the success of the FDI entry, how well Chinese TNCs will adapt to local environments – to overcome 'the liability of foreignness' – and how the public will eventually become acclimatized to Chinese products, brands and corporations (Milhaupt, 2009). With increasing awareness of a new investment-development paradigm and new TNC universe, Chinese TNCs should also ensure that their investment in the South, in the bottom of the pyramid in particular, is neither a showcase of philanthropy nor based on economic exploitation. Rather, China's OFDI should form part of a sustainable and beneficial business model in developing economies.

NOTES

1. However, a survey conducted by the Asia Pacific Foundation of Canada, in collaboration with the China Council for the Promotion of International Trade (CCPIT), revealed that respondents (CCPIT member companies) give much less weight to the importance of policy direction and incentives. 'Business potential', on the other hand, is seen as the primary driver (Woo and Zhang, 2005).

2. According to the International Energy Agency (IEA), China's net oil imports were 3.5 million barrels per day (mb/d) in 2006, and the projected net imports are anticipated to reach 7.1mb/d by 2015 and 13.1mb/d by 2030 in its reference scenario, implying that 64 percent and 79 percent of the total demand will have to depend on oil imports, respectively. Likewise, increasing demand for natural gas will drive China to rely increasingly on foreign gas imports, which will reach 37 billion cubic meters (Bcm) by 2030, constituting 29 percent of total natural gas consumption (162 Bcm) (Chen, 2008).

3. From 2002 onward, the Chinese government FDI statistics have been collected in accordance with the Organization for Economic Cooperation and Development (OECD) definitions and the International Monetary Fund's (IMF) balance-of-payments guidelines. Thus, if there were still discrepancies between the Chinese government and the United Nations Conference on Trade and Development's (UNCTAD) FDI statistics, the discrepancies from 2003 should be smaller than before (Cheng and Ma, 2007). The Chinese government FDI statistics provide information on the investment project, destination country/region, industry of the project and project of origin. Although they do not include project, job and investment expenditure in individual recipient economies, they are adequate to be used to identify trends and patterns in the sector/industry.

4. It can be argued that in the Chinese market, as foreign-invested companies usually enjoy a higher reputation, it might still be worthwhile for many domestic companies to take such a round trip.

5. Many analysts agree that Beijing's additional goal is to isolate Taiwan by luring the Latin American nations that still maintain diplomatic relations with Taiwan to shift their diplomatic attention to China. Some argue that China's involvement in the region could pose a future threat to the US influence (Dumbaugh and Sullivan, 2005).

6. In 2006, CNOOC acquired 45 percent of the shares of Nigerian National Petroleum Corp.

7. Technologies used by TNCs from developing countries are likely to be suitable for other developing countries and may therefore contribute to technological upgrading in host African countries. A significant amount of new machinery brought into host African countries – by both Chinese and Indian TNCs – was bought in China (Broadman, 2007).

8. For instance, by purchasing Germany's DA Company, which ranked third out of global industrial sewing machine manufacturing industries, the SGSB GROUP of Shanghai emerged as a world-class sewing equipment manufacturer (Jiang, 2006).

9. In 2005 the Department of Commerce of South Carolina opened its office in Shanghai. In 2008 the office was recognized by the Chinese government as one of the three foreign economic development and investment agencies for its efforts in assisting Chinese companies in investing abroad. The other two winners were the federal organizations of Sweden and Australia.

10. A study undertaken by a Chinese research institution estimates that 65 percent of Chinese FDI projects are losing money (http://news.9ask.cn/touzirongzi/dwtz/200907/169533.html) (accessed 4 October 2010).

11. The restrictiveness of Australia's FDI regime in mining is less than that in both OECD and non-OECD countries, and less than the overall average. On a scale of 0 (no restrictions) to 1 (prohibition of FDI), the OECD's index of FDI regulatory restrictiveness gives Australia a score of 0.1. See http://lowyinterpreter.org/post/2010/07/15/FDI-Less-restrictive-than-we-used-to-be.aspx (accessed 20 October 2010).

12. During financial crises, the stock market becomes unreliable. Nevertheless, in the initial stages of a crisis, investors are able to benefit from the collapse of the stock market to acquire more under-priced targets than before.

13. Recent crises, such as the turmoil in the financial markets and the impact of rising food prices, have also translated into a will to regulate specific industries.

14. For detailed information see http://www.theage.com.au/business/brakes-put-on-chinese-investment-20090924-g4p6.html (accessed 4 October 2010).

15. Despite its strength, greenfield investment can generate its own frictions. It can create excess capacity in an industry, resulting in the closure of local factories.
16. This section draws heavily on Milhaupt (2009).

REFERENCES

Broadman, H.G. (2007), *Africa's Silk Road: China and India's New Economic Frontier*, Washington, DC: The World Bank.

Bräutigam, D. (2010), 'Africa's Eastern promise: what the West can learn from Chinese investment in Africa', *Foreign Affairs*, 5 January, available at http://www.foreignaffairs.com/articles/65916/Deborah-brautigam/africa's-eastern-promise (accessed 4 October 2010).

Buckley, P.J., L.J. Clegg, A.R. Cross, X. Liu, H. Voss and P. Zheng (2007), 'The determinants of Chinese outward foreign investment', *Journal of International Business Studies,* **38**, 499–518.

Chen, S. (2008), 'China's outward FDI and energy security', EAI Working Paper No. 143 of annual meeting of the American Political Science Association, Boston, Massachusetts, USA.

Cheng, L. and Z. Ma (2007), 'China's outward FDI: past and future', mimeo, Hong Kong University of Science and Technology.

Davies, D. (2009), 'On China's rapid growth in outward FDI', *China Daily*, 3 August, available at http://www.chinadaily.com.cn/bw/2009-08/03/content_8506892.htm (accessed 6 October 2010).

Dumbaugh, K. and M.P. Sullivan (2005), 'China's growing interest in Latin America', *CRS Report for Congress*, Order Code RS22119, 20 April, pp. 1–6.

Dunning, J.H. (1993), *Multinational Enterprises and the Global Economy*, London: Addison Welsey.

Ferguson, A (2010), 'Attitudes towards China start to harden', *Sydney Morning Herald*, 29 January, available at http://www.smh.com.au/business/attitudes-towards-china-start-to-harden-20100128-n1vp.html (accessed 6 October 2010).

Gattai, V. (2009), 'EU–China foreign direct investment: a double-sided perspective', *European Studies: A Journal of European Culture, History and Politics*, **19**, 241–58.

Gu, J. (2009), 'China's private enterprises in Africa and the implications for African development', *European Journal of Development Research*, **21**(4), 570–87.

Havrylchyk, O. and S. Poncet (2007), 'Foreign direct investment in China: reward or remedy?', *Journal of World Economy*, **30**(11). 1662–81.

ITS Global (2008), 'Foreign direct investment in Australia', available at http://www.itsglobal.net (accessed 4 October 2010).

ITS Global (2009), 'Foreign investment in Australia: China and common sense', www.itsglobal.net.

Jiang, X. (2006), 'A new trend in China's FDI inflow and outflow', *China Economist*, 17 July, available at http://gr2.mofcom.gov.cn/article/china-news/200703/20070304487782.html (accessed 4 October 2010).

Kiggundu, M. (2008), 'A profile of China's outward foreign direct investment to Africa', paper submitted to the American Society for Business and Behavioral Sciences (ASBBS) Conference, Las Vegas, 22–24 February.

Krkoska, L. and Y. Korniyenko (2008), 'China's investments in Russia: where do they go and how important are they?', *China and Eurasia Forum Quarterly*, **6**(1), 39–49.

Ma, W. (2008), 'China's capital outflow: facing political risks and learning the ropes', 10 March, available at http://www.chinastakes.com/2008/3/ Chinas-Capital-Outflow-Facing-Political-Risks-and-Learning-the-Ropes.html (accessed 6 October 2010).

Milhaupt, C. (2009), 'Is the US ready for FDI from China? Lessons from Japanese experience in the 1980s', *Deloitte, Investing in the United States: A Reference Series for Chinese Investors*, Vol. 1, Vale Columbia Center on Sustainable International Investment.

National Bureau of Statistics of China (NBSC) (2010), *2009 Statistical Bulletin of China's Outward Foreign Direct Investment,* Beijing: China Statistics Press.

Nie, W. and A. Lu (2010), 'Why Chinese businesses invest abroad', *Jakarta Post*, 1 June, available at http://m.thejakartapost.com/news/2010/01/06/why-chinese-businesses-invest-abroad.html (accessed 4 October 2010).

Oisson, D. and X. Jin (2010), 'China outbound investment will impact on the Australian regulatory landscape', available at www.mallesons.com/publications/2010/Apr/10306748w.htm (accessed 4 October 2010).

Schüller, M. and A. Turner (2005), 'Global ambitions: Chinese companies spread their wings', *China Aktuell*, **4**, 3–12.

Sohlman, S. (2009), *Kina relationer med Afrika ur ett handelsperspektiv*, Stockholm: Kommerskollegium (Swedish National Board of Trade).

Stratfor Global Intelligence (2007), *'China: FDI as Political Risk Insurance'*, Stratfor Global Intelligence Database, available at http://www.stratfor.com/ china_fdi_political_risk_insurance (accessed 6 October 2010).

Thirlwell, M. (2010), 'FDI: China hearts Australia', available at http://lowyin-terpreter.org/post/2010/07/19/FDI-China-hearts-Australia.aspx (accessed 4 October 2010).

UNCTAD (2004), *World Investment Report 2004*, New York and Geneva: United Nations.

UNCTAD (2006), *World Investment Report 2006*, New York and Geneva: United Nations.

UNCTAD (2010), *World Investment Report 2010*, New York and Geneva: United Nations.

Wheatley, A. (2009), 'Why China will keep investing abroad', 20 July, available at http://www.nytimes.com/2009/07/21/business/global/21inside.html?_ r=1&pagewanted=2 (accessed 6 October 2010).

Woo, Y.P. and K. Zhang (2005), 'China goes global: the implications of Chinese outward direct investment for Canada', 23 November, available at http:// www.asiapacific.ca/analysis/pubs/pdfs/surveys/china_goes_global.pdf (accessed 4 October 2010).

APPENDIX

Table 4.A1 Chinese OFDI flows by major destination countries in 2009 (in US$ billion)

	Destination	OFDI flows		Destination	OFDI flows
1	Hong Kong (China)	35.60	17	Indonesia	0.23
2	Cayman Islands	5.37	18	Cambodia	0.22
3	Australia	2.44	19	Laos	0.20
4	Luxembourg	2.27	20	UK	0.19
5	British Virgin Islands	1.61	21	Germany	0.18
6	Singapore	1.41	22	Nigeria	0.17
7	USA	0.91	23	Kirghizstan	0.14
8	Canada	0.61	24	Egypt	0.13
9	Macau (China)	0.46	25	Iran	0.12
10	Burma	0.38	26	Turkmenistan	0.12
11	Russia	0.35	27	Brazil	0.12
12	Turkey	0.29	28	Venezuela	0.12
13	Mongolia	0.28	29	Vietnam	0.11
14	Korea	0.27	30	Zambia	0.11
15	Algeria	0.23	31	Netherlands	0.10
16	Democratic Republic of Congo	0.23			

Source: NBSC (2010).

Table 4.A2   Chinese FDI projects in South Carolina, USA, 2009

American Yuncheng Plate Making Inc., Spartanburg, 120 jobs
Parent Company: Dongguan Yuncheng Plate Making Group Co. Ltd,
 Guangdong
Bluestar Silicones USA Corp., Rock Hill, 50 jobs
Parent Company: China National Chemical Corp. aka ChemChina, Beijing
China Construction America of South Carolina Inc., Columbia, 25 jobs
Parent Company: China State Construction Engineering Corp., Beijing
Cosco Container Lines Americas Inc., Charleston, 8 jobs
Parent Company: China Ocean Shipping (Group) Company, Beijing
Cosco Logistics (Americas) Inc., North Charleston, 8 jobs
Parent Company: China Ocean Shipping (Group) Company, Beijing
E-P Equipment USA Corp., Inman, 8 jobs
Parent Company: E-P Equipment, Hangzhou
Fuyao North America Inc., Greenville, 5 jobs
Parent Company: Fuyao Glass Industry Group Co. Ltd, Fuzhou City
GSP North America Co. Inc., Spartanburg, 90 jobs
Parent Company: Guansheng Auto Parts Manufacture Co. Ltd, Wenzhou
Haier America, Camden, 225 jobs
Parent Company: Qingdao Haier Company Ltd, Qingdao
Techtronic Industries North America Inc. Anderson, Liberty, & Pickens, 1202
 jobs
Parent Company: Techtronic Industries Co. Ltd, Hong Kong
Total Employment: 1891

Source: South Carolina Department of Commerce, December 2009.

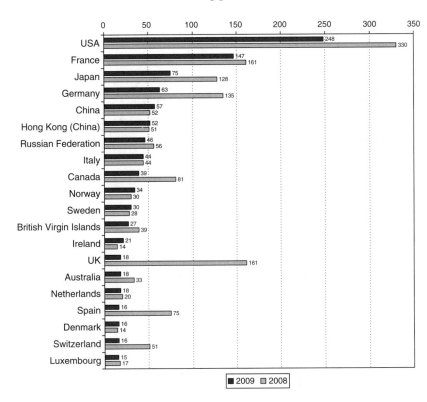

Source: UNCTAD (2010) and NBSC (2010).

Figure 4.A1   FDI outflows: top 20 home economies, 2008–09 (in US$
billion)

5. Determinants of investment intensity of source economies in China

Chunlai Chen

INTRODUCTION

One of the most prominent features of foreign direct investment (FDI) in China is the overwhelming dominance of developing economies. Comparing the two groups of developing and industrialized source economies at year-end 2008, investments from developing source economies accounted for 75.38 per cent of China's total inward FDI stock, while investments from industrialized source economies accounted for only 24.62 per cent of the total.[1]

Why has China been so successful in attracting FDI inflows from developing economies, especially from the Asian Newly Industrializing Economies (NIEs), but has not been as successful in attracting FDI inflows from industrialized economies, especially from the Western European economies, even though they are the major investors for world FDI? In other words, what factors explain the investment relations between economies? Braga and Bannister (1994) find that economic proximity, which includes geographic distance, cultural difference and regulatory barriers, affects the investment relations between countries. The investment levels are higher between countries which have higher economic proximity. For example, FDI flows among Association of South East Asian Nations (ASEAN) economies have increased dramatically since the 1990s. Markusen (1995) observes that the bulk of world FDI flows is among economies with similar per capita incomes and similar relative factor endowments. This observation is supported by the high levels of FDI flows among developed countries. Caves (1996) points out that languages and cultures shared between economies reduce multinational enterprises' (MNEs) transaction costs and that the bulk of foreign investments go where the transactional and information-cost disadvantages are least. Previous studies have made certain contributions to explaining the factors affecting investment relations between economies. However, there has been a lack of empirical studies linking the theoretical explanations with the empirical observations. Therefore, this chapter intends to fill the gap and contribute to the existing FDI literature. The chapter will investigate and analyse these issues empirically by using the concept of an investment intensity index. This index reveals the relative importance of an economy as a host for a source economy's investment as compared to the rest of the world as a host for the same source economy's investment.

The chapter is structured as follows. The next section presents a brief overview of the composition of FDI sources in China and the third section analyses the investment intensity of source economies in this country. The fourth section puts forward some hypotheses and discusses the factors which are thought to be important in determining the investment intensity of source economies in China. The fifth section uses regression analysis to test the hypotheses, and the conclusion is presented in the final section.

THE COMPOSITION OF FDI SOURCES

Since 1979 more than 170 economies have invested in China. However, who are the major investors? By the end of 2008, as shown in Table 5.1, FDI in China was overwhelmingly dominated by developing economies, which accounted for 75.38 per cent of the total accumulated FDI inflows, while industrialized economies accounted for only 24.62 per cent of the total. Among the developing economies, as a group the Asian NIEs[2] has been the largest investor, accounting for 56.64 per cent of the total. Within the Asian NIEs, Hong Kong has held the dominant position, accounting for 41.75 per cent of the total, followed by Taiwan (5.76 per cent), South Korea (4.74 per cent) and Singapore (4.39 per cent). The four ASEAN economies[3] accounted for 1.48 per cent of the total.

One notable feature is the large share held by the tax-haven economies. FDI inflows into China from these economies increased dramatically in the 1990s and particularly in the 2000s. As a result, their combined share in total FDI inflows increased to 13.64 per cent by the end of 2008. The Virgin Islands took the dominant position, accounting for 9.78 per cent of the total, followed by the Cayman Islands (1.78 per cent) and Samoa (1.30 per cent).

Among the industrialized economies, Japan and the USA are the most important investors in China, accounting for 7.78 per cent and 7.18 per cent respectivelyof the total, while the combined share of the European Union (EU) (15) was 7.19 per cent. Apart from the UK, Germany, the Netherlands and France, whose shares are 1.89 per cent, 1.76 per cent,

*Table 5.1   Accumulated FDI inflows into China by developing and
industrialized economies, 1983–2008 (calculated at constant
1990 US dollar prices)*

	Year 1983–2008	
	US$ (million)	(%)
Developing Economies	506 703	75.38
NIEs	380 719	56.64
Hong Kong	280 628	41.75
Taiwan	38 699	5.76
South Korea	31 861	4.74
Singapore	29 531	4.39
ASEAN (4)	9976	1.48
Malaysia	3853	0.57
Thailand	2644	0.39
Philippines	2002	0.30
Indonesia	1477	0.22
Tax-haven economies	91 700	13.64
Virgin Islands	65 709	9.78
Cayman Islands	11 990	1.78
Samoa	8759	1.30
Other developing economies	24 307	3.62
Industrialized Economies	165 506	24.62
Japan	52 320	7.78
USA	48 287	7.18
EU (15)	48 360	7.19
UK	12 698	1.89
Germany	11 816	1.76
Netherlands	7112	1.06
France	6915	1.03
Italy	3472	0.52
Other industrialized economies	16 538	2.46
Canada	4993	0.74
Australia	4566	0.68
New Zealand	626	0.09
Total	672 208	100

Source: National Bureau of Statistics of China (NBSC) (various years), and Ministry of
Commerce of China (MOFCOM).

1.06 per cent and 1.03 per cent, respectively, no other individual industrialized economy has contributed more than 1 per cent of the total accumulated FDI inflows into China.

Figure 5.1 presents the annual FDI inflows into China by developing

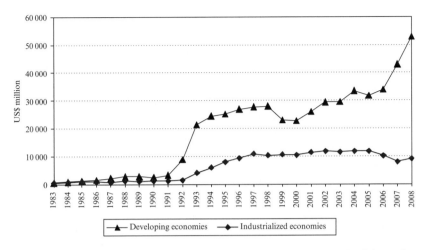

Source: National Bureau of Statistics of China (NBSC) (various years) and Ministry of Commerce of China (MOFCOM).

Figure 5.1   *FDI inflows into China by developing and industrialized economies (US$ million at 1990 constant prices)*

and industrialized economies during the period 1983–2008. In the sub-period 1983–91, FDI inflows into China were at a low level but increased steadily. Developing economies accounted for 66.75 per cent while industrialized economies accounted for 33.25 per cent of the total FDI inflows.

From 1992, FDI inflows into China surged. Both developing and industrialized economies increased their investments in China, but the rate of increase for developing economies was much higher than that of the industrialized economies from 1992 to 1997. However, during 1997–2000, FDI inflows from developing economies declined because of the Asian financial crisis but inflows from industrialized economies remained relatively stable. Despite the decline, the share of developing economies in total FDI inflows into China increased to 74.51 per cent while the share of industrialized economies declined to 25.49 per cent during the sub-period 1992–2000.

After its accession into the World Trade Organization (WTO), FDI inflows into China increased rapidly, almost all of which came from developing economies. Inflows increased from US$25.96 billion in 2001 to US$52.95 billion in 2008 (at 1990 constant US dollar prices). However, FDI inflows from industrialized economies only increased marginally during 2002–05 and even declined during 2006–08. As a result, the share of industrialized economies in total FDI inflows into China further declined to 23.41 per cent while the share of developing economies increased to 76.59 per cent during the sub-period 2001–08.

Obviously, FDI in China by source of economies, on the one hand, presents significant diversification in terms of the total number of investing economies; on the other hand, it reveals great concentration in terms of the magnitudes invested by the source economies. However, analysis of FDI sources in China requires caution. This is especially important in explaining the dominance of Hong Kong in China's FDI and the large increase in FDI inflows from the tax-haven economies, because of the 'round-tripping' issue.

Round-tripping involves the circular flow of capital out of China and the subsequent 're-investment' of this 'foreign' capital in China for the purpose of benefiting from fiscal entitlements accorded to foreign investors. Because the funds originate in the host economy itself, round-tripping inflates actual FDI inflows. According to UNCTAD (2007), a significant share of FDI inflows into China is round-tripping, mainly via Hong Kong and more recently and increasingly via some tax-haven economies — the Virgin Islands, Cayman Islands and Samoa. While official estimates by the Chinese government are not available, Guonan Ma suggested that round-tripping inward FDI accounted for 25 per cent of China's FDI inflows in 1992,[4] a figure supported by Harrold and Lall (1993). However, Xiao (2004) estimated that round-tripping FDI accounted for 40 per cent of China's total FDI inflows during 1994–2001.

Round-tripping typically involves three steps: (1) the accumulation of new capital in China, (2) the capital flight out of China; and (3) the round-tripping FDI back to China. Because of the fast economic growth and high savings rate, China has accumulated a large amount of new capital. However, a large part of the new capital has found its way abroad through miss-invoicing in international trade, smuggling and other channels of capital flight since those who are creating the new capital have strong incentives to diversify domestic risks and to seek better protection of property rights (Xiao, 2004). Some of this capital has stayed abroad waiting for opportunities to return to China. On average, the round-tripping FDI — the returning Chinese capital — is about 20–30 per cent of the capital flight (Xiao, 2004). The accumulated capital flight then forms the base for sustained round-tripping FDI when the opportunities to make profits and create new capital at home continue.

Round-tripping is driven by a number of incentives, in the case of China, preferential treatment offered to FDI and property rights protection being the main two. First, since the beginning of economic reform, the Chinese government has used tax incentives, tariff concessions and various preferential treatments intensively and selectively to attract FDI into designated areas and industries. Such preferential treatment is the primary incentive for domestic firms to engage in round-tripping. Second, China's property rights protection enforcement is weak and many private enterprises operate in an environment of restrictive regulations with loose protection of property rights. Thus, the private sector has strong incentives to move their profits out of China and then move them back in the form of FDI when they see potential profit opportunities as the Chinese government tends to give greater to the property rights of foreign investors. In addition, China's foreign exchange control regime, and better financial services overseas, influence FDI round-tripping.

After China's accession to the WTO, China strengthened property rights protection and gradually standardized national treatment of FDI firms, providing better protection of property rights and offering them greater market access. However, many of the preferential treatments offered to FDI firms were then reduced and eventually eliminated. In March 2007 China passed a new corporate income tax law, unifying the corporate income tax rates for foreign and domestic enterprises to 25 per cent. The unification of the corporate income tax rate, the elimination of preferential treatment of FDI firms and improved property rights protection will reduce the incentives for FDI round-tripping.

Another explanation for the rise in FDI into China from the tax-haven economies is the 'transit' investment in China from other economies via these economies in order to lower (or eliminate) their fiscal commitments. For example, the number of companies in Hong Kong that are incorporated in Bermuda and the Cayman Islands jumped 5.2 times from 178 in 1990 to 924 in 2000 (Wu et al., 2002). Partly to take advantage of the tax regime, but also to bypass the Taiwanese government's restrictions on investment in the mainland, the Virgin Islands and Cayman Islands rank second and third, respectively after China as the biggest recipients of Taiwan's outward investment (Breslin, 2003). This suggests that FDI in China from Hong Kong and Taiwan is more significant than the official data suggest.

Therefore, when we interpret the composition of FDI sources in China, we should acknowledge the data problems. However, since Hong Kong's investment is so dominant, even when we deduct its estimated investment of 25 per cent, it is still as high as 32 per cent of the adjusted total FDI stock, far ahead of any other investors. Therefore, despite the round-tripping problem, the general findings of FDI sources in China are still valid. The largest single investor in China is Hong Kong followed by Japan, the USA, Taiwan, South Korea and Singapore. As a group, the Asian NIEs are the largest investors in China followed by the tax-haven economies, the EU (15) and the four ASEAN economies.

THE INVESTMENT INTENSITY OF SOURCE ECONOMIES IN CHINA

Why has China been so successful in attracting FDI inflows from developing economies, especially from the Asian NIEs, but has not been very impressive in attracting FDI inflows from industrialized economies, especially from the Western European economies? In other words, what factors explain the investment relations between economies? One way to compare an economy's relative importance for its source economies' investments is to calculate the source economies' investment intensity indexes. The concept of investment intensity originated from the concept of trade intensity (see Drysdale and Garnaut, 1994).

Based on the concept of the trade intensity index, the investment intensity index can be calculated from the following equation:

$$III_{ij} = \left(\frac{\frac{I_{ij}}{I_{*j}}}{\frac{I_{i*}}{I_{**}}} \right) \times 100 \qquad (5.1)$$

where:

III_{ij} = investment intensity index of economy i's investment in economy j
I_{ij} = investment by economy i in economy j
I_{*j} = investment from the world in economy j
I_{i*} = investment from economy i in the world
I_{**} = total investment in the world

The index measures the relative importance of economy j as a host for economy i's investment as compared to the rest of the world. It can be interpreted as a measure of the relative resistances to FDI flows between economies reflected by the variations in the investment intensity index. An index above 100 per cent indicates that economy i's investment in economy j is more than the amount of its share of investment in the world. This implies that the relative resistance to FDI flows between economy i and economy j is lower than those between economy i and the rest of the world.

Table 5.2, which reports the investment intensity indexes between China and its major investors, reveals two interesting findings. First, the investment intensity indexes of Hong Kong, Taiwan, Singapore, South Korea, Thailand, Malaysia, Indonesia and the Philippines are all over 100 per cent, indicating that China is more important as a host for these economies' investments as compared to the rest of the world. In contrast, except for Japan, the investment intensity indexes are all below 100 per cent

Table 5.2   Investment intensity index of the major investors in China (%)

Economy	1992–95	1996–2000	2001–05	2006–08	1992–2008
Hong Kong	882	1122	1135	1255	1145
Taiwan	1038	1084	724	475	881
South Korea	280	671	1601	691	833
Philippines	486	3114	1482	278	748
Thailand	510	1072	854	152	540
Singapore	253	734	365	494	476
Japan	98	241	195	111	168
Malaysia	85	269	259	79	149
Indonesia	192	866	129	71	148
New Zealand	7	49	n.a.	133	86
Australia	54	147	207	41	83
USA	29	52	43	22	39
Germany	8	24	54	18	24
Canada	22	22	23	18	21
Italy	20	37	16	16	20
Netherlands	5	20	19	36	20
UK	15	18	18	12	16
Denmark	5	8	17	24	13
Austria	7	18	15	11	12
France	7	14	11	6	10
Switzerland	5	15	10	8	10
Finland	1	6	18	27	10
Sweden	3	9	8	11	9
Spain	4	2	4	6	4
Ireland	2	2	1	13	4
Portugal	1	3	4	4	4
Norway	2	7	2	3	3
Belgium	4	2	2	3	2

Note: n.a. = not available.

Source: Calculated from National Bureau of Statistics of China (NBSC) (various years), Ministry of Commerce of China (MOFCOM), *Invest in China*, FDI Statistics, and UNCTAD (various years).

for the industrialized economies. However, among these economies, the investment intensity indexes of Japan, the USA, Australia and New Zealand are relatively high compared with those of the Western European economies, which may reflect the regional biases of these economies' investments in the Asia-Pacific region.

Second, the investment intensity indexes are higher for those source economies in which the per capita income gaps between them and China are smaller. On the contrary, the investment intensity indexes are lower for those source economies in which the per capita income gaps between them and China are larger.

THE DETERMINANTS OF INVESTMENT INTENSITY — THE HYPOTHESES

What factors explain the differences in the investment intensity indexes of source economies? The investment intensity index is one of the indicators of economic proximity, which is a comprehensive conceptual measure of the overall similarities among economies. The factors affecting economic proximity include the geographic distance, cultural difference and regulatory barriers (Braga and Bannister, 1994). Since the investment intensity index is an indicator of economic proximity, the factors affecting economic proximity must affect the investment intensity index as well. In addition, there is apparent evidence that the bulk of world FDI flows is among economies with similar per capita incomes and similar relative factor endowments (Markusen, 1995), therefore we also take the economic and technological gap among countries as one of the important factors affecting the investment intensity index.

Can these factors explain the differences of the investment intensity indexes of the source economies in China? Based on the above discussion, we make the following hypotheses.

Hypothesis 1: The value of the investment intensity index of a source economy in China is negatively related to the gap in economic and technological development levels between China and that source economy.

Hypothesis 2: The value of the investment intensity index of a source economy in China is positively related to the levels of economic proximity between China and that source economy.

Based on Hypothesis 1, the differences in per capita income between China and the source economies are used as the proxy for the gap in economic and technological development levels between China and the source economies. The differences in per capita income, denoted as DPGDP, is the per capita GDP difference at 1990 constant US dollars. The DPGDP is expected to be negatively related to the investment intensity index.

Based on Hypothesis 2, the geographic distance between China and each of the source economies is used as a proxy for the transport and communication costs. The geographic distance, denoted as DIST, is expected to be negatively related to the investment intensity index. The distance between China and the other economies is the physical distance between the capital cities which is obtained from the Great Circle Calculator (at http://argray.com/dist/).

The cultural difference between China and each of the source economies is represented by a dummy variable defined as CCL. We give a value of one for the economies in which the main culture and language are Chinese, including Hong Kong, Macao, Taiwan and Singapore, and zero for the other economies. The cultural difference is expected to be positively related to the investment intensity index.

Another two dummy variables, East and South East Asia and the Asia-Pacific region, denoted as ESEA and AP, are used to test the regional effect on the investment intensity index. We give a value of one for the source economies within these regions and zero otherwise.

EMPIRICAL ANALYSIS AND EXPLANATIONS

The Empirical Model and Variable Specification

To test the hypotheses of investment intensity index of source economies in China, we use the following empirical model:

$$\ln III_{ij,t} = \beta_0 + \beta_1 \ln DPGDP_{ij,t} + \beta_2 \ln DIST_{ij} + \beta_3 CCL_i + \beta_4 ESEA_i$$

$$+ \beta_5 AP_i + v_i + \varepsilon_{i,t} \qquad (5.2)$$

The dependent variable, denoted as $III_{ij,t}$, is the investment intensity index of economy i in China (j) in time period t. The independent variables of DPGDP, DIST, CCL, ESEA and AP are hypothesized and defined in the above section. The dependent and independent variables are summarized in Table 5.3.

In this empirical study, we choose 34 source economies whose combined FDI accounted for 84 per cent of the total accumulated FDI inflows into China.[5] These economies are: Argentina, Australia, Austria, Belgium, Brazil, Canada, Denmark, Finland, France, Germany, Greece, Hong Kong (China), Indonesia, Ireland, Italy, Japan, Luxembourg, Macao (China), Malaysia, Netherlands, New Zealand, Norway, Philippines, Portugal, Singapore, South Africa, South Korea, Spain, Sweden, Switzerland, Taiwan (China), Thailand, the UK and the USA.

There are large annual fluctuations in the investment intensity index.

*Table 5.3   Variable list of the determinants of the investment intensity
index of source economies in China*

Variable name	Specification of variables	Sources and explanations
Dependent Variable		
$III_{ij,t}$	Investment intensity index of source economy i in China (j) in time period t.	Calculated from various issues of National Bureau of Statistics, *China Statistical Yearbook*; Ministry of Commerce of China, Invest in China, FDI Statistics; and various issues of United Nations, *World Investment Report*.
Independent Variables		
$DPGDP_{ij,t}$	Difference in per capita GDP between source economy i and China (j) in time period t. US dollars at 1990 prices.	Calculated from United Nations Statistical Division, National Accounts at http://unstats.un.org/unsd/snaama/dnllist.asp.
$DIST_{ij}$	Geographic distance between the capital cities of source economy i and China (j).	Obtained from the Great Circle Calculator (at http://argray.com/dist/).
CCL_i	Dummy variable for cultural difference.	One for Hong Kong, Macao, Taiwan and Singapore, zero for other source economies.
$ESEA_i$	Dummy variable for East and South East Asia region.	One for Hong Kong, Macao, Taiwan, Singapore, South Korea, Malaysia, Indonesia, Philippines, Thailand and Japan, zero for other source economies.
AP_i	Dummy variable for Asia and Pacific region.	One for Hong Kong, Macao, Taiwan, Singapore, South Korea, Malaysia, Indonesia, Philippines, Thailand, Japan, Australia, New Zealand, Canada and the USA, zero for other source economies.

Table 5.4   Ordinary least squares (OLS) regression results of investment intensity of source economies in China (1992–2008)

Variables	1	2
Constant	11.36	4.58
	(15.44)***	(4.86)***
LnDPGDP	–0.61	–0.19
	(–7.89)***	(–2.03)**
LnDIST	–0.62	–0.16
	(–13.05)***	(–6.11)***
CCL		0.72
		(2.45)**
ESEA		1.42
		(4.01)***
AP		1.70
		(6.73)***
R^2	0.55	0.78
No. of observations	136	136
F-statistics	127.21***	265.42***

Note: Standard errors are adjusted for White's heteroskedasticity; t-statistics are in parentheses. ** Statistically significant at 0.05 level (two-tail test); *** Statistically significant at 0.01 level (two-tail test).

To reduce the fluctuation, we use the average investment intensity index of four periods, 1992–95, 1996–2000, 2001–05 and 2006–08. Therefore, we have panel data of 34 source economies over four time periods ($t = 1, 2, 3$ and 4), containing 136 observations.

Regression Results and Explanations

We first estimate equation (5.2) by using the ordinary least squares (OLS) regression. The regression results are reported in Table 5.4. The regression performed very well; all the independent variables have the expected signs and are statistically significant.

For a robustness check, we also estimate equation (5.2) under random-effects panel regression so that we do not preclude the use of key fixed effect indicators which we wish to identify separately. The most obvious of these are the distance variable (DIST) – proxy for the transport and communication costs – and the cultural and language variable (CCL) – proxy for the cultural difference between China and each of the source economies – as well as the regional dummy variables (ESEA and AP), which may have an important bearing on the investment intensity of

Table 5.5   *Random-effects model regression results of investment intensity of source economies in China (1992–2008)*

Variables	1	4
Constant	11.28	5.00
	(8.48)***	(3.73)***
LnDPGDP	–0.60	–0.23
	(–4.33)***	(–1.76)*
LnDIST	–0.62	–0.17
	(–10.22)***	(–4.24)***
CCL		0.79
		(1.87)*
ESEA		1.31
		(2.62)***
AP		1.71
		(4.69)***
No. of observations	136	136
No. of groups	34	34
R^2: overall	0.55	0.78
Wald Chi^2	545.66***	5123.77***

Note: Standard errors are adjusted for clustering on group; t-statistics are in parentheses. * Statistically significant at 0.10 level (two-tail test); ** Statistically significant at 0.05 level (two-tail test); *** Statistically significant at 0.01 level (two-tail test).

source economies in China. The regression results of the random-effects model are reported in Table 5.5. The model performed very well and all the independent variables have the expected signs and are statistically significant. For our data set, the random-effects model produces essentially the same estimates as the OLS regression.

We now interpret the regression results. In general, the per capita income gap between China and the source economies has a negative impact on the investment intensity index. This implies that FDI flows are negatively related to the differences in the economic and technological development levels among economies. This result is consistent with the findings obtained by Markusen (1995) and Caves (1996, pp.46–56) that the bulk of FDI is among economies with similar per capita incomes and similar relative factor endowments. This partially explains the low levels of investment of the industrialized economies in China.

The distance between China and the source economies – the proxy of transport and communication costs – is an important constraining factor affecting the investment intensities of source economies in China. In contrast, the common Chinese culture and language and the existence of overseas Chinese relations have a positive impact on the investment intensities of source economies in China. Thus, our results have provided support for Caves's view that languages and cultures shared between economies reduce MNEs' transaction costs and that the bulk of foreign investments go where the transactional and information cost disadvantages are least (Caves, 1996, pp.46–56).

The positive East Asia, South East Asia and Asia-Pacific regional dummies show that the economies within these regions invested more in China than the economies outside these regions. This implies that economies tend to invest more in the region where they belong. The result also partially explains the relatively higher investment intensities in China of Japan, the USA, Australia and New Zealand as compared to other industrialized economies, especially from Western Europe.

In general, the regressions provided strong support for our hypotheses set out above. The investment intensities in China of the source economies are negatively related to the gap in the economic and technological development levels and are positively related to the levels of economic proximity between China and the source economies.

The regression results allow us to explain the differences of investment intensities and provide some implications for future investment in China of the major source economies.

Since the Asian NIEs' investments, particularly from Hong Kong, have been the largest part of the story of FDI in China, it is worth looking at these investments in a little more detail. Their remarkable intensities are well explained by the factors of the gap in economic and technological development levels and the levels of economic proximity between China and the Asian NIEs.

First, it is generally agreed that the economic and technological development level of the Asian NIEs is above that of China but lower than that of the industrialized economies. In the last four decades the economies of the Asian NIEs have developed relatively faster than other developing countries. This has led to both a rapid accumulation of human and physical capital and a rapid rise in their real wages. The changes in resource endowments of production factors have led to a process of economic restructuring and technological upgrading in the Asian NIEs. Consequently, many labour-intensive industries lost competitiveness, and realized that investment abroad was a means of utilizing accumulated managerial and technical expertise and established export markets. Coincidently, China, with its abundant labour supply, has a comparative advantage in labour-intensive activities. The labour-intensive production technology and the well-established international export markets of the Asian NIEs are well suited to China's need to realize its comparative advantages and to promote its international exports. Therefore, China is a good location for the Asian NIE investors to explore overseas investment opportunities.

The second factor is the high proximity of Hong Kong, Taiwan and to a less extent Singapore and South Korea with China. The common Chinese culture, language and close geographical distance greatly reduces the costs of doing business in China for these investors.

The rapid increase and the high investment intensities in China from ASEAN economies (Thailand, the Philippines, Malaysia and Indonesia) in the 1990s and the 2000s resembled the early pattern of the Asian NIEs' investments in most aspects. In general, the changing domestic economic structures, the extensive Chinese business networks[6] and the close geographical location have led to and facilitated the companies in the ASEAN economies to venture into China.

China, with its relatively abundant labour resources and a comparative advantage in labour-intensive activities, is an attractive location for developing economy investors to explore overseas investment opportunities, particularly for export-oriented FDI. Since its accession to the WTO, China has, on the one hand, reduced trade and investment barriers and improved the investment environment, while, on the other, its export markets have been greatly enlarged as WTO member economies – particularly industrialized economies – have opened domestic markets to China's exports. Therefore, there are great incentives for developing economy investors to increase FDI in China in general and to increase export-oriented FDI in particular. It is expected that China will remain an important host economy for investments from developing economies well into the future.

Investments from industrialized economies are somewhat different from that of the Asian NIEs and other developing economies. This is because, first, the economic and technological gap between the industrialized economies and China is relatively large and the transfer of technology is hampered, to a certain extent, by the appropriateness of the technology. Second, firms in industrialized economies usually possess more advanced technology and production techniques. Since the legal framework for protecting intellectual property rights in China is relatively weak, firms in industrialized economies that have advanced technology and production techniques are reluctant to invest in China. Third, the industrialized economies, especially the Western European economies, have little proximity with China, therefore the costs for their firms to do business in China are relatively high. As a result, they are very prudent in setting up ventures in China. Fourth, the services sector in industrialized economies is advanced and has recorded the highest growth rates in global FDI flows over the last three decades. Most of China's services industries were closed to FDI before its 2001 accession to the WTO. Fifth, the large MNEs are the main carriers of FDI from industrialized economies and cross-border mergers and acquisitions (M&As) are an increasingly important means by which they carry out FDI. However, cross-border M&As transactions by foreign investors in China have only been allowed in an experimental fashion in recent years. All these have negative impacts on the investment decisions of industrialized economy investors. Consequently, the magnitude and the intensity of investment from industrialized economies in China are very low compared with their total investments in the world. However, compared with other industrialized economies, especially the Western European economies, the intensities of investments in China from Japan, the USA, Australia and New Zealand are relatively high. This shows the regional investment bias of these economies towards the Asia-Pacific region.

Obviously, the current composition of FDI sources in China needs to be diversified if China wants to benefit more from FDI. The diversification of FDI sources not only is necessary for China to attract a greater quantity of FDI, but also is very important for it to attract high quality FDI. In general, enterprises from industrialized economies with high technological and innovative capabilities have advantages in high technology, product differentiation, managerial and entrepreneurial skills, and knowledge-based intangible assets. Because of these advantages, FDI from industrialized economies is more interested in the Chinese market. The general implication is that host economies with larger market size, faster economic growth and higher income will attract more market-oriented FDI. China's huge domestic market, fast growth and rising income are very attractive to market-oriented FDI from industrialized economies. Therefore, China has a great potential to attract FDI from industrialized economies. However, to realize its potential, China should fulfil its commitments to the WTO in trade and investment liberalization, particularly in strengthening the protection of intellectual property rights, opening more of the services sector to FDI and relaxing restrictions in cross-border M&As.

CONCLUSION

In this study we analysed the difference in investment intensity of the source economies, and tested the determinants affecting the variations of the investment intensity indexes of the source economies in China. The investment intensity index measures the investment relations between China and its source economies by comparing the relative importance of

China as a host for the source economies' investments as compared to the rest of the world as hosts for these economies' investments. The investment intensity index provides a useful method to analyse the resistance factors influencing investment flows between economies. The study reveals several main findings.

First, the investment intensity index of the source economies in China varies enormously. However, comparing the two groups of the developing economies and the industrialized economies, the investment intensity indexes of the developing economies are all above 100 per cent and are much higher than those of the industrialized economies. This implies that China is more important as a host for the developing economies' investments than for the industrialized economies' investments.

Second, what factors explain the differences in the investment intensities of the major investors in China? The regression analyses provide strong support for our hypotheses. In general, the economic and technological development gaps and the levels of economic proximity are important factors affecting FDI flows between economies.

Third, on the one hand, since economic proximity is positively related to investment intensity between economies, the high economic proximity between China and the East Asian and South East Asian economies, particularly Hong Kong and Taiwan, implies that China will remain an important host economy for investments from these economies. On the other hand, with the sustained and fast economic growth in China, combined with the huge inflows of FDI and technology into its domestic economy, the economic and technological development gaps between China and the industrialized economies will be reduced. As a result, China will become a more important host economy for FDI from the industrialized economies in the near future. However, to realize its potential, China should fulfil its commitments to the WTO in trade and investment liberalization, particularly in strengthening the protection of intellectual property rights, opening more of the services sector to FDI and relaxing restrictions in cross-border M&As.

NOTES

1. The calculation is based on 1990 constant US dollar prices.
2. The Asian NIEs include Hong Kong, Singapore, South Korea and Taiwan.
3. The four ASEAN economies are Indonesia, Malaysia, Philippines and Thailand.
4. Personal communication to the author from Dr Guonan Ma at the 'China Update 2007' conference held at the Australian National University in 2007. Dr Ma advised that he estimated in 1993 that round-tripping FDI accounted for 25 per cent of China's total FDI inflows in 1992.

5. The tax-haven economies of the Virgin Islands, the Cayman Islands and Samoa, are excluded from the sample because of the 'transit' investment issue discussed in the previous section.
6. For more detailed analysis on overseas Chinese business networks, see EAAU (1995).

REFERENCES

Braga, C. and G. Bannister (1994), 'East Asian investment and trade: prospects for growing regionalisation in the 1990s', *Transnational Corporations*, **3**(1), 97–136.

Breslin, S. (2003), 'Foreign direct investment in China: what the figures don't tell us', paper presented at Asia-Link Conference, Regional Governance: Greater China in the 21 Century, 24–25 October, University of Durham, available at http://www2.warwick.ac.uk/fac/soc/pais/staff/breslin/research/fdi.pdf (accessed 17 June 2010).

Caves, R. (1996), *Multinational Enterprise and Economic Analysis*, 2nd edn, Cambridge: Cambridge University Press.

Drysdale, P. and R. Garnaut (1994), 'Trade intensities and the analysis of bilateral trade flows in a many-country world: a survey', in R. Garnaut and P. Drysdale (eds), *Asia Pacific Regionalism: Readings in International Economic Relations*, Sydney, Australia: Harper Educational Publishers.

East Asia Analytical Unit (EAAU) (1995), *Overseas Chinese Business Networks in Asia*, Canberra, Australia: EAAU, Department of Foreign Affairs and Trade.

Harrold, P. and R. Lall (1993), 'China: reform and development in 1992–93', World Bank Discussion Paper, No. 215, The World Bank, Washington, DC.

Markusen, J. (1995), 'The boundaries of multinational enterprises and the theory of international trade', *Journal of Economic Perspectives*, **9**(2), 169–89.

Ministry of Commerce of China (MOFCOM), 'Invest in China, FDI Statistics', available at http://www.fdi.gov.cn/pub/FDI_EN/Statistics/FDIStatistics/default.htm (accessed 17 June 2010).

National Bureau of Statistics of China (NBSC) (various years), *China Statistical Yearbook*, Beijing: China Statistics Press.

United Nations Conference on Trade and Development (UNCTAD) (various years), *World Investment Report*, New York and Geneva: United Nations.

United Nations Conference on Trade and Development (UNCTAD) (2007), 'Rising FDI into China: the facts behind the number' UNCTAD Investment Brief, No. 2, available at http://www.unctad.org/en/docs/iteiiamisc20075_en.pdf (accessed 19 April 2010).

United Nations Statistical Division, National Accounts, available at http://unstats.un.org/unsd/snaama/dnllist.asp.

Wu, F., P. Siaw, Y. Sia and P. Keong (2002), 'Foreign direct investments to China and Southeast Asia: has ASEAN been losing out?', *Economic Survey of Singapore* (Third Quarter), 96–115, available at http://unpan1.un.org/intradoc/groups/public/documents/apcity/unpan010347.pdf (accessed 17 June 2010).

Xiao, G. (2004), 'People's Republic of China's round-tripping FDI: scale, causes and implications', ADB Institute Discussion Paper, 7, available at http://www.adbi.org/files/2004.06.dp7.foreign.direct.investment.people.rep.china.implications.pdf (accessed 15 April 2010).

6. Foreign strategic investment and banking efficiency in China

Ying Xu[1]

INTRODUCTION

China's banking sector has traditionally been under heavy government regulation and control and foreign participation in the banking sector has been restricted. However, since its accession to the World Trade Organization (WTO) in 2001, China has gradually lifted these restrictions and substantially opened up the banking sector to foreign investors. In recent years, attracted by China's huge market potential, foreign bank participation has increased significantly. Moreover, encouraged by the government, the majority of foreign investors have adopted a unique form of foreign entry: foreign strategic investment.

Foreign strategic investment (FSI) is 'medium-to-long-term' foreign investment based on minority equity participation and agreements on the transfer of know-how (CBRC, 2003). Compared to traditional forms of foreign entry, FSI has two important features. First, FSI is minority equity participation, currently under the ceilings ensured by the authorities of 20 percent ownership by a single foreign investor and 25 percent by the combined share of all foreign investors in one bank (CBRC, 2003). Through this form of participation foreign investors can therefore only own up to 20 or 25 percent of any local bank. This contrasts with foreign direct investment (FDI), which is characterized by foreign investors holding controlling ownership stakes of a domestic bank (OECD, 1996).[2] Second, FSI also differs from international portfolio investment. The latter involves only equity participation, whereas FSI entails long-term business cooperation, managerial involvement and technology transfer. In almost all cases of FSI, foreign investor equity purchase is accompanied by agreements on transfer of information technology and management expertise. Furthermore, a key term often included in these agreements is that local banks award one or multiple places on the board of directors to representatives of foreign investors.

The debate among policy-makers and within academia on the potential

impact of FSI on China's banking performance represents two opposing views. The government is the main advocate for FSI, believing that
foreign strategic investment holds the prospect of significant benefits for
the domestic banking industry. Through technology transfer in particular,
FSI helps improve the performance of local banks in terms of corporate
governance and management, and helps strengthen their competitive position (CBRC, 2006). The authorities encourage this form of foreign participation and assist in the selection of prestigious international banks and
financial institutions to be local banks' strategic investors. Nevertheless,
quite a number of scholars, both internationally and within China, have
been critical of the potential impact of strategic investment. They argue
that because all foreign investors are minority shareholders within the
FSI scheme, their involvement is marginal and their influence over the
management and business decisions of domestic banks limited (Leigh and
Podpiera, 2006; Peng and Zhang 2007).

This debate remains inconclusive as there is little systematic empirical
evidence on the impact of FSI on domestic banks,[3] apart from a number
of descriptive accounts such as that provided by He and Fan (2004).
Berger et al. (2009) and Garcia-Herrero and Santabarbara (2008) are
among the few researchers to have undertaken empirical study in this
area. They present evidence that foreign participation is associated with
efficiency improvement in domestic banks. In particular, the improvements observed relate to cost efficiency (Berger et al., 2009) and profit
efficiency (Garcia-Herrero and Santabarbara, 2008). However, Berger et
al.'s (2009) analysis of the cost efficiency impact of FSI was limited by
the short time period covered by their data sample, which ended in 2003.
This is the year in which the authorities officially began to encourage
FSI and since then a significant number of FSI agreements have been
signed.

This study examines the impact of FSI on the performance of China's
banking system with a focus on cost efficiency. It makes three contributions to the literature. First, data on 86 Chinese commercial banks over
the period 1999–2006 are used. Compared to the existing quantitative
research on Chinese banks' performance, this analysis has the merit of
employing the largest bank coverage in China for a recent time period
in which FSI activities have been most rigorous and prevalent in the
banking sector. Second, it separates the complex impacts from different
components of the FSI scheme on the cost structure and cost efficiency
of domestic banks using stochastic frontier models. More specifically, it
distinguishes the impacts of managerial cooperation on cost efficiency
from the impacts of foreign investors' equity participation, and the key
results show a statistically significant positive correlation between foreign

board member involvement and local banks' cost efficiency levels, whereas foreign equity participation fails to deliver such impact.

The remainder of the chapter is structured as follows. The next section briefly reviews the banking industry in China and the trends and characteristics of FSI. The third section introduces the conceptual framework that describes the relation between FSI and cost efficiency. The fourth section presents the empirical analysis using the stochastic frontier approach. The fifth section discusses the results of the regression analysis. Finally, the chapter concludes with a discussion of policy implications and possible directions for future research.

THE CHINESE BANKING SYSTEM AND FSI

The commercial banking system in China exhibits significant diversity in terms of ownership structure. It consists of five state-owned commercial banks (SOCBs), 12 joint-stock commercial banks (JSCBs),[4] 113 city commercial banks and 36 302 rural and urban credit cooperatives. SOCBs, owned by the central government, are the largest banks in China, holding more than half of all total banking assets. They provide nationwide wholesale and retail banking services and their traditional customers are large and medium-sized enterprises. JSCBs are banks that are partly owned by the state, and partly owned by state-owned enterprises, private enterprises and individuals. They offer retail and wholesale banking services in medium and large cities. JSCBs, together with SOCBs, make up the majority (66.1 percent) of total financial assets and 76.8 percent of total commercial banking assets in China. The remaining two groups of commercial banks, city commercial banks and urban and rural credit cooperatives, include banks that are small in size relative to the SOCBs and JSCBs, despite their large numbers. Furthermore, unlike national and regional banks, they have area-based commercial bank operations, by and large in one city or one village. In addition, they offer limited area-specific banking services (Figure 6.1).

Historically, state ownership and government involvement in the management of the banking industry have caused serious problems, such as poor asset quality and dysfunctional corporate governance, resulting in an uncompetitive and inefficient industry driven by social responsibility instead of market mechanism. Policy lending and direct credit have blocked competition among state-owned banks in particular, which directs a large amount of financial resources into loss-making state-owned firms (MGI, 2006). Banks are usually overstaffed, with extensive branch networks contributing to high operating costs. Furthermore, bank

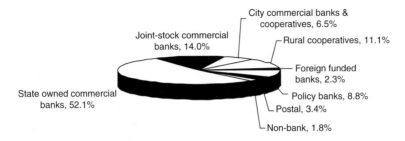

Note: The percentages are shares of different groups' total assets in the whole financial industry.

Source: Chinese Banking Regulatory Commission (CBRC) (2008).

Figure 6.1   Chinese financial industry structure, 2008

portfolios owe little to market-based assessments of the creditworthiness of their borrowers. Shirai (2002) identified a steady deterioration in cost efficiency, which reflects an increase in operating costs driven by rises in personnel expenditure and a decline in operating income, caused by a falloff in net interest income.

Financial reforms initiated by the government started in 1979. However it is only since the Asian financial crisis and especially since the accession to the WTO in December 2001, when China committed to fully opening up its banking sector by 2006, that the government embarked on a series of far-reaching banking reforms to prepare Chinese banks for the harsh competition from foreign banks predicted to occur after 2006. These reform efforts included termination of credit plans, recapitalization of three large SOCBs and opening to foreign competition. An important strategy aimed at fundamental reform of the domestic banking sector has been market liberalization, and the FSI promotion scheme has been among the most highlighted policies.

The term 'strategic' reflects the strategic decisions both by the Chinese authorities and by foreign investors. FSI is one of the government's latest strategies to reform its incompetent banking sector (WTO, 2008). The Chinese government expects that foreign banks' entry to China will entail the benefit of improving the quality of domestic banking through the transfer of know-how. Nevertheless, it endeavors to maintain majority state ownership in its banking industry for ideologically based reasons. Hence minority equity participation is encouraged, rather than wholly foreign-funded banks, or foreigners' majority shareholding of Chinese banks. FSI is also a strategic decision for foreign investors. Despite the continuing opening up of the banking sector, merger and acquisition by

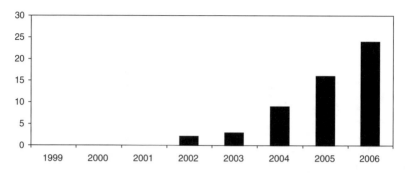

Source: Various studies including Hope and Hu (2006), Leigh and Podpiera (2006), and Okazaki (2007); the latest deals are updated by the author based on public announcements.

Figure 6.2   Number of Chinese banks receiving FSI

foreign banks is not yet officially allowed in China's banking industry. Moreover, extensive business and geographical limitations on the activities of wholly foreign-owned and joint-venture banks remain in China. In addition, domestic banks, particularly state-owned banks, have well-established branch networks throughout the country. Even if all of the restrictions on foreign banks were eliminated, direct market penetration would still not be easy (Leigh and Podpiera, 2006). Hence, FSI is the most cost-effective option because with a relatively small amount of investment foreign investors can have immediate access to the broad branch network built by the domestic banks and thus reap the profits.

Compared to other forms of foreign entry in the Chinese banking sector, FSI has a relatively short history. Nevertheless, its size has increased dramatically since 2001 (Figure 6.2). Almost all major banks in China now have foreign strategic investors (Cui, 2008). Despite offering minority equity participation, FSI offers a significant prospect of the transfer of international best practice to China's local banks, as reflected in the mutual agreements.

Foreign investment in Chinese banks has undergone three phases. First, in the pre-WTO phase there were only isolated transactions, involving niche players of small banks such as the China Everbright Bank and the Bank of Shanghai. Foreign investors were mainly multinational financial institutions like the Asian Development Bank (ADB) and the International Financial Corporation (IFC). These are in some cases defined as FSI in the literature, but are not counted as FSI in this empirical analysis because of the nature of their portfolio investment.[5] Second, with WTO accession in December 2001 and China making the most comprehensive commitment to opening up its banking system, the second phase has seen prestigious international banks like HSBC and Citibank enter China's banking industry. Yet foreign bank participation during this period remained in JSCBs and city banks in major cities. Third, after the China Banking Regulatory Commission (CBRC) updated guidelines in December 2003 to encourage foreign share purchase, FSI intensified, and extended to SOCBs. At the same time, participation in smaller banks also began to increase substantially. Table 6.A2 in the Appendix provides a brief overview of FSI in 2006 (Leigh and Podpiera, 2006).

As a result of the strong momentum observed since 2004, FSI has become the most dominant form of foreign entry in the Chinese banking sector. By the end of 2007, it reached into every stratum of the Chinese banking sector, including four of the five SOCBs, ten of the twelve JSCBs, eight city banks and three rural banks. The banks involved constitute roughly 80 percent of China's total banking assets. This total strategic investment amounted to US$21.25 billion.

Furthermore, foreign entry in the Chinese banking sector is an ongoing process in China so the list of banks that receive FSI continues to grow and the proportion of foreign stakes is increasing. For instance, in a recent strategic investment in June 2008 the United Overseas Bank of Singapore agreed to purchase a 15.38 percent stake in the Evergrowing Bank, one of the last two joint-stock banks that had not yet found foreign strategic partners. Moreover, investors continue to increase their shares. In many Chinese banks, foreign stakes have already reached the 25 percent ceiling prescribed by the government.[6]

Another feature of FSI in China is that it involves a large variety of foreign institutions, ranging from universal banks or ordinary commercial banks, to specialized commercial or government investment institutions, to non-bank multinational companies.[7] In particular, international banks and financial institutions like HSBC, Citibank, Bank of America and Standard Chartered are the owners and practitioners of the most advanced banking technologies and skills in the world.[8] Their participation in China's bank management and business activities offers great opportunities for domestic banks to learn and improve their performance.

Given the restrained level of equity participation, FSI is expected to be a catalyst for technology transfer, which will in turn enhance domestic banking performance. The CBRC has made it clear that the introduction of FSI is aimed at helping domestic banks adopt good corporate governance and risk management policies (CBRC, 2007). Accordingly, these objectives are the guiding principles of the agreements signed by foreign investors when purchasing their stakes in Chinese banks. Key mechanisms for transferring know-how include assigning board seats to foreign

partners, personnel training, information technology and technical assistance, and business cooperation (Table 6.A3 in Appendix). In these agreements, 17 out of 25 Chinese banks have agreed to award board seats to
foreign investors.

ANALYTICAL FRAMEWORK

In measuring bank efficiency, this study adopts cost efficiency to gauge
changes in domestic bank efficiency performance. Cost efficiency is defined
as the bank managers' ability to employ the optimal level of inputs given
input prices and output quantities.

There are three channels through which cost efficiency effects can be realized. The first is through personnel training. FSI is associated with the direct
secondment of skilled officers and the adoption of management expertise of
investors in the business operations of the Chinese banks. For instance,
eight HSBC experts worked in the Bank of Communication in 2005 and
three more joined in 2006. Moreover, the agreement between the two banks
specifies that at least 150 hours of technical assistance is to be provided by
HSBC each year. In the case of the China Construction Bank (CCB), more
than 500 employees from the Bank of America, the strategic partner of
CCB, are expected to come to provide consulting services (Hope and Hu,
2006). Second, state-of-the-art facilities and technologies are introduced to
local banks following FSI agreements. Terms of transfer of information
technology (IT) can be found in many technical assistance plans accom-
panying strategic investment deals. Third, foreign board members are
another important source of efficiency improvement for local banks insofar
as their contribution to management shows directly how decision-making
and internal management processes are undertaken in a modern corporate
entity and therefore boosts domestic banks' efficiency performance.

The potential benefits of cost efficiency can be substantial. Hope and
Hu (2006) argue that FSI is a strong force improving cost efficiency of
domestic banks. Employees of domestic banks can learn directly and first
hand the best international industry practices. Supported by IT systems
and programs, they can perform their banking business more efficiently,
and react effectively to interest and credit risks, and avoid excessive costs
otherwise. Indirectly, FSI strengthens internal control, streamlines management processes and upgrades human resources to ensure greater cost
efficiency. Management information systems can provide accurate and
timely information about a bank's performance and the performance of
a bank's personnel, out of which incentives can be created to induce and
reward better performance. This whole process raises the awareness of all

employees and management of the need to maintain these new standards and prevents the bank from investing in excess and redundant inputs. Together with the supervision provided by foreign board members, imported technology and best practice ensure domestic banks operate at a sustainable level of cost efficiency. In sum, FSI's potential impact on cost efficiency is complex. It would be preferable therefore to distinguish among the effects of different components in the FSI scheme, including personnel transfer and IT, yet the data only allow for singling out the effect of foreign board members.

Nevertheless, these are the potential benefits of FSI on cost efficiency which are institutionalized by mutually signed agreements. Whether these benefits exist will be examined in the following empirical analysis.

STOCHASTIC COST FRONTIER MODEL

The stochastic frontier methodology is employed. The methodology was developed by Aigner et al. (1977) and Meeusen and van den Broek (1977). It has been widely applied to the measurement of banking efficiency (Kim, 1986; Berger et al., 2009) and has also become the most commonly used technique to model banking efficiency and to analyse factors that account for individual bank's efficiency variations (Berger and Mester, 1997). In essence, the method involves the estimation of a stochastic frontier cost function (model 1) and an inefficiency model (model 2). The first model is a cost function, representing the cost structure of Chinese domestic banks, and including a composite error term. This composite error term consists of a conventional random error term and a newly added error term, often called the inefficiency term, used to capture the inefficiencies observed among individual banks. The separation of the inefficiency term from the conventional error is made possible by the distribution assumptions made on the inefficiency term. This inefficiency term can then be modeled to identify factors that influence cost inefficiency.

The stochastic frontier approach contains two important advantages for this study. First, it is one of the few methodologies that can be used to analyse cost efficiency. Furthermore, unlike Data Envelope Analysis, its parametric structure fulfils the aim of identifying factors that influence cost efficiency. Second, its two-model structure and the imposed distribution assumption on the inefficiencies term allow for disentangling other cost effects from the highlighted cost efficiency impact of FSI.

The nature of FSI in China's banking industry indicates that it can influence local bank cost structures in a range of ways. In addition to its potential effect on individual bank cost efficiency, FSI might change the cost function of the banking industry because FSI is linked closely with substantial new investments for the purchase of IT facilities and systems, personnel training, the establishment of new departments and institutions for monitoring performance and capacity building, and the setting up of new businesses. These investments increase costs, which counteract FSI's potential effects of reducing cost or increasing cost efficiency resulting from personnel training or the presence of foreign board members. As a result, the different effects on costs pulling in opposite directions may cancel each other out and remain indistinguishable if estimated using a conventional cost estimation method. By introducing the FSI variable in the frontier cost function (model 1) and the foreign board member dummy in the inefficiency model (model 2), and simultaneously estimating the two models, the stochastic frontier approach can distinguish the cost efficiency effects of FSI from its other cost augmenting impacts on China's banks.

Cost Frontiers (Model 1)

A translog functional form is specified to estimate the cost function of China's banks. This is a commonly used functional form for modeling financial firms (Lawrence and Shay, 1986; Garcia-Herrero and Santabarbara, 2008; Berger et al., 2009). Compared to Cobb-Douglas or Constant Elasticity of Substitution (CES) specifications that are restricted to monotonically increasing or decreasing shapes, translog cost curves are a second-order approximation to an arbitrary cost function and provide greater flexibility[9] (Denny and Pinto, 1978; Berger and Mester, 1997).

Furthermore, a formal test, the generalized likelihood ratio (LR) test, is used to confirm the choice of the translog functional form. The correct critical values for the test statistics come from a mixed χ-squared distribution drawn from Kodde and Palm's (1986) research.[10] A Cobb-Douglas specification is initially estimated,[11] but the null hypothesis of the translog as the correct functional form cannot be rejected. This suggests that the translog functional form offers a better fit for the data.

Thus, the stochastic frontier cost function to be estimated for the panel data of China's banks takes the translog functional form. Based on Berger et al.'s (2009) study, it is specified as:

$$\ln\left(\frac{C_{it}}{Z_{it}w_{2it}}\right) = \alpha_0 + \alpha_j \sum_{j=1}^{4} \ln\left(\frac{Y_{jit}}{z_{it}}\right) + \beta_1 \ln\left(\frac{w_{1it}}{w_{2it}}\right) + \phi_1 T$$

$$+ \frac{1}{2}\alpha_{jk} \sum_{j=1}^{4} \sum_{k=1}^{4} \ln\left(\frac{Y_{jit}}{z_{it}}\right) \ln\left(\frac{Y_{kit}}{z_{it}}\right) + \frac{1}{2}\beta_{11} \ln\left(\frac{w_{1it}}{w_{2it}}\right) \ln\left(\frac{w_{iit}}{w_{2it}}\right)$$

$$+ \frac{1}{2}\phi_2 T^2 + \frac{1}{2}\gamma_j \sum_{j=1}^{4} \ln\left(\frac{Y_{jit}}{z_{it}}\right) \ln\left(\frac{w_{1it}}{w_{2it}}\right) + \psi_j \sum_{j=1}^{4} \ln\left(\frac{Y_{jit}}{z_{it}}\right) T$$

$$+ \psi_5 \ln\left(\frac{w_{1it}}{w_{2it}}\right) T + Z'\theta + u_{it} + v_{it} \tag{6.1}$$

where C_{it} is the total cost of bank i at time t,[12] which is the sum of the bank's total interest expenses and total non-interest expenses. Total non-interest expenses include personnel expenses and other overheads. There are four output variables,[13] Y, which denotes total loans, total deposits, liquid assets and other earning assets of each bank. Two input price variables, w, are constructed as interest expenses to total deposits (w_1) and non-interest expenses to fixed assets (w_2). One fixed input, z, is defined as total earning assets.[14]

Following Berger et al. (2009), this general form of the translog function is normalized twice. First, bank outputs and total costs are divided by total earning assets, z, to reduce the heteroscedasticity that is likely to exist among banks of different sizes. A further normalization of the total cost and the first input price, w_1, by the second input price, w_2, ensures the linear homogeneity of input prices, which is a basic assumption of the cost function.[15]

In addition to output quantity and input price variables, the cost function includes environmental variables. In principle, these variables represent factors that influence the 'environment' of the banking industry – factors that may fundamentally change the average trend of total costs, such as technological changes or a change in regulatory or business environment (Coelli et al., 2005). The time trend given by T is often included to capture such general changes. As the translog functional form is essentially a second-order transformation of average cost curves, T^2 is added accordingly as well as its interaction terms. A key variable introduced in the environment vector is FSI, as is bank type. Bank type is constructed as a vector of dummy variable (SOCBs, JSCBs and city banks).[16]

Inefficiency Model (Model 2)

The inefficiency model[17] captures the variables that influence cost efficiency, which explain the varied cost efficiency performance among individual banks. The inefficiency model can be specified as:

$$u_{it} = \delta_0 + \delta_1 LIST + \delta_2 FBM + \omega_{it} \tag{6.2}$$

The dummy variable of foreign board members, *FBM*, a component of FSI, is introduced to the inefficiency model to address the central question of whether the presence of foreign board members included in some of the FSI schemes helps local banks to improve their cost efficiency.

A dummy variable 'listing', where listed banks are denoted as 1, and 0 otherwise, is also included in the inefficiency model for two reasons. First, the Initial Public Offering (IPO) has favorable effects: improvement in disclosure and the creation of market pressure, which are potentially linked to efficiency improvement. Evidence suggests that the directors and managers of the listed banks are keen to subject bank performance to market appraisals of efficiency and profitability (Dobson and Kashyap, 2006). Second, the IPO is closely related to FSI as many Chinese banks seek foreign strategic investors as a first step on the path to going public (Okazaki, 2007). So it is important to control and distinguish the effect of IPO from that of FSI.

Interaction terms of *FBM* with bank type dummies are also included to test whether the presence of foreign board members induces different cost efficiency effects for banks of different types. The model is specified as:

$$u_{it} = \delta_0 + \delta_1 LIST + \varphi TYPE * FBM + \omega_{it} \qquad (6.3)$$

Hypothesis Matrix

A hypothesis matrix is constructed to help elucidate the complexity of correlations between components of FSI and both cost and cost efficiency, respectively, and a criterion is used to help determine whether a factor influences average cost and cost inefficiency (Table 6.1). If a factor induces technological change and influences average cost, then it should be included in the cost frontier or model 1; if a factor influences the management skills of bankers, then it is a factor of the cost efficiency model and should be included in model 2.

As a component of FSI, introducing new products and services is likely to increase the average cost of a bank, but not likely to impact on bankers' management skills. Thus it should be included in the cost frontier model. IT/personnel training will induce technological change and reduce average costs, but only in the long term, whereas in the short term it will instead add to fixed costs. Therefore cost efficiency improvement is expected to occur in the long run. However, the sample under observation will presumably catch those short-run effects. Lastly, but most importantly, the presence of a foreign board member is likely to help local bankers' improve their management skills and hence reduce cost inefficiency, but is not likely to change the average cost or the cost function. So it is more appropriate to include foreign board membership in the inefficiency model. LIST, a bank that is listed in the stock market, is another factor that might produce

Table 6.1   Hypothesis matrix

	Cost frontiers (technological change)	Cost inefficiency (managerial skills)
FSI		
1. new products or services	+	
2. IT/personnel training	+ (ST); − (LT)	− (LT)
FBM		−
Other		
1. LIST		−
2. TYPE	yes	yes

gains in cost efficiency, but might not influence the average costs of a bank. Bank type, however, might make a difference to both average costs and cost efficiency. In addition to these conceptual intuitions, the choice of variable for each model was also confirmed by a set of specification (LR) tests, following the study of Coelli et al. (1999).

Data

The sample employed in this study is an unbalanced panel consisting of annual data of 86 Chinese banks over the period 1999–2006. This represents the largest bank coverage among the existing quantitative studies of Chinese banking efficiency and a good sample of Chinese banks. All the SOCBS and JSCBS, more than half of the 112 city commercial banks and 11 of the rural cooperatives are included in the sample, accounting for over 80 percent of total banking assets.[18] However, not all of these banks had information available for every year. Some banks were merged or closed while at the same time new banks were established; so the number of banks varies from a minimum of eight banks in 1999 to a maximum of 74 in 2005. Furthermore, additional observations are dropped because they contain missing data for the variables necessary for the regression models. In sum, the final data set has a total of 341 observations.

All the bank data are obtained from Fitch's International Bank Database, Bankscope. This is a global database that contains information on banks around the world and includes comprehensive data and information on Chinese banks. Data in the Bankscope database are mostly compiled from income statements, balance sheets and applicable notes found in audited annual reports. This database provides adequate micro statistics of Chinese banks required for this econometric analysis. Macro data such as total banking assets used to calculate banks' market share are obtained from the CBRC.[19] Finally, data for the main variables of interest – FSI[20] and foreign board members – are compiled by the author, based on bank announcements, annual reports and other references.[21]

ESTIMATION AND RESULTS

The computer program FRONTIER 4.1 (Coelli, 1996) is used to obtain maximum likelihood estimates of the cost frontier and inefficiency models. The program estimates the two models simultaneously in one step. To save space, only the estimation results of the cost frontier (model 1) for the environmental variables, bank type dummy and FSI are presented, which have important implications for the main research question. The results are reported in Tables 6.A5 and 6.A6 in the Appendix. And they mainly report the estimation results of the inefficiency model (model 2), which is the focus of the analysis.

It could be argued that bank type influences both the average cost and cost efficiency of a bank. However, the results of the specification test only indicate its influence on the former. Bank type dummies are therefore included in the cost frontier. All models in Table 6.A6 in the Appendix show similar results for the three bank type dummies. SOCBs and city banks enter all equations negatively and are found to be statistically significant, indicating that SOCBs and city banks outperform JSCBs and rural banks in terms of banking cost. Moreover, SOCBs are associated with higher significance levels and larger coefficient sizes. SOCBs appear to be the most cost-efficient group relative to all other types of banks in China. This result conflicts with the conventional wisdom that state-owned institutions are relatively inefficient (Fu and Heffernan, 2005), but does resemble the findings of Berger et al.'s (2009) analysis, who explain this as due to SOCBs' different accounting practices. Berger et al. also emphasize that all state-owned banks receive cost subsidies from other government agencies – a privilege not shared by other banks.

In the first model specification (b-1), FSI is included in the inefficiency model to test its overall impact on cost efficiency. As expected, FSI shows no significant results because, apart from equity participation, FSI involves a bundle of agreements that potentially have a range of effects on cost structure and cost efficiency. For instance, business expansion and investment in IT and capacity building in the FSI scheme may increase costs, at least in the short run; conversely, in the long run improved management skills may reduce costs and increase cost efficiency. The inclusion of foreign partners on local banks' board of directors also entails potential gains in cost efficiency.

To disentangle these different effects, and more importantly to emphasize the distinctive role of a foreign board member (FBM) on banking performance improvement, the dummy variable of foreign board member is constructed and tested in the inefficiency model along with FSI in the cost frontier (b-2). FSI displays a significant and positive coefficient, thus capturing its cost-increasing influence. However, FBM in the inefficiency model displays a highly significant, negative correlation with cost inefficiency, at a 5 percentage level. This implies that the presence of foreign board members is an important contributor to cost efficiency in a domestic bank.

Listing (dummy variable indicating whether a bank is listed on a stock market) is added to the equation (b-3) to control and distinguish the effect of IPO from that of FBM. As expected, the coefficient of listing is highly significant and is a factor contributing to banks' cost efficiency improvements. Listing on a stock market indeed appears to be driving disciplined Chinese banks to make efforts to increase their efficiency levels. More importantly, with the variable of listing included, the size of the FBM's coefficient shrinks while its significance level goes up notably, from the 5 percentage level to a high 1 percentage level, which indicates that listing's effects are separated out and the coefficient of FBM becomes more robust. In sum, this result confirms the key finding of this analysis that the presence of foreign board members is an important factor associated with improvements in domestic banks' cost efficiency. As hypothesized, it is very likely that foreign board members' participation in the management of Chinese domestic banks directly influences the banks' internal management process and boosts their efficiency performance.

Interacting bank ownership types with the variable of foreign board member shows no significant results and no effects are discernible from the data set. However, the different signs associated with state-owned banks (positive) and joint-stock banks (negative) offer a hint that the power and influence of foreign board members may be more constrained in state-owned banks than in joint-stock banks, because the control and influence of the state prevail in the former group. Nevertheless, the coefficients are not sufficiently significant to provide solid evidence.

Three time dummies are introduced to capture the effects of important events on the cost and cost efficiency of Chinese banks. The WTO dummy compares the pre-WTO and post-WTO periods. The post-WTO period is further divided into two periods to identify the general trend. They all seem to have a greater impact on cost reduction rather than influencing the cost efficiency of individual banks (Table 6A.6 in Appendix), reflecting that a change in the banking industry environment supports banks' efforts to reduce costs.

The trend of cost reduction has largely been a response to the increasing competitive pressure resulting from WTO accession. The Chinese government made its commitment on financial liberalization to the WTO in December 2001, and appealed to domestic banks to prepare themselves for a more competitive industry environment. The pressure quickly intensified following WTO accession when the government removed the barriers towards foreign banks operating in China. The competitive pressure peaked when the government granted foreign competitors equal treatment to their domestic counterparts at the end of 2006.

Compared to the government-initiated reform programs, the competitive pressure exerted by foreign entry seems to have been a more powerful force in mobilizing changes in the domestic banking sector. As the World Bank (2001, p. 20) observed, 'the very threat of entry has often been enough to galvanize the domestic banks into overhauling their cost structure and the range and quality of their service'. Facing such pressure, many domestic banks undertook full-scale structural reforms, and cost reduction was one of their main priorities (Okazaki, 2007).

Sensitivity Analysis

The results of the analysis are robust, as is indicated by highly significant gamma statistics, which suggests that stochastic effects and cost inefficiency are important factors underlying bank performance. Endogeneity might be an issue for cost and FSI variables. One could argue that the correlation between the two is not only one way from FSI to cost, but also works in the other direction. In other words, the efficiency of a local bank may influence investors' entry decision and foreign investors might target banks with lower costs. However, this is not supported by the situation in China. First, the entry of foreign investors has been carefully guided by the authorities. Second, given some space for selection, cost efficiency is not an important criterion for foreign investors, compared to asset size and financial strength (Hope and Hu, 2006).

In addition to including listing and time dummies to separate impacts from other reform strategies on cost and cost efficiency, the outliers – 'the big five' state-owned banks – are excluded from the sample to test the robustness of the results. In principle, the main results hold.

CONCLUSION

The opening up of the banking sector to foreign participation is part of a broader strategy by China's authorities to enhance the efficiency of the banking sector and to achieve deepened integration with the global economy. Unlike in other emerging markets or transition economies, foreign participation takes a unique form in China – as foreign strategic investment or foreign minority shareholding of domestic banks under a ceiling specified by the government. FSI is also characterized by comprehensive agreements signed by foreign investors to cooperate with local partners on new business development, technology transfer and personnel training. Another important term in these agreements is that local banks award seats on the board of directors to foreign investors.

Two opposing views dominate the debate on the potential impact of FSI on domestic banking performance. One is held by the Chinese government, which believes that FSI and particularly the associated technological cooperation agreements offer the prospect of huge benefits to local banks. However, in contrast many scholars are critical of the influence that foreign investors can exert, given their minority ownership position.

This study employs data on 86 Chinese commercial banks over the period 1999–2006 to empirically examine the impact of FSI on the cost efficiency of the Chinese banking industry. Recognizing the multiple impacts of FSI on cost structure and cost efficiency, the study distinguishes between the effect of the presence of foreign board members' effects and the overall effects of FSI. By using the stochastic frontier approach, the research captures the significant correlation between the presence of foreign board members and local banks' cost efficiency improvements. The results confirm the influence of foreign partners, through the mechanism of board membership, on the operation of Chinese banks.

The findings provide some support for current government policies encouraging FSI, but also highlight the importance of the influence of foreign investors. Foreign board members are one of the channels through which foreign investors can convey this influence. Indirectly, the result also suggests that the government should lift the cap on foreign equity participation. In this way, foreign investors could have a greater share of domestic banks and accordingly more influence on decision-making. It is encouraging to see some positive sign in this direction. In 2007, the government agreed that foreign investors could purchase up to an 85.6 percent stake in the Guangdong Development Bank thereby allowing foreign majority ownership of this Chinese bank.

Instead of intervening in the micro management of banks, the government should play a more supportive role to strengthen the institutional structures within the banking industry. Only then might domestic banks benefit from a higher level of foreign participation (Peng and Zhang 2007).

Such structures include rating agencies, accounting and audit bodies, and credit and collateral registries. Finally, and most importantly, any initiatives aimed at improving the learning capacity of the banking industry, such as those related to personnel training, information system or other information technology, should be adopted and maintained.

Despite its significant findings, this study was subject to several limitations. First, the data sample ends in 2006, whereas most of the FSI entered in 2004 and 2005, so the analysis is an immediate assessment. The results therefore show short-term effects, and long-term influences could not be captured. Second, apart from the component of the presence of foreign board members, FSI's other components such as IT facility purchase and joint-venture establishment are not separable due to a lack of data and information; therefore FSI's effects on cost and cost efficiency are not fully explained. It remains unclear whether introducing new business and products is the main reason that FSI increases average costs, yet, if this is the case, the cost will 'pass through' to profits collected by banks. So the next step of this research is to examine profit efficiency of those banks to justify the hypothesis.

In sum, continuous data collection and more extensive observation of the development of FSI and its impact on domestic bank performance are crucial. After the end of 2006, foreign-funded banks in China were granted the same treatment as local banks. The banking system is now facing new challenges, resulting from the heightened direct competition between local and foreign banks. Future studies are expected to develop further insights on the liberalization process of the banking sector.

NOTES

1. The author would like to thank Jenny Corbett, Kalippa Kalirajan, Ligang Song, Philippa Dee, Lilai Xu, Yiping Huang and Yu Su for their helpful comments.
2. The guideline adopted in China prior to 2005 stipulated that FDI meant foreign investors could hold more than 25 percent of the ownership stakes of a local firm. Since 2005, this share has been changed to 10 percent to conform to the international (Organization for Economic Cooperation and Development (OECD)) benchmark (NBSC and MCC 2004).
3. In reviewing the literature on the impact of foreign entry on the Chinese banking industry, it is important to distinguish the studies on FSI from a group of general foreign entry studies (Ye, 2006; Chen and Xiao, 2007; Chen and Tu, 2008; Jiao, 2008). The common features of the latter group are as follows. First, they adopt Claessens et al.'s (2001) framework to examine the impact of foreign entry on various aspects of banking performance. Second, foreign entry is measured by annual changes in the share of the number of foreign financial institutions in total domestic financial institutions or the share of the total assets of foreign institutions in total domestic banking assets. Third, the shares are then included in the model as industry environment variables. Hence, a key disadvantage of these studies is that, while they may capture the industry-wide

impact of foreign entry on the domestic banking industry, they are unable to test the direct impact of foreign investment on each recipient bank, for which the cost efficiency methodology adopted by this study proves more helpful.

4. In the literature, references to state-owned commercial banks normally relate to four main banks: the Industrial & Commercial Bank of China (ICBC), the Bank of China (BOC), the China Construction Bank (CCB) and the Agriculture Bank of China (ABC). These are the four biggest banks in China, often termed the 'big four'. Yet the Bank of Communication (BOCOM), the fifth largest bank, has recently been included in this group by the China Banking Regulatory Commission (CBRC), the central supervisory committee on banking in China. This study follows this new categorization. In the empirical analysis, a comparison of regressions with the BOCOM counted as one of the state-owned commercial banks and joint stock commercial banks shows that its inclusion does not notably influence the main results.

5. Refer to the discussion on the differences between FSI and international portfolio investment in the introductory section.

6. As an exceptional case, in 2007 the government gave its approval for foreign investors to purchase up to an 85.6 percent stake in the Guangdong Development Bank and allowed foreign majority ownership.

7. Due to limited data, it is difficult to distinguish between the impacts from institutions of different types in this empirical analysis. Further case studies might help shed some light on this important dimension.

8. Refer to Table 6.A1 in the Appendix for a list of foreign banks that are FSI investors.

9. Fourier-flexible functional form is an even more flexible functional form. It uses Fourier trigonometric terms to approximate virtually any cost function. However it consumes more degrees of freedom so is not deemed suitable for this study.

10. Due to the one-sided nature of the inefficiency term, the common test statistics are not valid.

11. The estimated Cobb-Douglas frontier cost function is

$$\ln\left(\frac{C_{it}}{z_{it}w_{2it}}\right) = \alpha_0 + \alpha_j \sum_{j=1}^{4} \ln\left(\frac{Y_{jit}}{z_{it}}\right) + \beta \ln\left(\frac{w_{1it}}{w_{2it}}\right) + \phi_1 T + \; + u_{it} + v_{it}$$

with notation following the translog frontier cost function introduced below.

12. To save space, the time dimension is omitted below from other variable explanations.

13. There is no consensus in the literature on the definition of bank outputs and their factor inputs. There are two main approaches: the production approach and the intermediation approach (Wheelock and Wilson, 1995). For the purpose of this study, the production approach is adopted, so banks are viewed as producers of loans and deposit accounts and other non-interest banking services using labor and capital. For reference, the intermediation approach views banks as institutions that generate loans from the deposits they collect. According to this approach, loans are outputs but deposits are inputs.

14. Table 6.A4 in the Appendix provides complete definitions of the variables.

15. The duality or the unique correspondence between the production function and cost function requires that the cost function to be homogeneous of degree one. This implies that the factor share must sum to one, or $\Sigma_i \beta_i = 1$. Normalization by the last price is one method used to satisfy the linear endogeneity assumption.

16. By including bank type dummies, it is expected that banks of various types will show cost curves of different intercepts, but it is also suspected that banks of different types will show varied slopes of cost curves. An expended model is estimated including interaction terms of all the bank variables with bank type. The specification test result suggests that the extended model is not superior to the unexpended model. In other words, bank type influences the intercepts rather than the slopes.

17. The efficiency model and inefficiency model are used interchangeably. They represent

the same idea in which factors that are positively associated with cost inefficiency are
negatively correlated with cost inefficiency.
18. In particular, the data set includes 5 state-owned commercial banks, 12 joint-stock
     commercial banks, 58 city commercial banks, and 11 rural cooperatives.
19. CBRC reports the official macro statistics of total assets and total liabilities of the
     banking industry on its website, (http://www.cbrc.gov.cn/chinese/info/twohome/index.
     jsp?itemCode=9) (accessed, March 2009).
20. It includes the date of the agreement and characteristics of the agreement
     associated with each FSI deal, and the percentage of shares purchased by strategic
     investors.
21. The references include Garcia-Herrero and Santabarbara (2008), Leigh and Podpiera
     (2006), Hope and Hu (2006) and He and Fan (2004).

REFERENCES

Aigner, D., P.S. Lovell and I. Materov (1977), 'Formulation and estimation of
    stochastic frontier production models', *Journal of Econometrics*, **6**, 21–37.
Berger, A.N. and L.J. Mester (1997), 'Inside the black box: what explains differ-
    ences in the efficiencies of financial institutions?' *Journal of Banking and Finance*,
    21(7), 895–947.
Berger, A.N., I. Hasan and M. Zhou (2009), 'Bank ownership and efficiency in
    China: what will happen in the world's largest nation?', *Journal of Banking and
    Finance*, **33**, 113–30.
CBRC (2003), *Administrative Rules Governing the Equity Investment in Chinese
    Financial Institutions by Overseas Financial Institutions*, Beijing: China Banking
    Regulatory Commission.
CBRC (2006), *CBRC 2006 Annual Report*, Beijing: China Banking Regulatory
    Commission.
CBRC, (2007), *CBRC 2007 Annual Report*, Beijing: China Banking Regulatory
    Commission.
CBRC, (2008), *CBRC 2008 Annual Report*, Beijing: China Banking Regulatory
    Commission.
Chen, F. and W. Tu (2008), 'Effect of foreign bank entry on the host country's
    banking efficiency: Eastern European countries' experience and China's prac-
    tice', *World Economy Study* (in Chinese), **1**, 26–35.
Chen, W.G. and J. Xiao (2007), 'Waizi yinhang jinru xiaoying shizheng yanjiu',
    (The empirical analysis of foreign bank entry in China), *The Economist* (in
    Chinese), 96–103.
Claessens, S., A. Demirguc-Kunt and H. Huizinga (2001), 'How does foreign
    entry affect domestic banking markets?' *Journal of Banking and Finance*, **25**,
    891–911.
Coelli, T.J. (1996), *A Guide to FRONTIER Version 4.1: A Computer Program for
    Stochastic Frontier Production and Cost Function Estimation*, CEPA Working
    Papers 7, Armidale, Australia: University of New England.
Coelli, T.J., S. Perelman and E. Romano (1999), 'Accounting for environmental
    influences in stochastic frontier models: with application to international air-
    lines', *Journal of Productivity Analysis*, **11**, 251–73.
Coelli, T.J., D.S.P. Rao, C.J. O'Donnell and G.E. Battese (2005), *An Introduction
    to Efficiency and Productivity Analysis,* New York: Springer.

Cui, K. (2008), 'Challenges facing Chinese banks in the post-WTO period and strategies', *Special Zone Economy* (in Chinese), March.

Denny, M. and M.C. Pinto (1978), 'An aggregate model with multi-product technologies', in M. Fuss and D. MacFadden (eds), *Production Economies: A Dual Approach to Theory and Applications*, Amsterdam: North Holland, pp. 248–67.

Dobson, W. and A.K. Kashyap (2006), 'The contradiction in China's gradualist banking reforms', in W.C. Brainard and G.L. Perry (eds), *Brookings Papers on Economic Activity* 2, Washington, DC: Brookings Institution Press, pp. 103–48.

Fu, X. and S. Heffernan (2005), *Cost X-efficiency in China's Banking Sector*, Cass Faculty of Finance Working Paper, WP-FF-14, City University, London.

Garcia-Herrero, A. and D. Santabarbara (2008), *Does the Chinese Banking System Benefit from Foreign Investors?*, BOFIT Discussion Papers 11, Bank of Finland, Finland.

He, L. and X. Fan (2004), 'Foreign banks in post-WTO China: an intermediate assessment', *China & World Economy*, **12**(5), 3–16.

Hope, N. and F. Hu (2006), 'Reforming China's banking system: how much can foreign strategic investment help?', Working Paper 276, Stanford University.

Jiao, J. (2008), 'The impact of foreign entry on China's banking performance', *Market Weekly* (in Chinese), **2**, 117–18.

Kim, M. (1986), 'Banking technology and the existence of a consistent output aggregate', *Journal of Monetary Economics*, **18**, 181–95.

Kodde, D.A. and F.C. Palm (1986), 'Wald criteria for jointly testing equality and inequality restrictions', *Econometrica*, **54**, 1243–8.

Lawrence, C. and R.P. Shay (1986), 'Technology and financial intermediation in a multiproduct banking firm: an econometric study of U.S. banks 1979–82', in C. Lawrence and R.P. Shay (eds), *Technological Innovation, Regulation and Monetary Economy,* Cambridge, MA: Ballinger, pp.53–92.

Leigh, L. and R. Podpiera (2006), 'The rise of foreign investment in China's banks: taking stock', IMF Working Paper 292.

McKinsey Global Institute (MGI) (2006), *Putting China's Capital to Work: The Value of Financial System Reform*, New York: McKinsey Global Institute.

Meeusen, W. and J. van den Broek (1977), 'Efficiency estimation from Cobb-Douglas production function with composed error', *International Economic Review*, **8**, 435–44.

NBSC and MCC (2004), *Statistical Rules on Direct Foreign Investment in China, 645,* Beijing: National Bureau of Statistics of China (NBSC) and Ministry of Commerce of China (MCC).

OECD (1996), OECD Benchmark Definition of Foreign Direct Investment, Paris: OECD.

Okazaki, K. (2007), 'Banking system reform in China: the challenges of moving toward a market-oriented economy', Occasional Paper, RAND.

Peng, Z. and N. Zhang (2007), 'Foreign strategic investors cannot change corporate governing structure in China's state owned commercial banks', *Jingji Zongheng* (in Chinese), **1**, 15–17

The Banker (2006), 'Top 1000 world banks 2006'.

Shirai, S. (2002), 'Banking sector reforms in the case of the People's Republic of China: progress and constraint', in *Rejuvenating Bank Finance for Development in Asia and the Pacific*, New York: United Nations, pp. 49–98.

World Bank (2001), *Finance for Growth: Policy Choices in a Volatile World*, Oxford: Oxford University Press.
Wheelock, D.C. and P.W. Wilson (1995), 'Evaluating the efficiency of commercial banks: does our view of what banks do matter?', *Review*, July/August.
World Trade Organization (WTO) (2008), *Trade Policy Report 2008: China*, Washington, DC: World Trade Organization.
Ye, X. (2006), 'The empirical analysis of the impact of foreign entry on China's banking efficiency', *Research on Financial and Economic Issues*, **2**, 61–4.

APPENDIX

Table 6.A1   Foreign strategic investors: banks

Foreign banks	Nationality	World ranking	Home country ranking
Citibank	USA	1	1
Bank of America	USA	3	2
HSBC	UK	2	1
Royal Bank of Scotland	UK	7	2
Standard Chartered Bank	UK	61	7
Deutsche Bank	Germany	23	1
Bank of Nova Scotia	Canada	38	2
BNP Paribas	France	24	2
ANZ	Australia	52	2
UBS	Switzerland	18	1
ING Group NV	Netherlands	22	3
Rabobank Group	Netherlands	20	2

Note: Ranking by tier 1 capital ratio (*The Banker*, 2006).

Table 6.A2   FSI in Chinese banks: a snapshot of 2006

No.	Domestic banks	Foreign investors	Investment (US$ Million)	Share acquired %	Foreign board member
1	Industrial and Commercial Bank of China	Goldman Sachs & Allianz & American Express	3800	8.50	Yes
2	Bank of China	Royal Bank of Scotland & Merrill Lynch & Li Ka Shing Foundation, Temasek, UBS, Mitsubishi UFJ Financial Group	5252	16.80	Yes
3	China Construction Bank	Bank of America, Temasek	3966	14.20	Yes
4	Bank of Communication	HSBC	1747	19.90	Yes
5	Shanghai Pudong Development Bank	Citibank	878	19.90	Yes
6	Minsheng	Temasek, Hang Seng Bank	275.1	12.55	No
7	Huaxia	Deutsche Bank, Pangaea Capital Management	450	20.90	Yes
8	Industrial	Hang Seng Bank, GIC	258	20.98	Yes
9	Shenzhen Development Bank	Newbridge Capital, GE Consumer Finance	249	25.00	Yes
10	Guangdong Development Bank	Citigroup, IBM	895	24.74	Yes
11	CITIC	BBVA	639.8	5.00	No
12	Bo Hai	Standard Chartered Bank	123	19.90	Yes
13	Bank of Shanghai	HSBC	83	11.00	Yes
14	Bank of Beijing	ING Group NV	215	19.90	Yes
15	Tianjin CCB	ANZ Banking Group	120	19.90	Yes
16	Nanjing CCB	BNP Paribas	87	19.20	No
17	Xi'an CCB	Bank of Nova Scotia	20.2	12.50	No
18	Jinan CCB	Commonwealth Bank of Australia	17	11.00	Yes

Table 6.A2 (continued)

No.	Domestic banks	Foreign investors	Investment (US$ Million)	Share acquired %	Foreign board member
19	Hangzhou CCB	Commonwealth Bank of Australia	76	19.90	Yes
20	Nanchong CCB	German Investment & Development Bank	5	13.30	No
21	Ningbo CCB	OCBC	71	12.20	No
22	Dalian CCB	SHK financial group	19.3	10.00	No
23	Hangzhou RCB	Rabobank Group	20	10.00	No
24	Shanghai RCB	ANZ	252	19.90	Yes

Source: Various studies including Hope and Hu (2006), Leigh and Podpiera (2006) and Okazaki (2007); the latest deals are updated by the author based on public announcements.

Table 6.A3   *Two examples of the agreement terms*

Chinese banks	Foreign investor	Agreement terms
China Construction Bank (CCB)	Bank of American (BOA) Temasek	1. BOA obtains a seat on the CCB board of directors. 2. BOA provides assistance in areas of corporate governance, risk management, information technology, human resource management, and retail banking (including credit cards). 3. BOA provides 50 people to advise CCB. 4. Temasek assists CCB to improve corporate governance. 5. Temasek has right to nominate candidates for the CCB board of directors.
Hangzhou United Rural Cooperative Bank	Rabobank	1. First overseas investor in a Chinese rural cooperative bank. 2. Rabobank provides management expertise and technical assistance in business management, distribution policy, product management, risk management and information technology. 3. Rabobank will send a senior staff member.

Source: Hope and Hu (2006).

Table 6.A4   Variable definitions and sources

Variables	Description	Source
Deterministic components		
Total cost – C	total interest expenses plus total non-interest expenses	Bankscope
Output (1) – $Y1$	total loans	Bankscope
Output (2) – $Y2$	total deposits	Bankscope
Output (3) – $Y3$	liquid assets	Bankscope
Output (4) – $Y4$	other earning assets	Bankscope
Fixed input – Z	total earning assets	Bankscope
Input price (1) – $w1$	interest expenses to total deposits	Bankscope
Input price (2) – $w2$	non-interest expenses to fixed assets	Bankscope
Foreign investment		
FSI	percentage of a domestic bank's foreign ownership by foreign strategic investment	various sources
FBM	there are foreign board members = 1; otherwise = 0	various sources
Bank type		
SOCB	state-owned commercial banks = 1; otherwise = 0	
JSCB	joint-stock commercial banks = 1; otherwise = 0	
CCB	city commercial banks = 1; otherwise = 0	
Other bank specific variable		
LIST	domestic bank is listed = 1; otherwise = 0	Bankscope

Table 6.A5   Estimation of cost frontiers and cost inefficiency model: 86 Chinese banks (1999–2006) (a)

Stochastic frontier
Dependent variable: ln(C/Z*W2)

	(b-1)	(b-2)	(b-3)	(b-5)
Cost frontier				
...	...	...	...	...
SOCB	−0.3003**	−0.3512***	−0.3577***	
	(0.1221)	(0.1178)	(0.1162)	
JSCB	−0.1357	−0.1200	−0.0542	
	(0.1051)	(0.1008)	(0.1059)	
CITY	−0.1624*	−0.2038**	−0.2162**	
	(0.0939)	(0.0915)	(0.9581)	
FSI		0.0199**	0.0213***	0.0181***
		(0.0044)	(0.0041)	(0.0046)
Cost inefficiency model				
Constant	−9.5020	0.0749***	0.3160*	−0.0010
	(25.1440)	(0.3204)	(0.1622)	(0.2876)
FSI	−0.0882			
	(0.2853)			
FBM		−5.5401**	−3.1173***	−1.7954**
		(2.6684)	(0.9815)	(0.9041)
LIST			−1.938***	−1.6787**
			(0.6687)	(0.7122)
SOCB*FBM				0.1968
				(0.1358)
JSCB*FBM				−3.5050
				(2.4114)
CITY*FBM				0.0000
				(0.1001)
Sigma-squared	3.8577	−0.5104***	0.3693***	0.4328***
	(9.0394)	(0.1263)	(0.0630)	(0.1001)
Gamma	0.9821***	0.9138***	0.8997***	0.8905**
	(0.0434)	(0.0326)	(−0.0301)	(0.0361)
Ln (likelihood)	−184.84	−173.51	−166.37	−172.36

Note: *, ** and *** denote statistical significance level at 10 percent, 5 percent and 1 percent respectively. Numbers in parentheses are asymptotic standard errors.

Table 6.A6   *Estimation of cost frontiers and cost inefficiency model: 86 Chinese banks (1999–2006) (b)*

Stochastic frontier
Dependent variable: ln(C/Z*W2)

	(b-6)	(b-7)	(b-8)	(b-9)
Cost frontier				
. . .	. . .	. . .	. . .	. . .
SOCB	−0.3524***	−0.3529***	−0.3540***	−0.3518***
	(0.1154)	(0.1181)	(0.1167)	(0.1192)
JSCB	−0.0570	−0.0507	−0.0523	−0.0535
	(0.1082)	(0.1057)	(0.1071)	(0.1076)
CITY	−0.2201**	−0.2121**	−0.2137**	−0.2128**
	(0.0950)	(0.0964)	(0.0942)	(0.0957)
FSI	0.0215***	0.0211***	0.0213***	0.0289***
	(0.0041)	(0.0042)	(0.0042)	(0.0044)
WTO	−0.2119*			
	(0.1270)			
Yr02-04			−0.2199*	
			(0.1281)	
Yr05-06			−0.2951*	
			(0.1655)	
Cost inefficiency model				
Constant	0.3334**	0.3704	0.3268*	0.3509
	(0.1572)	(0.2442)	(0.1754)	(0.2376)
FBM	−3.0907***	−3.1548***	−3.1125***	−3.1075 ***
	(0.8743)	(1.1032)	(1.0739)	(0.9848)
LIST	−1.9430***	−1.8941***	−1.9366***	−1.9283 ***
	(0.6279)	(0.7139)	(0.7037)	(0.6819)
WTO		−0.0617		
		(0.2104)		
Yr02-04				−0.0639
				(0.2139)
Yr05-06				−0.0272
				(0.2255)
Sigma-squared	0.3695***	0.3692***	0.3654***	0.3709***
	(0.0622)	(0.0715)	(0.0774)	(0.0680)
Gamma	0.9057***	0.9003***	0.9030***	0.8993***
	(0.0312)	(0.0354)	(0.0417)	(0.0383)
Ln (likelihood)	−165.13	−166.35	−164.83	−166.32

Note: *, ** and *** denote statistical significance level at 10 percent, 5 percent, and 1 percent respectively. Numbers in parentheses are asymptotic standard errors.

7. The role of geographical proximity in FDI productivity spillovers in China

Sizhong Sun, Ligang Song and Peter Drysdale

INTRODUCTION

The subject of productivity spillovers from foreign direct investment (FDI) to domestic firms has attracted considerable attention since the pioneering work of Caves (1974). It is argued that FDI can positively affect domestic industries and firms' productivity, namely that there exist positive productivity spillovers to domestically owned industry from FDI through three channels, that is, the backward and forward linkage between FDI-invested firms and domestic firms, labour mobility, and demonstration and competition effects (Blomstrom and Kokko, 1998). However, empirical exercises do not yield consensus support to the existence of positive productivity spillovers. Some researchers find positive productivity spillovers while others find negative or insignificant spillovers (see, for example, Blomstrom and Kokko, 1998; Saggi, 2002; Gorg and Greenaway, 2004; Smeets, 2008 for surveys).

However, many of these studies do not consider the impact of domestic firms being geographically close to FDI-invested firms in measuring the productivity spillovers. This omission might contribute to the mixed findings reported in previous studies. It is intuitively straightforward that the closer domestic firms are to foreign firms, the more likely the positive spillovers will occur, as the channels through which the productivity spillovers occur, for example, through the demonstration and competition effects, will be more effective. Only a few researchers have recently empirically investigated the role of geographical proximity in FDI productivity spillovers, for example, Barrios et al. (2006) in the Irish manufacturing sector from 1983 to 1998, Girma and Wakelin (2007) in the UK electronics sector from 1980 to 1992, Resmini and Nicolini (2007) in European countries, Halpern and Murakozy (2007) in Hungary, Gaelotti (2008) in the Czech Republic and Crespo et al. (2007) in Portugal. These studies generally confirm that geographical proximity to FDI-invested firms promotes productivity spillovers to domestic firms.

It can be argued that the geographical distance between domestic and FDI-invested firms could play an implicitly important role in the occurrence of productivity spillovers through all the three channels just mentioned. This is because the geographical proximity is likely to affect the costs as well as ease of domestic firms' activities in absorbing spillovers. A number of previous studies have shown that knowledge spillovers are spatially bounded, for example, theoretically Baldwin et al. (2001), Martin and Ottaviano (1999) and Fujita and Thisse (2002), and empirically Audretsch and Feldman (1996), Bottazzi and Peri (2003), Jaffe and Trajtenberg (2002), Jaffe et al. (1993) and Keller (2002). First, for the channel of backward and forward linkage, direct contacts with suppliers and distributors that are located closely to each other are most convenient in that transportation costs will be minimized and communication among them is relatively easily facilitated (Girma and Wakelin, 2007). Second, geographical proximity also facilitates labour mobility as job search costs are likely to be lower. Third, geographical proximity enables domestic firms to closely observe, and therefore better learn and imitate FDI-invested firms, and also tends to increase face-to-face competition.

In this chapter, utilizing a comprehensive manufacturing sector data set that accounts for over 85 per cent of China's total industrial output, we test the impact of geographical proximity on FDI productivity spillovers in the Chinese context. This comprehensive data set allows us to capture the geographical locations of the firms more accurately using the unique zip code information reported in the data set.

The chapter is organized as follows. The next section reviews the literature on productivity spillovers focusing primarily on China. The third section presents the FDI inflow at the firm level in China aimed at providing some background information for the subsequent empirical exercises. The fourth section sets up the empirical model and estimation strategy, presents the data and constructs the variables. The findings are reported and discussed in the fifth section and the final section concludes.

LITERATURE REVIEW

Comprehensive surveys on FDI productivity spillover studies can be found in Blomstrom and Kokko (1998), Saggi (2002), Gorg and Greenaway (2004) and Smeets (2008). Compared with studies of other countries, researchers have found much more consistent positive productivity spillovers from FDI in China.

Using the third industrial census data in 1995, Li et al. (2001) examine the FDI productivity spillovers in China's manufacturing sector, and find positive spillovers, with the magnitude depending on the types of domestic firm ownership and different sources of FDI. For example, state-owned firms increase their technology level through competing with FDI-invested firms. Several researchers explored this industrial census data set providing further evidence of positive productivity spillovers. For example, Buckley et al. (2002) confirm that collectively owned firms are more capable of absorbing productivity spillovers from FDI than state-owned firms. Chuang and Hsu (2004) also confirm the evidence of positive FDI productivity spillovers. Moreover, Buckley et al. (2007) find a curvilinear productivity spillover effect from FDI, namely the positive productivity spillovers exist first but decline beyond a critical point.

Using the more comprehensive firm level panel data in the Chinese manufacturing sector from 1995 to 1999, Liu (2008) finds that an increase in FDI lowers domestic firms' short-term productivity levels, but raises their long-term rates of productivity growth. Sun (2011), using a simultaneous equation estimation approach based on a large firm level data set in 2003 to accommodate for the potential endogeneity of FDI, finds substantial positive productivity spillovers from FDI.

Similar studies have also been carried out on regional China. Using an industry level panel data set in the manufacturing sector of Shenzhen City from 1993 to 1998, Liu (2002) tests the intra-industry and inter-industry productivity spillovers of FDI finding a significantly positive relationship between FDI in the manufacturing sector and the level and growth rate of productivity in component industries, which is interpreted as positive FDI spillovers. Sun (2009b), using a stochastic production frontier approach, investigates the FDI productivity spillovers in Gansu Province, one of the least developed regions in China, and finds positive spillovers in the sense that the presence of FDI-invested firms positively and significantly affect domestic firms' technical efficiency.

Although these studies find positive productivity spillovers, none of them have incorporated the role of geographical proximity in their model estimations, possibly due to lack of data on geographical locations (or distances) of the firms. This chapter fills in this gap.

To capture the impact of geographical proximity, previous studies have adopted three approaches: namely, to construct a measurement of FDI that incorporates geographical information; to examine the productivity spillovers in regions/industries where co-agglomeration between domestic and FDI-invested firms exists; and to calculate geographical distance between domestic and FDI-invested firms. Halpern and Murakozy (2007), Girma and Wakelin (2007) and Crespo et al. (2007) adopt the first approach, by using a foreign presence weighted by a function of geographical distance and constructing foreign presence at the regional level. Barrios et al. (2006) take the second approach by examining the spillovers in the industries in which there exists co-agglomeration between domestic and FDI-invested firms. The third approach handles the geographical proximity directly. Gaelotti (2008) constructs a geographical distance in kilometres between a domestic firm and its closest FDI-invested firm as an explanatory variable, which, however, does not capture the possible impact of FDI-invested firms that are farther away.

Different from these three approaches, in this study we try to measure the geographical proximity as to whether a domestic firm is geographically located in the same zip code region, a unique information provided in our data set, as a FDI-invested firm. The approach allows us to match a domestic firm that is geographically close to FDI-invested firms with a similar domestic firm that is not, and compare the differences in their level of productivity, which, after controlling for other factors, can be attributed to the impact of being geographically close to FDI-invested firms.

FIRM LEVEL FDI

This section presents a description of firm level FDI in the Chinese manufacturing sector from 2005 to 2007, providing some background information for subsequent empirical exercises. We report both the level of foreign presence (FDI) and firm labour productivity at the overall and regional distribution levels.

Table 7.1 presents the overall distribution of foreign presence and labour productivity during the period under study. The level of foreign presence appears to be on a declining trend, decreasing from the mean of 0.35 in 2005 to 0.33 in 2007, although the reduction is small. This slightly declining trend is also confirmed by the percentage of the number of FDI-invested firms in the total number of firms, which reduces from 27.87 per cent in 2005 to 25.57 per cent in 2007. In contrast, the average firm level labour productivity rises significantly in this period increasing from 3.92 in 2005 to 4.22 in 2007. Both foreign presence and labour productivity exhibit significant variations in that they have substantial standard deviations and the differences between their minimum and maximum values are large. In all three years, there are some industries which are almost monopolized by FDI (namely, the level of foreign presence is 0.99), and meanwhile there are industries where there is no FDI at all (namely, the level of foreign presence is 0).

Table 7.2 reports the regional picture. Not surprisingly, the level of

Table 7.1 FDI and firm labour productivity 2005–07

Variable	Mean	Standard deviation	Min.	Max.	No. of firms	Percentage*
2005					192 786	27.87
fpo	0.35	0.19	0	0.99		
lnlp	3.92	1.06	−2.84	8.41		
2006					216 146	26.60
fpo	0.34	0.18	0	0.97		
lnlp	4.07	1.05	−1.33	8.36		
2007					245 401	25.57
fpo	0.33	0.18	0	0.99		
lnlp	4.22	1.05	−1.60	8.23		

Note: fpo denotes the level of foreign presence in four-digit industries measured in output term; lnlp denotes labour productivity in natural logarithm form; * is the percentage of number of FDI-invested firms in the total number of firms in the sample.

Source: Author's own calculations.

Table 7.2 FDI and firm labour productivity 2005–07

Variable	Mean	Standard deviation	Min.	Max.	No. of observations	Percentage*
Coastal China					470 001	34.11
fpo	0.36	0.18	0	0.99		
lnlp	4.06	1.04	−2.83	8.41		
Western China					65 181	7.42
fpo	0.26	0.17	0	0.99		
lnlp	4.06	1.15	−2.84	8.36		
Central China					119 151	7.37
fpo	0.27	0.17	0	0.99		
lnlp	4.21	1.12	−2.58	8.41		

Note: fpo denotes the level of foreign presence in four-digit industries measured in output term; lnlp denotes labour productivity in natural logarithm form; * is the percentage of number of observations that are FDI-invested firms in the total number of observations in the sample.

Source: Author's own estimation.

foreign presence in Coastal China is significantly higher than those of Central and Western China, with the average foreign presence being 0.36 in Coastal China while only 0.26 and 0.27 in Central and Western China, respectively, while the standard deviations are approximately the same across the three regions. This feature is more obvious if we look at the percentage of number of observations that belong to FDI-invested firms in the total number of observations. This percentage is 34.11 in Coastal China, while in contrast it is only 7.42 in Central China and 7.37 in Western China. The labour productivity does not display such a pattern. It appears to have similar distributions across the three regions, although the average labour productivity in Central China is higher than those of Coastal and Western China. Regarding the standard deviations of labour productivity, Coastal China has the smallest standard deviations, while Western China has the biggest one, to some extent reflecting that Coastal China is more developed than Western and Central China.

In summary, there exist two distinct features regarding the FDI and labour productivity in the Chinese manufacturing sector from 2005 to 2007. First, the level of foreign presence appears to decline slightly and a large proportion of FDI flows into Coastal China. Second, firm labour productivity appears to be on an increasing trend, with no significant differences across the three regions in China.

EMPIRICAL MODEL AND DATA

We evaluate the impact of geographical proximity to FDI-invested firms on the productivity of domestic firms, treating the geographical proximity as a treatment. Let an indicator variable $dclose_{it} \in \{0, 1\}$ denote that a domestic firm i is geographically located close to FDI-invested firms at time t if it takes a value of one and zero otherwise. We are interested in the impact of geographical proximity on domestic firms' productivity level (y_{it}) which is defined as:

$$y_{it}^1 - y_{it}^0$$

where the superscript 1 and 0 denote $dclose = 1$ and $dclose = 0$, respectively.

However, we cannot observe the same firms' productivity in both situations, that is, if a firm is located close to FDI-invested firms we do not observe its productivity when it is not located close to FDI-invested firms and vice versa. Thus the individual impact is unidentified. Instead we look at the average impact of geographical proximity, which, following the previous literature on microeconometric evaluation (for example, Roy, 1951; Rubin, 1974; Heckman et al., 1997; Dehejia and Wahba, 2002), is defined as:

$$E\{y_{it}^1 - y_{it}^0 | dclose_{it} = 1\} = E\{y_{it}^1 | dclose_{it} = 1\} - E\{y_{it}^0 | dclose_{it} = 1\}$$

where the unobserved average productivity that firms would have experienced if they had not been located close to FDI-invested firms is estimated by applying the average productivity of those that are not close to FDI-invested firms $E\{y_{it}^0 | dclose_{it} = 0\}$. This approach, however, requires that we control for the self-selection bias possibly caused by the factors that simultaneously determine both domestic firms being geographically located close to FDI-invested firms and their levels of productivity.

One way to do so is to construct an appropriate counterfactual comparison group. We adopt the coarsened exact matching (CEM) technique proposed by Iacus et al. (2008) to construct such a control group. The CEM algorithm is a non-parametric matching method, assuming that conditional on a set of observable factors (the unconfoundedness assumption), the outcome (labour productivity) is independent of the treatment (geographical proximity). The CEM first coarsens each variable into categories, in which the variable takes substantively indistinguishable values. These categories then stratify the data set. At each stratum, every geographically close domestic firm is matched to a domestic firm that is not geographically close to FDI-invested firms by the exact matching algorithm. To estimate the impact of geographical proximity, the uncoarsened data of the matched observations are used.[1]

Applying the matched sample, we conduct an econometric analysis to estimate the treatment effect, using other explanatory variables of firm productivity to control for the remaining imbalance between geographically close domestic firms and their control groups. The econometric model is as follows:

$$
\begin{aligned}
\ln (lp) = {} & \lambda_0 + \lambda_1 firmsize + \lambda_2 age + \lambda_3 k + \lambda_4 averagewage \\
& + \lambda_5 ownership + \lambda_6 western + \lambda_7 middle \\
& + \lambda_8 herfindahl + \lambda_9 oic + \lambda_{10} lec + \lambda_{11} sei \\
& + \lambda_{12} fp + \lambda_{13} fp \times firmsize + \lambda_{14} fp \times age + \lambda_{15} fp \times k \\
& + \lambda_{16} fp \times averagewage + \lambda_{17} fp \times ownership \\
& + \lambda_{18} fp \times western + \lambda_{19} fp \times middle \lambda_{20} nooffdi \\
& + \lambda_{21} dclose + \lambda_{22} dindustry + \lambda_{23} dyear + v
\end{aligned}
\tag{7.1}
$$

where v denotes the independent and identically distributed (i.i.d.) normal error terms; lp is the labour productivity; *firmsize* denotes firm size and is equal to the number of employees in 1000 unit; k is the capital intensity, which is proxied by fixed assets per employee; *age* is the number of years since a firm first started its business; *averagewage* denotes firm average wage and is equal to total salary divided by the number of employees, which captures both the labour quality and labour costs; *ownership* is a dummy variable that takes a value of 1 if a firm is privately owned and 0 if state and collectively owned; *western* and *middle* are two regional dummy variables, which take a value of 1 if a firm is located in Western and Central China, respectively; the Herfindahl index, *herfindahl*, captures the market structure; *oic* denotes the overall industrial concentration, which is computed as the ratio of province-industry (four digit) share of national industry employment against the province share of national manufacturing employment, and captures the possible spillover effect from industrial concentration, which otherwise may be mistakenly attributed to the impact of FDI; *fp* denotes the level of foreign presence, and is equal to the share of FDI-invested firms' output in the four-digit industries,

$$fp = \frac{\sum_{i \in I} x_i}{\sum_{j \in J} x_j},$$

where x denotes a firm's output, I denotes the set of FDI-invested firms in the industry, J denotes the set of all firms in the industry and $I \subset J$. Moreover, *fp* is interacted with such firm characteristics as firm size, age and capital intensity to accommodate for the heterogeneity of FDI productivity spillovers; *nooffdi* is the number of FDI-invested firms in the same zip code divided by the total number of FDI-invested firms; *dclose* is a dummy variable, taking the value of 1 if a domestic firm is geographically close to FDI-invested firms and 0 otherwise; *dindustry* and *dyear* are one set of two-digit industry dummies and one set of three-year dummies, respectively.

The variable of interest is *dclose*. Its coefficient measures the treatment effect of being geographically close to FDI-invested firms. The other two measurements of FDI also capture other aspects of FDI impact, and they are the relative number of FDI-invested firms that are located in the same zip code (*nooffdi*) measuring the impact of FDI-invested firms within the same region (zip code), and the foreign presence (*fp*), a commonly used measurement of FDI, measuring the impact of FDI within the same industry. The rest of the variables included in the model control for other factors that can affect a firm's productivity level. These variables are selected following previous studies including Aitken and Harrison (1999), Aitken et al. (1997), Sun (2009b) and Sun (2011). These variables can be classified into two categories, namely, the firm characteristics (firm size, age, capital intensity, average wage, ownership structure and geographical region) and industry variables (the Herfindahl index and the overall industry concentration).

The data set used in this exercise is a firm level data set that accounts for over 85 per cent of China's total industrial output from 2005 to 2007, which was collected annually by China's National Bureau of Statistics to compile the 'Industry' section of the *China Statistical Yearbook*. A number of previous studies have utilized data from this source to study various aspects of Chinese industrial economy. For example, Hu et al. (2005) examine the research and development (R&D) and technology transfer in China's large and medium-size enterprises. Jefferson et al. (2008) investigate the productivity growth in the Chinese industrial economy. Sun (2009a) tests the export spillovers of FDI in a two-digit industry from 2000 to 2003. Sun (2011) explores the productivity spillovers in the manufacturing sector in 2003.

Following Jefferson et al. (2008) to clean the data, we exclude the firms that employ less than eight workers as they may not have reliable accounting systems, report negative net values of fixed assets, non-positive outputs and wages, and are located in the upper and lower tails (more than four standard deviations from the mean) of the productivity (measured by value added per employee) distribution. The data set contains firm zip codes, which have six digits with the first two digits denoting the province, the third digit representing postal zones within the province, the fourth digit denoting the county (city) and the fifth and sixth digits identifying postal offices in towns or suburbs. Since the zip code reveals detailed geographical information, we can define the geographical proximity as a domestic firm being located within the same zip code as FDI-invested firms, namely, if in the zip code where a domestic firm is located there exists at least one FDI-invested firm, then this domestic firm is geographically close to FDI-invested firms. In the sample, nearly 80 per cent of firms are located close to FDI-invested firms.

Table 7.3 reports the statistics that describe the variables used in the econometric exercises, where all monetary variables, such as the value added, which are used to construct labour productivity, are deflated to 2000 prices, using the producer price index for manufactured goods obtained from the *China Statistical Yearbook 2008*.

ESTIMATION AND EMPIRICAL RESULTS

We conduct the empirical analysis applying a two-step procedure, namely, first to implement a CEM procedure, which matches domestic firms that are geographically close to FDI-invested firms to those that are not to construct an appropriate control group; second, to carry out an ordinary least squares estimator over the matched firms to estimate equation (7.1).

Table 7.3   Descriptive statistics

Variables	Mean	Standard deviation
ln(lp)	4.09	1.04
firm size	0.19	0.76
firm age	9.39	9.75
capital intensity	77.82	155.63
average wage	13.18	10.27
ownership	0.66	0.47
Herfindahl index	0.02	0.03
oic	34.91	168.85
western	0.10	
middle	0.18	
dclose	0.75	
foreign presence	0.31	0.17
nooffdi	0.0003	0.0006

Note: *western, middle* and *dclose* are dummy variables, where their mean indicates the percentage of firms that take a value of 1, for example, 10 per cent of firms are located in Western China while 18 per cent of the sample firms are located in the Central region.

Source: Calculated using the Enterprise Data, National Bureau of Statistics, China, 2005–07.

We use a procedure provided by Blackwell et al. (2008) to conduct the CEM, which is made over such firm characteristics as firm size, age, capital intensity, average wage and ownership structure, and in addition the matching is implemented such that a geographically close domestic firm is matched to a domestic firm that is not geographically close to FDI-invested firms within the same two-digit industry, in the same year and in the same province.

All together the CEM procedure produces 1884 strata in the data set, of which 848 strata are matched where 491 103 domestic firms that are geographically close to FDI-invested firms are matched with 161 298 domestic firms that are not. One aim of the CEM is to reduce the imbalance between the distributions of the treated and control groups. As suggested by Iacus et al. (2008), the imbalance for individual variables is measured by the absolute difference in means of the treated and control groups as $I_1^{(j)} = |\overline{X}_{mt}^{(j)} - \overline{X}_{mc}^{(j)}|$, where $\overline{X}_{mt}^{(j)}$ and $\overline{X}_{mc}^{(j)}$ denote the weighted means of the group of *mt* treated units and *mc* matched control units for variable *j*, and the multivariate differences between the distribution of the treated and control groups is measured by a $L_1 - type$ distance, $L_1(f, g) = \Sigma_{l_1 \cdots l_k} |f_{l_1 \cdots l_k} - g_{l_1 \cdots l_k}|$, where *k* is the number of variables used in the matching, f and g denote k-dimensional relative frequency of the treated and control units, respectively, which is obtained from discretizing and cross-tabulating the k variables, and $l_1 \cdots l_k$ denote the number of bins used in the discretization of continuous variables or levels of categorical variables. A high value of L1 distance indicates larger imbalance between treated and control groups, with a zero L1 distance implying balanced distributions. The multivariate L1 distance obtained is 1.979, and the univariate imbalance measurements for firm size (*firmsize*), age (*age*), capital intensity (k) and average wage (*averagewage*) are 0.06, 0.19, 0.11 and 0.41, respectively. Therefore the matching does not completely eliminate the imbalance between treated and control groups.

To control for the residual imbalance, we conduct the econometric exercise over the matched sample, using both the firm and industry level control variables (equation 7.1). Equation (7.1) is estimated using the ordinary least squares estimator over the matched sample. Table 7.4 presents the estimation results, where adjust R^2 is 0.2 and F statistic is 3238.24, indicating a relatively good fit and overall significance of the explanatory variables.

The treatment (being geographically close to FDI-invested firms) effect for the domestic firms' productivity is significantly negative, with being geographically close to FDI-invested firms causing the labour productivity of domestic firms to reduce by approximately 9.3 per cent over the period under study. The negative impact of geographical proximity on domestic firms' productivity level is a little bit surprising, but can occur if the negative effect of fiercer competition owing to geographical proximity (particularly in the short run) outweighs the positive effect of geographical proximity on the backward and forward linkages and labour mobility. Regarding the other two measurements of FDI, the relative number of FDI-invested firms in the same zip code is found to exert a significantly negative impact, which implies that the increased competition due to the existence of a larger number of FDI-invested firms in the same region also does harm to domestic firms. The coefficients of foreign presence, which captures the impact of FDI in the same industry, and its interaction terms with firm characteristics are all statistically significant at the 5 per cent level. The firm size is found to negatively affect the magnitude of productivity spillovers from foreign presence (*fp*), which occurs possibly due to the competition effects. Firm age, capital intensity and average wage exert significantly positive effects on the spillover magnitude, indicating the importance of experience, capital intensity and worker quality. Firms located in Western and Central China appear to receive bigger productivity spillovers from FDI-invested firms, again reflecting less competition from FDI-invested firms as FDI is more concentrated in Coastal China.

Table 7.4 Estimation results

Regressors	Labour Productivity	
	Coefficient	Robust standard error
firmsize	−0.0614	0.0052
age	−0.0107	0.0003
k	0.0016	0.00002
average wage	0.0192	0.0003
ownership	0.1562	0.0055
western	−0.3211	0.0080
middle	−0.0737	0.0063
herfindahl	0.2171	0.0452
oic	−0.0001	0.00001
fp	−0.5765	0.0209
fp × *firmsize*	−0.1577	0.0153
fp × *age*	0.0051	0.0008
fp × *k*	0.0012	0.0001
fp × *average wage*	0.0100	0.0007
fp × *ownership*	−0.2739	0.0153
fp × *western*	0.7069	0.0242
fp × *middle*	0.4859	0.0185
nooffdi	−47.2273	2.1142
dclose	−0.0928	0.0029
industry dummies	yes	
year dummies	yes	
constant	4.2007	0.0094
Number of observations	644 399	
$F(49\,644\,349)$	3238.24	
Adj R-squared	0.2	

Note: The coefficients of all variables are statistically significant at the 5 per cent level.

Source: Author's own estimation.

Compared with the state- and collectively owned firms, privately owned firms benefit less from the productivity spillovers of FDI.

The other control variables also exert a significant impact on domestic firms' labour productivity. For firm characteristics, since they are interacted with the foreign presence (*fp*), their impact on labour productivity depends on the level of foreign presence. In an industry where there is no FDI inflow, bigger and older firms are less productive, while in contrast firms that are more capital intensive, tend to have higher average wage, and those that are privately owned tend to have higher labour productivity. In addition, firms that are located in Western and Central China are significantly less productive, which is not surprising given the fact that Coastal China is more developed than Western and Central China. The market structure, captured by the Herfindahl index, is found to exert significantly positive effect on domestic firms' labour productivity, while in contrast the impact of the concentration of manufacturing activities (*oic*) is significantly negative. It may be due to the fact that the concentration of manufacturing activities increases the competition among firms, which can subsequently hurt firms' performance in the short run.

CONCLUSION

In this study, using a comprehensive firm level data set, we have investigated the impact of geographical proximity to FDI-invested firms on domestic firms' labour productivity, and found that domestic firms being geographically close to FDI-invested firms might negatively affect their labour productivity. A possible reason for this might be due to the competition effect resulting from the increased FDI presence at least in the short run. It would be interesting in future studies to apply the same approach developed in this study to the data covering a longer period to see whether domestic firms' labour productivity could be improved resulting from their responses to the competition effects. We also find that the magnitude of intra-industry productivity spillovers from FDI, namely, the impact of foreign presence (*fp*), depends on such firm characteristics as firm size, age, capital intensity, average wage, ownership structure and geographical location, confirming that heterogeneity exists in the productivity spillovers associated with FDI.

NOTE

1. See Iacus et al. (2008).

REFERENCES

Aitken, B. and A. Harrison (1999), 'Do domestic firms benefit from direct foreign investment? Evidence from Venezuela', *American Economic Review*, **89**, 605–18.

Aitken, B., Hanson, H.G. and A.E. Harrison (1997), 'Spillovers, foreign investment, and export behaviour', *Journal of International Economics*, **43**, 103–32.

Audretsch, D.B. and M.P. Feldman (1996), 'R&D spillovers and the geography of innovation and production', *American Economic Review*, **86**, 630–40.

Baldwin, R.E., P. Martin and G. Ottaviano (2001), 'Global income divergence, trade and industrialization: the geography of growth track-off', *Journal of Economic Growth*, **6**, 5–37.

Barrios, S., L. Bertinelli and E. Strobl (2006), 'Coagglomeration and spillovers', *Regional Science and Urban Economics*, **36**, 467–81.

Blackwell, M., S.E. Iacus, G. King and G. Porro (2008), 'CEM: Coarsened Exact Matching in Stata', Harvard University, Cambridge, Massachusetts.

Blomstrom, M. and A. Kokko (1998), 'Multinational corporations and spillovers', *Journal of Economic Survey*, **12**, 247–77.

Bottazzi, L. and G. Peri (2003), 'Innovation and spillovers in regions: evidence from European patent data', *European Economic Review*, **43**, 915–23.

Buckley, P.J., J. Clegg and C. Wang (2002), 'The impact of inward FDI on the performance of Chinese manufacturing firms', *Journal of International Business Studies*, **33**, 637–55.

Buckley, P.J., J. Clegg and C. Wang (2007), 'Is the relationship between inward FDI and spillover effects linear? An empirical examination of the case of China', *Journal of International Business Studies*, **38**, 447–59.

Caves, R.E. (1974), 'Multinational firms, competition, and productivity in host-country markets', *Economica*, **41**(162), 176–93.

Chuang, Y. and P. Hsu (2004), 'FDI, trade, and spillover efficiency: evidence from China's manufacturing sector', *Applied Economics*, **36**, 1103–15.

Crespo, N., I. Proença and M.P. Fontoura (2007), 'FDI spillovers at regional level: evidence from Portugal', Working Papers 2007/28, Department of Economics at the School of Economics and Management (ISEG), Technical University of Lisbon.

Dehejia, R.H. and S. Wahba (2002), 'Propensity score matching methods for nonexperimental causal studies', *Review of Economics and Statistics*, **84**, 151–61.

Fujita, M. and J.F. Thisse (2002), *Economics of Agglomeration. Cities, Industrial Location and Regional Growth*, Cambridge: Cambridge University Press.

Gaelotti, E. (2008), 'Do domestic firms benefit from geographic proximity with FDI? Evidence from the privatization of the Czech glass industry', Working Papers IES, Faculty of Social Sciences, Institute of Economic Studies, Charles University, Prague.

Girma, S. and K. Wakelin (2007), 'Local productivity spillovers from foreign direct investment in the U.K. electronics industry', *Regional Science and Urban Economics*, **37**, 399–412.

Gorg, H. and D. Greenaway (2004), 'Much ado about nothing? Do domestic firms really benefit from foreign direct investment?', *World Bank Research Observer*, **19**, 171–97.

Halpern, L. and B. Murakozy (2007), 'Does distance matter in spillovers?', *Economics of Transition*, **15**, 781–805.

Heckman, J., H. Ichimura and P. Todd (1997), 'Matching as an econometric evaluation estimator: evidence from evaluating a job training programme', *Review of Economic Studies*, **64**, 605–54.

Hu, A.G.Z., G.H. Jefferson and J. Qian (2005), 'R&D and technology transfer: firm-level evidence from Chinese industry', *Review of Economics and Statistics*, **87**, 780–86.

Iacus, S.M., G. King and G. Porro (2008), *Matching for Causal Inference Without Balance Checking*, Cambridge, MA: Harvard University.

Jaffe, A.B. and M. Trajtenberg (2002), *Patents, Citations and Innovations: A Window on the Knowledge Economy*, Cambridge, MA: MIT Press.

Jaffe, A.B., M. Trajtenberg and R. Henderson (1993), 'Geographic localization of knowledge spillovers as evidenced by patent citations', *Quarterly Journal of Economics*, **108**, 577–98.

Jefferson, G.H., G.R. Thomas and Y. Zhang (2008), 'Productivity growth and convergence across China's industrial economy', *Journal of Chinese Economic and Business Studies*, **6**, 121–40.

Keller, W. (2002), 'Geographic localization of international technology diffusion', *American Economic Review*, **92**, 120–42.

Li, X., X. Liu and D. Parker (2001), 'Foreign direct investment and productivity spillovers in the Chinese manufacturing sector', *Economic System*, **25**, 305–21.

Liu, Z. (2002), 'Foreign direct investment and technology spillover: evidence from China', *Journal of Comparative Economics*, **30**, 579–602.

Liu, Z. (2008), 'Foreign direct investment and technology spillovers: Theory and evidence', *Journal of Development Economics*, **85**, 176–93.

Martin, P. and G. Ottaviano (1999), 'Growing locations: industry location in a model of endogeneous growth', *European Economic Review*, **43**, 281–302.

Resmini, L. and M. Nicolini (2007), 'Productivity spillovers and multinational enterprises: in search of a spatial dimension', Papers DYNREG10, Economic and Social Research Institute (ESRI).

Roy, A. (1951), 'Some thoughts on the distribution of earnings', *Oxford Economic Papers*, **3**, 135–45.

Rubin, D. (1974), 'Estimating causal effects to treatments in randomised and non-randomised studies', *Journal of Educational Psychology*, **66**, 688–701.

Saggi, K. (2002), 'Trade, foreign direct investment, and international technology transfer: a survey', *World Bank Research Observer*, **17**, 191–235.

Smeets, R. (2008), 'Collecting the pieces of the FDI knowledge spillovers puzzle', *World Bank Research Observer*, **23**, 107–38.

Sun, S. (2009a), 'How does FDI affect domestic firms' exports? Industrial evidence', *World Economy*, **32**, 1203–22.

Sun, S. (2009b), 'Testing technology spillovers of FDI: a stochastic frontier approach', *Empirical Economics Letters*, **9**, 933–40.

Sun, S. (2011), 'Foreign direct investment and technology spillovers in China's manufacturing sector', *The Chinese Economy*, **44**, 25–42.

PART III

Price determinants and policy challenges

8. Fluctuations of prices in the world grain market: policy responses by the Chinese government

Wei-Ming Tian and Zhang-Yue Zhou

INTRODUCTION

The grain price hikes in the international market during 2007–08 were most astonishing and attracted much attention all around the world.[1] In mid-2007 the prices of wheat and corn started to increase sharply. In early 2008, the price of rice also started to rise steeply. According to the data published by the World Bank, the price of wheat peaked by March 2008 to reach US$440 per tonne. In April 2008, the price of rice reached its climax, at US$907 per tonne, while the price of corn peaked in June, at US$287. Compared to the price level in May 2007, the month before the price hikes started, the peak prices were, respectively, 125 percent, 186 percent and 52 percent higher for wheat, rice and corn. In response, governments in many countries took interventionist measures over the food prices in their domestic markets in order to achieve urgent socioeconomic objectives, such as food security and social stability. However, with the deepening of the global financial crisis, the prices of grains declined sharply in the latter half of the year. By the end of 2008, the prices of wheat, rice and corn fell from their respective peaks by 50 percent, 41 percent and 36 percent (World Bank, 2009).

The fluctuations in grain prices at such a speed during such a short time span is most detrimental to the management of food economies of many countries, especially those developing countries whose food security has been an ongoing concern such as China. As such, it is imperative to examine policy responses by governments of countries whose food security may be significantly affected by such price fluctuations and to evaluate the efficacy of their policy responses.

In this chapter, we examine the policy responses by the Chinese government during the 2007–08 world grain price fluctuations. We first, in the next section, display the dramatic price changes in the world grain market and discuss the likely consequences of such erratic price variations. In the third section, we examine what caused the price hikes. We then survey what policy measures were undertaken by the Chinese government and evaluate their efficacy in the fourth section. In the fifth section, we delineate issues to which attention should be given in order to better prepare China for any future erratic price movements in the world grain market. The last section concludes the chapter.

ERRATIC FLUCTUATIONS IN WORLD GRAIN PRICES AND RESULTANT CONSEQUENCES

Since the early 2000s, movements of prices of major grain crops in the world market had been modest until mid-2007 although corn price experienced some major changes in early 2004 and mid-2006 to mid-2007. However, from mid-2007, the price increase of major grain crops, led by wheat, was dramatic. The prices of major crops dropped in the latter half of 2008 (Figure 8.1).

Despite the fact that the 2007–08 grain price boom was short-lived, it nonetheless generated a series of undesirable consequences.

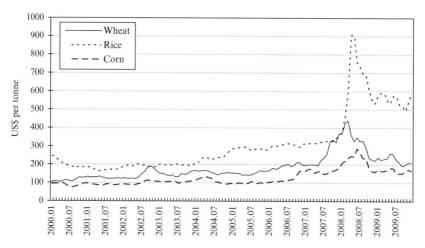

Note: Wheat price refers to US no. 1 hard red winter, ordinary protein, export price delivered at the Gulf; corn price refers to US no. 2 yellow corn, f.o.b. US Gulf ports; rice price refers to Thai 5 per cent broken white rice, milled, indicative price based on weekly surveys.

Source: World Bank (2009).

Figure 8.1   World grain price fluctuations during 2007–08

Wastes in Policy Efforts

The sharp increases in food prices coupled with rapid rises in energy and mineral resource prices created enormous inflationary pressure in many economies in the first half of 2008. This forced many governments to deviate policy resources to prevent or control inflation. When the price boom busted in the latter part of 2008 coupled with the deepening of the global financial crisis, many governments had to relax their monetary policies in order to stimulate their economies. Not only had the price boom and bust led to wastes in policy efforts, it could perhaps have also misled governments' macroeconomic policies or delayed policy efforts in combating the upcoming economic slides resultant from the global financial crisis.

Reduced Food Supply in Some Countries

Some developing countries, such as Haiti, Kenya, Nepal, Bangladesh and Côte d'Ivoire, rely upon imports to ensure domestic food supply. When food prices soared in late 2007 and early 2008 (by as much as two to three times in nominal prices), these countries had great difficulties in securing sufficient foreign exchange to afford the imports, leading them to having to reduce food imports. This further pushed up their domestic food prices, detrimental to poor consumers. Import bills increased sharply in 2008 (FAO, 2009a).

Social Unrest

The supply shortages and price hikes resulted in social unrest in a number of countries. According to *The Economist* (2008), 'food riots have erupted in countries all along the equator'. Countries that experienced social unrest resulting from the food crisis include, for example, Haiti, Cameroon, Egypt, the Philippines, Côte d'Ivoire and Nepal.

Restrictive Food Trade Policies

The 2007–08 food price hikes led many countries to adopt restrictive policies in their food trade, which in turn further aggravated the price hike problem in the world market. Governments around the globe implemented measures, such as export bans, export taxes or import subsidies, to try to isolate domestic prices from world prices. According to a report released in June 2008 by the International Monetary Fund (IMF), some exporters of key food products introduced quantitative restrictions on food exports or introduced or increased food export taxes in order to stabilize or reduce domestic food prices (IMF, 2008). In December 2008, the Food and Agriculture Organization (FAO) also published a comprehensive list of policy measures taken by governments to reduce the impact of soaring prices (FAO, 2008a). Such taxes and quotas are highly distortionary and they reduce the gains from higher prices for exports. On the other hand, lower domestic prices discourage producers who should instead be encouraged to increase food production. Such policy responses further exacerbated the price hike problem. The price fluctuations and the associated policy interventions also erode confidence on multilateral trade negotiations under the World Trade Organization (WTO).

Given that food security has been an ongoing concern for the Chinese government, the price fluctuations in the world grain market certainly had gained its attention. Not unexpectedly, the government heavily intervened in its food trade and also in domestic grain production and marketing. Before we turn to survey the policy responses by the Chinese government, however, it is useful to examine the causes that have led to the world grain price hikes. Understanding such causes helps the discussion in the rest of the chapter on what China has done and what it should do in the future.

FACTORS RESPONSIBLE FOR PRICE FLUCTUATIONS

The wild price fluctuations in the world grain market caught many people by surprise. There have been numerous writings that try to pin down the causes that were responsible for the price volatility.[2] Some examples include ADB (2008), FAO (2008b) Heady and Fan (2008), IMF (2008), ODI (2008), OECD/FAO (2008), Timmer (2008) and von Braun (2008). Here, we provide a brief account of our own delineations of the major causes that have led to the price hikes during 2007–08.

Price variations are a normal phenomenon in agricultural markets. What disturbs people most about the 2007–08 price hikes is the sharp rises (and falls) by significant margins within a relatively short time span, involving nearly all major food and feed commodities. Many factors would have contributed to the price hikes.

Supply Side

In the past two decades or so, global grain supply growth had been slower. Figure 8.2 demonstrates the slow increase in world cereal production until

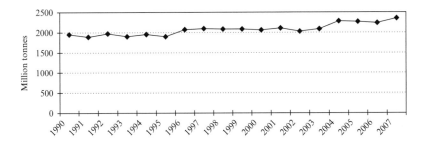

Source: FAO (2009c).

Figure 8.2 Slow increase in world cereal production

2007. A number of factors have contributed to the slower increase in grain supply.

1. A number of developing economies such as China and India have experienced faster economic growth. This resulted in faster indus- trialization and urbanization in these countries, which in turn led to increased agricultural resources being deviated to non-agricultural use. For example, in China during 2000–08, an average of 186 000 hec- tares of arable land was used each year for non-agricultural purposes (urban expansion, roads, industrial facilities and so on) (Ministry of Land and Natural Resources, 2009).

2. Reduced investment in grain production research, development and extension in many countries, partly due to low prices during the two decades prior to 2006, resulted in slower improvements in grain pro- duction technologies (Pardey et al., 2006; World Bank, 2007; Pardey et al., 2008; Beintema and Elliott, 2009).

3. Low grain prices prior to 2006 also induced European Union (EU) countries and the USA to increase their level of land set idle. Under the 'Grain for Green' program, the Chinese government also encouraged for some marginal land to be set aside for environmental rehabilitation purposes. During 2000–04, altogether about 5.75 million hectares of cultivated land were set aside; 2003 alone saw 2.24 million hectares set aside. The grain price increase in late 2003 led to the scale-down of this program since 2004 (in 2008, only 7600 hectares were set aside under this program) (Ministry of Land and Natural Resources, 2009).

4. As a result of the WTO movement, markets in developing economies have become increasingly open. This facilitated the structural adjust- ments of their agricultural production. Agricultural activities have

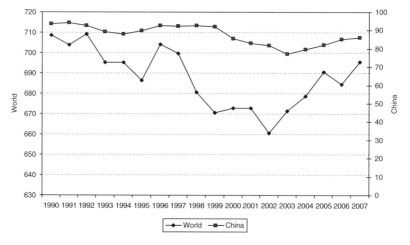

Source: Based on FAO (2009c).

*Figure 8.3   Declining harvested area of cereals, China and the world,
1990–2006 (million ha)*

been carried out more so based on comparative advantages. Where possible, farmers shifted resources to produce more higher-valued agricultural products, with less input for grain production. Figure 8.3 shows the declining trends in areas sown to cereals in China and the world during 1990 and 2008. The area sown to cereals in China declined steadily in the late 1990s and early 2000s. The trend has been arrested since 2004 due to strong government interventions in response to the domestic grain price hikes started in late 2003. The Chinese government treated the 2003 grain price hikes as warning signals of food insecurity (Government of China, 2004). Some developing countries, such as Afghanistan, Somalia, Sudan and Zimbabwe, had low grain production output, suffering from prolonged domestic political and social instabilities (FAO, 2008c).

5.   The soaring prices of oil after the invasion of Iraq resulted in higher prices for agricultural inputs. This leads to higher production costs, also contributing to higher output prices (FAO, 2009b).

Demand Side

While the above factors have resulted in a slower increase in global grain supply, some other factors have contributed to increased demand for grains.

1. In developing countries, improved income as a result of faster economic growth in the past few decades has led to increased grain consumption, especially among those lower income consumers. Further, income growth as well as population growth and urbanization have gradually changed the structure of food demand. Diets are moving away from starchy foods towards more meat and dairy products, which intensify demand for feed grains (Cranfield et al., 1998; Wu, 1999; Regmi et al., 2001; Ishida et al., 2003; Gandhi and Zhou, 2007).

2. Production of bio-fuel also raised the demand for grains. According to an estimate by the United States Department of Agriculture (USDA), in 2001/02, the proportion of corn used in the USA for the production of ethanol out of total domestic corn consumption was less than 10 percent. By 2008/09, this proportion, however, jumped to about 35 percent (USDA, 2008). Other countries, for example some EU members, supported by their governments, also used grains or rapeseeds to produce ethanol and bio-diesel. Brazil makes use of mainly sugarcane to produce bio-ethanol. Indonesia and Malaysia also use palm oil to produce bio-diesel. The production of bio-fuel raw materials competes for land for cereal production (FAO, 2008d; OECD, 2008; Saunders et al., 2009).

Other Important Factors

Clearly, the slower increase in supply but faster rise in demand would have placed an upward pressure on grain prices. However, none of the above demand or supply factors experienced drastic changes during 2007–08 on a global scale although the use of corn had a major increase in the USA. Hence, except for the use of corn for bio-fuel being an important contributing factor affecting world grain prices, most of the above-mentioned factors cannot be held responsible for the steep rise in grain prices in 2007–08 and the major causes must be found elsewhere.

We believe speculation and manipulation by some financial groups in the world agricultural market is the major cause. Most agricultural markets are thin markets, especially the world rice market. In effect, it does not need a huge sum of money to disturb the world agricultural markets. Some speculators shifted their hot money into the agricultural market. They are also in a position to access or manipulate market information. It is their speculation and manipulation that triggered and fueled the price hikes. The speculation and manipulation, in turn, must have influenced the underlying spot markets to the extent that they affected the decisions of grain producers, traders and processors (Irwin et al., 2007; Sanders et al., 2008; Aulerich et al., 2009; FAO, 2009b).

Several other important factors would have also contributed significantly to the 2007–08 price boom. Production shortfalls in major exporting countries in 2005–06 caused by adverse weather conditions were another trigger for the price hikes. In these major exporting countries, cereal production declined by 4 percent in 2005 and 7 percent in 2006. Yields in Australia and Canada fell by about one fifth in aggregate, and yields were at or below trend in many other countries (FAO, 2008b).

The gradual reduction in the level of stocks, mainly cereals, since the mid-1990s, is another factor that would have impacted on the market. Since the previous high-price event in 1995, global stock levels have declined, on average, by 3.4 percent per year as demand growth has outstripped supply (FAO, 2008b). The low level of stocks in conjunction with a reduced production level in 2005–06 would psychologically influence the decisions of major players in the grain market, and would have contributed to set the stage for rapid price hikes.

Short-term policy actions by national governments also made things worse. As noted earlier, after the start of price hikes, some governments introduced measures to reduce the impact of higher prices on their domestic markets, such as export bans and increased export tariffs. Such policy responses exacerbated the short-run volatility of international prices. The impact of such short-term policy responses is especially obvious in the international rice market, which is a well-known thin market, as shown by the extremely steep price increases in early 2008 when important exporting countries introduced export bans to protect their own consumers (see the rice price hike in Figure 8.1) (for more details about trade-oriented policy measures taken by various governments, see FAO, 2008a).

It is noted that changes in exchange rates would have also affected the world grain price levels. Most agricultural commodity prices are quoted in US dollars. The significant decline in its value in the past few years would mean higher prices for commodities denominated in US dollars.[3] The price hikes during 2007–08 also reflected the incapability of handling emergencies by major international organizations, including the FAO, WTO, World Bank and IMF. They failed to institute a mechanism that could prevent such market turmoil from happening and when the turmoil took place during 2007–08, failed to play a role to stabilize the world grain market in a coordinated manner. Generally, they all predict upward trends of cereal prices in the long run. Their prediction is not wrong, but such information does have an impact on traders' expectation and behavior. Therefore, to some extent, their predictions also help to fuel speculations in the futures market.

The above discussion clearly shows that the changes in those 'normal' demand and supply factors are not the main causes of the sudden price spike during 2007–08. Market speculation and manipulation by large financial groups in the agricultural market is the major cause. In the next section, we survey how the Chinese government has reacted to the global grain price hikes.

POLICY RESPONSES BY THE CHINESE GOVERNMENT

Food security has been an ongoing issue in China due to the huge population and limited agricultural resources. The Chinese government has always been sensitive to any major price hikes in the market and has almost always reacted or quite often overreacted to price hikes (Zhou and Chen, 1995; Zhou and Tian, 2005). The sharp increases in grain prices in 2007–08 in the world market would be expected to affect grain price levels in China's domestic market if no intervening measures were undertaken. This is because China is now a member of the WTO and there are fewer restrictions on the grain trade between China and the rest of the world. As expected, the Chinese government did indeed intervene in China's grain trade, both domestically and internationally. Reported below are some major policy responses undertaken by the Chinese government.

In response to the rapid price increase in the world market, the Chinese government decided to abolish, from 20 December 2007, VAT rebates applied to the exports of rice, wheat, corn and soybean and their flours, in order to discourage exports (Ministry of Finance, (2007a). Such rebates were introduced earlier to increase China's grain export competitiveness in the world market. In 2003, the rate of rebates for processed products out of wheat, corn and so on was 13 percent (Ministry of Finance and State Taxation Bureau, 2003).

The government implemented policies that made imports of certain food items cheaper or easier but exports of them more difficult. A temporary grain export tariff was introduced effective from 1 January 2008, ranging between 5 percent and 25 percent, for a total of 57 categories of grain products. Flours of certain cereals (for example, flours of wheat, corn and rice) could be exported only under export quota permits (Ministry of Finance, 2007a, 2007b). The nominal 1 percent import tariff (obliged tariff is 3 percent, reduced temporally to 1 percent in 2008) for soybean was continued from the beginning of 2008. Starting from 1 June 2008, the import tariff for frozen pork was reduced from 12 percent to 6 percent. The import tariff for coconut oil and olive oil was reduced from 10 percent and 9 percent, respectively, to 5 percent. For some important feedstuff, for example, soybean cakes and peanut cakes, the import tariff

Table 8.1   Increases in government floor prices for grain crops (¥ per kg)

Crop	2007	2008 February	2008 March	2008 October	2009
White wheat	1.44	1.50	1.54		1.74
Red wheat	1.39	1.40	1.44		1.86
Early rice (indica)	1.40	1.50	1.54		
Mid and late rice (indica)	1.44	1.52	1.58	1.88*	
Japonica rice	1.50	1.58	1.64	1.84#	
Corn				1.50#	

Note: * South China only, # Northeast China only.

Source: NDRC (2008b) and various previous notices.

was reduced from 5 percent to 2 percent. On 13 June 2008, VAT rebates for exports of vegetable cooking oils were abolished. Starting from 1 August 2008, the Ministry of Commerce asked that imports of all soybean, soybean cakes, soybean oil, rapeseeds, rapeseeds oil and palm oil should be reported to the Ministry and the Ministry would regularly publicize the information regarding such imports. The purpose of introducing this reporting mechanism was to enable the government to monitor trade activities more closely.[4]

By the end of 2008, world grain prices regressed and were comparable to, or not significantly higher than, those before the hikes, except for rice. Thanks to a good harvest, on 1 December 2008, the Chinese government removed or reduced the export tariffs for wheat, rice, corn, some miscellaneous grains and their flours (State Council, 2008a).

In addition to the introduction of policy measures controlling food imports and exports, in the domestic market, interventions into prices of various foods also took place. These foods included milled grains and processed foods derived from them, cooking oil, pork, beef and mutton and their processed foods, dairy products and eggs. Some large agribusiness companies that wished to increase the price for any of these foods were required to report to the government before they did so (NDRC, 2008a). On 1 December 2008, this policy ceased in response of eased food supply.

In the domestic market, there were also the increases in grain floor procurement prices and the implementation of government buy-in. In view of the rapid steep increase in world grain prices in early 2008, the government raised the grain floor procurement prices several times (Table 8.1). In the latter half of 2008, the markets for grains, cooking oil and sugar became a bit sluggish in the domestic market, partly due to the good

Table 8.2   Agricultural subsidy in China 2002–08 (billion yuan)

	2002	2003	2004	2005	2006	2007	2008
Direct subsidy	–	–	11.60	13.20	26.20	42.70	63.30
Improved seeds subsidy	0.10	0.30	2.85	3.87	4.07	6.61	12.07
Farm machine subsidy	–	0.04	0.07	0.30	0.60	2.00	4.00
Total	0.10	0.34	14.52	17.37	30.87	51.31	103.00

Note: – Data do not exist or are not available.

Source: Calculated by authors from Ministry of Finance publications.

domestic harvest and partly due to the decline in world grain prices which had become lower than domestic prices (except for rice, whose world price was still higher, but close to China's domestic price). The government implemented a temporary buy-in plan to stop the prices from declining too much in order to protect farmers' interests. Under this plan, the government bought from the market 11.78 million tonnes of paddy rice and 8.52 million tonnes of corn at market prices (NDRC, 2009).

The other policy measures introduced by the government were to keep the input price under check and in the meantime to ensure an adequate supply of some key inputs, chiefly chemical fertilizers. On 15 February 2008, the government increased the export tariff for some phosphate fertilizers from 20 percent to 30–35 percent (State Council, 2008b). Starting from 20 April 2008, an additional 100 percent special export duty was added to the exports of all chemical fertilizers and also some raw materials used in the production of chemical fertilizers (State Council, 2008c). From 1 September 2008, the special additional export duty for nitrogen chemical fertilizers and ammonia was further increased to 150 percent, while the special additional export duty for other chemical fertilizers and raw materials was to remain at 100 percent (Xinhua Net, 2008). On 1 December 2008, the government decided to lower the export duty for all chemical fertilizers and raw materials in response to changed market situations (State Council, 2008a).

During 2008, central government's fiscal expenditure on agriculture also increased significantly, amounting to ¥595 billion from ¥432 billion in 2007, an increase of 38 percent. Out of this total expenditure, the amount used for 'three agricultural subsidies' (direct subsidy to grain production, subsidy to the adoption of improved seeds and subsidy to the acquisition of farm machinery) reached ¥103 billion, doubling that of 2007 (Table 8.2).

Clearly, all the major policy responses aimed at (1) increasing China's domestic grain production; (2) ensuring a stable grain supply and thus a stable price level; and (3) reducing exports at a time when there could be, or at least was perceived to be, the potential of a severe global grain shortage. The support for grain production indeed helped to increase the output level. Total grain output amounted to 529 million tonnes in 2008, an increase of 5.4 percent over 2007. It was the fifth year in a row that grain production registered a growth. All other agri-foods, for example, rapeseeds, horticultural products, meats, poultry eggs, milk and aquatic products, registered positive growth.

The measures undertaken by the Chinese government also succeeded in keeping domestic grain prices in check. Indeed, these measures had successfully isolated the domestic market from the world market. This is evidenced by the stable price levels as exhibited in China's domestic market (Figure 8.4).

Reduced export supports or increased export tariffs were meant to discourage grain exports so that domestic grain supply can be ensured and prices could be kept insulated from international influences. In 2008, China's grain exports indeed declined dramatically (Table 8.3). It is noted that soybean is a different story. The government reduced the in-quota tariff to 1 percent during 2008 from 3 percent in the previous years and the import rose to a new record level.

It is noted, however, although those measures were successful in curtailing grain exports, the restrictions on exports disadvantaged China's grain producers. We believe that China should have allowed more grains to be exported to take advantage of higher grain prices in the world market.

Exporting grains during 2007–08 when the world prices were high might raise domestic prices to some extent but should not have caused too much worry. Indeed, whether the exports would lead to higher domestic grain prices or the general CPI depends on many factors, including the volume of exports, domestic level of production and consumption, and the size of reserve stocks and also the availability of such information to the trading community and the general public. Should the domestic prices be pulled up as a result of more exports, the higher prices would help producers increase their income, a major policy objective the government has kept emphasizing in recent years. Surely, increased grain prices will increase the cost of living, chiefly of urban consumers. However, for the majority of urban consumers, the increase as a share in their total consumption expenditure will be very nominal. For the urban poor, the increase as a proportion of their total consumption is likely to be large. What the government needed to do here was to ensure that the welfare of the few poor was taken care of whilst not completely depriving a large number of Chinese farmers from benefiting from higher produce prices. Ironically, before China joined the WTO, many were concerned that cheaper imports would hurt farmers. But when the world market offered the Chinese farmers a rare opportunity to benefit from China joining the WTO, farmers were refused the opportunity.

Not only were the farmers losers from the government's export restrictions, the government itself was also a loser in that it missed a great opportunity to let the food price in China go higher, thus letting farmers enjoy higher income and boosting China's domestic market.[5] Further, the government's rigid export restrictions could not completely stop China's grains from flowing into the international market via grain smuggling. The huge difference between the world price and China's price (see Figure 8.4) was a huge temptation, resulting in some individuals smuggling grains from China to the overseas market (*China Business News*, 2008).

On the input price side, the government did try to exercise its control over agricultural input price levels, chiefly chemical fertilizers. Nonetheless, in 2008, the prices for agricultural inputs still increased greatly, by 20.3 percent. Although agricultural output prices also increased by an impressive 14.1 percent, it was 6 percentage points lower than the increase in input price, leading to worsening agricultural terms of trade (SSB, 2009).

HANDLING FUTURE SHOCKS: STRATEGIES CHINA SHOULD TAKE

China's population will continue to increase until about 2030, leading to increasing demand for grains. On the other hand, it has been widely accepted that due to rapid industrialization and urbanization, China's agri-food supply potential will be further strained. Future deviation of limited resources away from agricultural uses will only see reduced or, at its best, stabilized supply from domestic production, unless there are significant technological breakthroughs that will dramatically lift the yields. As such, some imports of grains from the world market will be unavoidable. However, relying on imports from the international market is not without risks, given the many unknowns that can emerge at any time just as had happened in 2007–08. Hence, China needs to be better strategically prepared in case any future market turmoils happen again and also to make a contribution to avoid such turmoils from taking place. Here we delineate a number of strategies to which attention should be given.

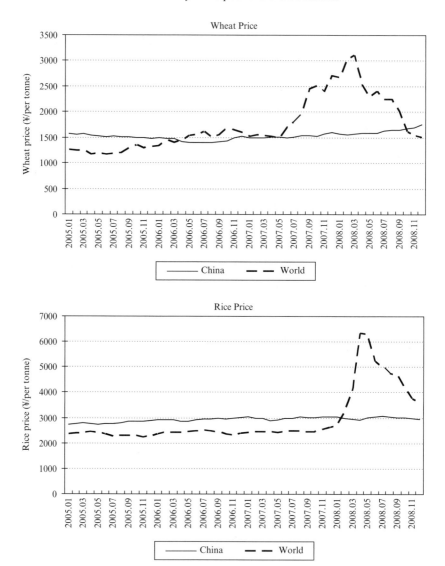

Note: International grain prices (in US$) were obtained from the World Bank Commodity Price. Grain prices in China were based on Zhengzhou Wholesale Market prices. Monthly average exchange rates between Chinese Renminbi yuan (¥) and the US dollar were used to convert the international price into Chinese yuan.

Figure 8.4   Grain prices, China and the world (2004–08)

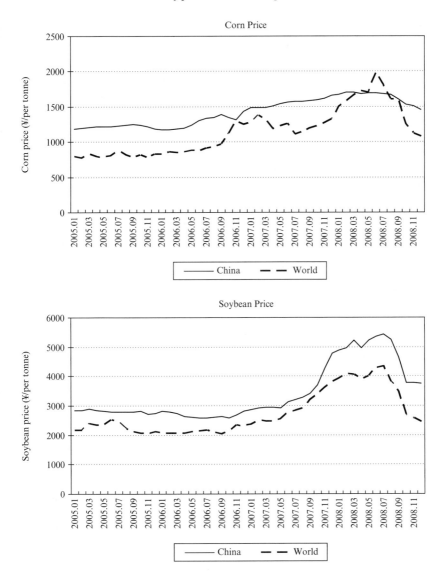

Figure 8.4   (continued)

Table 8.3   China's grain trade, 2000–08 (000 tonnes)

Part A: Imports

	Imports by Crops					Total Imports	
	Wheat	Rice	Barley	Corn	Soybean	Without Soybean	With Soybean
2000	880	240	1970	0	10930	3150	14080
2001	690	270	2370	0	13990	3440	17430
2002	600	240	1910	8	11321	2849	14170
2003	430	371	1360	1	20742	2191	22933
2004	7260	770	1710	0	20230	9750	29980
2005	3538	522	2179	4	26591	6272	32863
2006	613	730	2140	65	28270	3548	31818
2007	101	487	913	35	30821	1536	32357
2008	43	330	1076	50	37436	1499	38935

Part B: Exports

	Exports by Crops					Total Exports	
	Wheat	Rice	Barley	Corn	Soybean	Without Soybean	With Soybean
2000	188	2950	0	10470	210	14350	14560
2001	713	1860	0	6000	250	9480	9730
2002	699	1990	0	11670	280	15680	15960
2003	2514	2610	0	16391	270	24103	24373
2004	1089	910	0	2320	330	4730	5060
2005	605	686	4	8642	413	9761	10175
2006	1509	1253	6	3099	395	5867	6262
2007	3073	1343	118	4918	475	9452	9927
2008	3098	973	15	273	484	4359	4843

Part C: Net Imports

	Net Imports by Crops					Total Net Imports	
	Wheat	Rice	Barley	Corn	Soybean	Without Soybean	With Soybean
2000	692	−2710	1970	−10470	10720	−11200	−480
2001	−23	−1590	2370	−6000	13740	−6040	7700
2002	−99	−1750	1910	−11662	11041	−12831	−1790

Table 8.3 (continued)

	Net Imports by Crops					Total Net Imports	
	Wheat	Rice	Barley	Corn	Soybean	Without Soybean	With Soybean
2003	−2084	−2239	1360	−16390	20472	−21912	−1440
2004	6171	−140	1710	−2320	19900	5020	24920
2005	2934	−164	2176	−8638	26177	−3489	22688
2006	−896	−523	2134	−3034	27875	−2319	25556
2007	−2972	−856	795	−4883	30346	−7916	22430
2008	−3055	−643	1061	−223	36952	−2860	34092

Source: Ministry of Commerce (2009).

Smarter Use of the World Grain Market

Being a member of the WTO, China's grain markets are expected to become further integrated with the world market. Let the domestic market integrate with the world market but be prepared for any turmoils in the world market. When world grain prices are temporarily lower than China's, legitimate measures as allowed by the WTO rules may be used to prevent any glut of cheaper imports from coming to China in order to protect producers' interests. When world grain prices are higher than China's, grain exports may be allowed, if such surplus is available, for higher returns for producers. To help the Chinese farmers to avail themselves of any opportunities in the world market, a social safety net must be in place soon to protect the interests of the poor.

Being Proactive in Promoting and Establishing Regional and Global Collaboration

Rice will continue to be a staple for many Chinese. It is also the staple for many consumers in many parts of Asia. Rice plays a major role in ensuring food security in this region. It is advantageous for China to take a leading role in calling for the establishment of a regional rice safety net, say, for example, 'ASEAN + China', or 'ASEAN + 3' (China, South Korea and Japan), or even further extending to include India and Australia. China, South Korea and Japan should assume greater responsibility in maintaining higher volumes of buffer stock.

China could also take a leading role in promoting global collaborations under the WTO. China could advocate the inclusion of special clauses

that help ensure food security in developing countries in WTO trade negotiations and call for greater restraints on the use of exporting policies by
member countries that could aggravate volatile world food markets.

In addition, it is also beneficial for China to be proactive, to engage
in more bilateral free trade agreements with major food exporting countries such as Australia, Argentina and Brazil. Also, China may consider
producing more grains by investing in countries where grain production
resources are abundant. It is noted that such investment can be politically
sensitive if it is done by China's state-owned enterprises. On the other
hand, private enterprises may be more concerned with the high financial
requirements and political risks. Government supports, similar to the
Japanese External Trade Organization (JETRO) and the Australian Trade
Commission (Austrade), may be instituted to assist private enterprises in
embarking on such investments. Grains so produced do not have to be
exported to China but can be consumed anywhere in the world. Increase
in world grain supply will ease the food shortage situation anyway, no
matter who consumes it. This will benefit China's grain supply, directly
or indirectly, and will also represent a contribution from China towards
world grain security. In addition, this will also help to improve host countries' rural income and rural development, and help to transfer China's
agro-technologies to less developed countries to help them increase their
agricultural outputs in general.

Greater Investment in Agricultural and Rural Development

Limited, and most likely shrinking, resources available for agricultural
production in China will be the major challenge for China to increase its
domestic grain supply. This constraint can only be conquered, to some
extent, by innovating yield-augmenting techniques. The importance of
increasing investment in agricultural research and development (R&D)
and extension cannot be overemphasized in the case of China. Studies
have shown that the return from agricultural R&D and extension investment is quite promising as shown by a number of studies on the returns
of China's agricultural R&D and extension (see, for example, Fan et al.,
2001a; Fan et al., 2001b, Fan et al., 2002).

Great investment is also needed to build new, or improve, existing
agricultural and rural infrastructural facilities. Such facilities include,
for example, roads, electricity, irrigation, health, vocational education
and training, and communication. The quality and availability of such
infrastructural facilities will in the long run have an important impact on
China's grain production potential.

Empowering Farmers by Allowing Them to Establish Independent Farmer Organizations

China's small-scale household-based production renders the large number of producers little negotiating power in the market and also in the political system. To a great extent, they have to pay whatever the price they are asked to pay for production inputs and have to accept whatever the price they are offered for their outputs. More often they suffer from the price-cost squeeze. Farmers must be allowed to form their own organizations in order to better represent themselves in the input and output markets. Their own organizations will also help them to have their voice heard in the wider society. If farmers are continuously marginalized both economically and politically, China's grain production potential will be negatively affected. After all, grains are produced by farmers.

Building Market Research Capacity to Provide Essential Intelligence Inputs for Policy Responses

In the past three decades or so, the Chinese government has almost always reacted to changes in the grain markets hastily (for example, in late 1993, 2003 and 2008). This is a reflection of the fact that the government does not possess the essential market intelligence to help it work out sensible policy responses. This is attributable to the lack of a research team that is capable of carrying out regular, forward-looking and dependable market research at both the national and international levels. The Chinese government really needs to invest in this area by forming a research team at the national level that can provide the government with reliable market intelligence.

Transparency of Grain Reserve Management

How the country's grain reserve is managed is still shrouded in secrecy. No one knows exactly how much grain is in the nation's grain reserve. Secrecy makes it difficult to stabilize the Chinese grain market as well as the world grain market due to the speculation problem. Speculation is, as noted earlier, the major cause that resulted in the 2007–08 world grain market turmoils. The Chinese government should publicize the level of grain reserves (as well as other information regarding China's food economy management) to the market on a regular basis, as does the Indian government (Zhou, 1997, pp. 73–5). This would discourage speculation and in the meantime help producers and traders from both China and the rest of the world to adjust their production and business activities in response to China's reserve stock changes. Reduced speculation would help not only China to stabilize its grain market but also the whole international community to stabilize the world grain market.

We believe the use of the above strategies will help China to significantly boost its capability in handling any future grain market turmoils, domestic or international, thus leading to greatly improved food security for China. China's adoption of the above strategies will not undermine global food security, instead it will make a contribution to help the world to achieve better food security. In addition, speculation in domestic grain markets will also be curtailed. As far as discouraging speculation in the world grain market is concerned, China's action alone will not be able to achieve it; broader international cooperation is required. Nonetheless, should China allow its management of grain reserves to be transparent, it will make a significant contribution towards curtailing future speculation in the global grain market.

CONCLUSION

A number of factors, but chiefly speculation, resulted in the sharp fluctuations in the world grain market during 2007–08. The world market turmoil led to many governments implementing restrictions on grain trade in order to stabilize their domestic markets. The Chinese government, without exception, also undertook a number of measures to make grain exports more difficult and expensive and grain imports easier and cheaper. Domestically, it also intervened in the market by influencing input and output prices.

The policy responses undertaken by the Chinese government did successfully insulate the domestic market from the world market. The government was less successful in curtailing input price hikes in China, leading to worsening terms of trade for agriculture. Export restrictions hurt the farmers' interests and deprived them of the rare opportunity to benefit from higher world grain prices. Export restrictions also resulted in grain smuggling.

Although the 2007–08 price boom is over, the forces that resulted in the boom are still present, especially speculation due to the large amount of liquidity traveling around the globe. The possibility of future market turmoils cannot be excluded. For China to be better prepared for any future world market fluctuations, a number of areas deserve particular attention. These include: establishing a social security system as a matter of urgency to look after the welfare of the poor but allowing grain prices to rise as appropriate to benefit farmers, thus encouraging them to produce; taking a leading role in promoting and establishing regional and global food security systems; increasing investment for developing and extending yield-augmenting technologies to increase China's grain production potential; allowing farmers to establish their independent organizations in order to boost their negotiating powers in the market and in the country's political systems; building a national-level market research team to provide essential intelligence inputs for policy formulation; and ensuring transparency in grain reserve management to reduce the impact of speculation on grain market stability.

NOTES

1. The term 'grain' refers to cereals only and does not include soybeans and tuber crops as the term is used in China's official statistics.
2. Interesting and useful discussions about the food price crisis by researchers at the International Food Policy Research Institute (IFPRI) can be found at its website, http://www.ifpri.org/themes/foodprices/foodprices.asp (accessed 16 June 2009).
3. The change in the value of US dollars also has other effects on agricultural markets, for example, altering trade patterns. For more details, see the FAO report (FAO, 2008b, pp. 13, 20).
4. It is noted that some measures were undertaken to also combat inflation. China experienced higher inflation in late 2007 and early 2008. The Consumer Price Index (CPI) grew by more than 6 percent between August 2007 and July 2008, with the peak of 8.7 percent in February 2008.
5. One of the biggest mistakes in China's past three decades of economic reforms is the neglect of the development of the rural market, keeping in mind that some 70 percent of consumers are rural dwellers. Policies biased in favor of urban consumers kept the purchasing power of the rural community very low, leading to their inability to buy many products produced in the urban system. One serious consequence of this neglect is the over-dependence of the country's economy upon overseas markets. When facing global economic crises as happened in 2007–08, the problem of lacking rural purchasing power becomes acute, directly curbing the growth of the economy. The price boom in the world grain market was a golden opportunity to increase rural income but it has been lost forever. The government should let the agricultural market integrate with the world market, either when the market is sluggish or when it is booming. When sluggish, the government should consider using its support policies (for example, buy in the market to increase buffer stock) to protect farmers. When booming, let the farmers benefit from the higher world prices. If urban consumers need to be protected, use other policy instruments (for example, release of the buffer stock, social safety net targeting the poor) but not deny farmers the chance to increase their income.

REFERENCES

Asian Development Bank (ADB) (2008), *Soaring Food Prices: Response to the Crisis*, Manila, the Philippines.

Aulerich, N., L. Hoffman and G. Plato (2009), 'Issues and prospects in corn, soybeans, and wheat futures markets: new entrants, price volatility, and market performance implications', USDA, FDS-09G-01, Washington, DC.

Beintema, N. and H. Elliott (2009), *Setting Meaningful Investment Targets in Agricultural Research and Development: Challenges, Opportunities and Fiscal Realities*, FAO: Rome.

China Business News (2008), 'Exposing China's largest case of grain smuggling', available at http://hi.baidu.com/56cun/blog/item/2f448c171d5eba084b90a7fb.html (accessed 3 March 2009).

Cranfield, J.A.L., T.W. Hertel, J.S. Eales and P.V. Preckel (1998), 'Changes in the structure of global food demand', Staff Paper 98-05, GTAP Centre, Purdue University.

Economist, The (2008), 'Food and the poor', 17 April, available at http://www.economist.com/world/international/displaystory.cfm?story_id=11049284 (accessed 3 March 2009).

Fan, S., C. Fang and X. Zhang (2001a), 'How agricultural research affects urban poverty in developing countries: the case of China', EPTD Discussion Paper 80, IFPRI, Washington, DC.

Fan, S., L. Zhang, X. Zhang and X. Ma (2001b), *Regional Priorities of Public Investment in Rural China: A County-level Analysis*, Report prepared for the project Priorities of Public Investments in Chinese Agriculture, IFPRI, Washington, DC.

Fan, S., L. Zhang and X. Zhang (2002), *Growth, Inequality, and Poverty in Rural China: The Role of Public Investments*, IFPRI Research Report No. 125, Washington, DC.

Food and Agriculture Organization (FAO) (2008a), 'Policy measures taken by governments to reduce the impact of soaring prices (as of 15 December 2008)', available at http://www.fao.org/giews/english/policy/ (accessed 18 March 2009).

Food and Agriculture Organization (FAO) (2008b), 'Soaring food prices: facts, perspectives, impacts and actions required', High-Level Conference on World Food Security: The Challenges of Climate Change and Bioenergy, Rome, April.

Food and Agriculture Organization (FAO) (2008c), *Crop Prospects and Food Situation*, various issues, FAO: Rome.

Food and Agriculture Organization (FAO) (2008d), *Bioenergy, Food Security and Sustainability – Towards an International Framework*, FAO: Rome.

Food and Agriculture Organization (FAO) (2009a), *Crop Prospects and Food Situation*, FAO: Rome, April.

Food and Agriculture Organization (FAO) (2009b), 'High Food Prices and the Food Crisis – Experiences and Lessons Learned', FAO: Rome.

Food and Agriculture Organization (FAO) (2009c), FAOSTAT, available at http://faostat.fao.org/default.aspx (accessed 1 July 2009).

Gandhi, V.P. and Z.Y. Zhou (2007), 'Rising demand for livestock products in India: nature, patterns and implications', paper presented at the ABARE in-house seminar series, Canberra, Australia, 13 July.

Government of China (2004), '2004 government report', *People's Daily*, 16 March.

Heady, D. and S. Fan (2008), 'Anatomy of a crisis – the causes and consequences of surging food prices', IFPRI Discussion Paper 00831, IFPRI, Washington, DC.

International Monetary Fund (IMF) (2008), Food and Fuel Prices – Recent Developments, Macroeconomic Impact, and Policy Responses, IMF Report, Washington, DC.

Irwin, S.H., P. Garcia and D.L. Good (2007), 'The performance of Chicago Board of Trade corn, soybean, and wheat futures contracts after recent changes in speculative limits', selected paper presented at the American Agricultural Economics Association, Annual Meeting, Portland, Oregon, 29–31 July.

Ishida, A., S.H. Law and Y. Aita (2003), 'Changes in food consumption expenditure in Malaysia', *Agribusiness*, **19**, 61–76.

Ministry of Commerce (2009), 'Monthly bulletin of Chinese agricultural import and export statistics', available at http://www.mofcom.gov.cn (accessed 15 June 2009).

Ministry of Finance (2007a), 'VAT export rebates for grains and flours are to cease from 20 December 2007', available at http://www.mof.gov.cn/caizhengbuzhuzhan/zhengwuxinxi/caizhengxinwen/200805/t20080519_27896.html (accessed 17 November 2008).

Ministry of Finance (2007b), 'Tariffs to be levied for grains and flour exports in 2008', available at http://www.mof.gov.cn/caizhengbuzhuzhan/zhengwuxinxi/bulinggonggao/tongzhitonggao/200805/t20080519_27999.html (accessed 17 November 2008).

Ministry of Finance and State Taxation Bureau (2003), 'Notice on adjustments of tax rebates of exports', 13 October, available at http//:www.ahhpcpa.com.cn (accessed 5 July 2006).

Ministry of Land and Natural Resources (2009), 'The 2008 communiqué of land and natural resources', Government of China, Beijing, available at http://www.mlr.gov.cn/zwgk/tjxx/200912/t20091215_129769.htm (accessed 9 August 2009).

National Development and Reform Commission (NDRC) (2008a), 'Commodity categories and names of companies that are required to report to NDRC when their prices are to be increased, Public Notice No. 2', available at http://www.zzdarc.gov.cn/news/zcfg/2008/117/08117101516G399218HIFKG6IB9AFD3.html (accessed 25 May 2009).

National Developement and Reform Commission (NDRC) (2008b), 'Increased support from the government for the production of grains and other agricultural products', available at http://www.ndrc.gov.cn/xwfb/t20081020_241014.htm (accessed 21 November 2008).

National Developement and Reform Commission (NDRC) (2009), 'Report on the implementation of the plan for national economy and social development in 2008 and the draft plan for national economy and social development in 2009', available at http://news.xinhuanet.com/newscenter/2009-03/15/content_11014900.htm (accessed on 12 June 2009).

Organization for Economic Cooperation and Development (OECD) (2008), 'Biofuel support policies: an economic assessment', Paris: OECD.

Organization for Economic Cooperation and Development/Food and Agriculture Organization (OECD/FAO) (2008), *Agricultural Outlook: 2008–2017*, Paris and Rome: Organization for Economic Cooperation and Development and Food and Agriculture Organization.

Overseas Development Institute (ODI) (2008), 'Rising food prices: a global crisis', Brief Paper 37, London, April.

Pardey, P.G., J.M. Alston and R.R. Piggott (eds) (2006), *Agricultural R&D in the Developing World: Too Little, Too Late?* Washington DC: International Food Policy Research Institute.

Pardey, P.G., J.M. Alston and J.S. James (2008), 'Agricultural R&D policy: a tragedy of the international commons', Department of Applied Economics, University of Minnesota.

Regmi, A., M.S. Deepak, J.L. Seale and J. Bernstein,(2001), 'Cross-country analysis of food consumption patterns', in A. Regmi (ed.), *Changing Structure of Global Food Consumption and Trade*, ERS WRS No. 01-1, USDA, Washington, DC.

Sanders, D.R., S.H. Irwin and R.P. Merrin (2008), 'The adequacy of speculation in agricultural futures markets: too much of a good thing?', Marketing and Outlook Research Report 2008-02, Department of Agricultural and Consumer Economics, University of Illinois at Urbana-Champaign, June, available at http://www.farmdoc.uiuc.edu/marketing/morr/morr_archive.html (accessed 9 October 2009).

Saunders, C., W. Kaye-Blake and S. Cagatay (2009), 'Analysing drivers of world food prices: weather, growth, and biofuels', paper presented at the 27th Conference of the International Association of Agricultural Economists, Beijing, 16–22 August.

State Council (2008a), 'On the adjustments of export tariffs by the Tariff Administration Commission of the State Council', available at http://jjs.mof. gov.cn/guanshuisi/zhengwuxinxi/zhengcefabu/200811/t20081113_89940.html (accessed 1 June 2009).

State Council (2008b), 'On the adjustments of export tariffs of some chemical fertilisers by the Tariff Administration Commission of the State Council', available at http://policy.mofcom.gov.cn/section/claw!fetch.html?id=g000059171 (accessed 23 June 2009).

State Council (2008c), 'Notice on the imposition of special export tariffs of chemical fertilisers by the Tariff Administration Commission of the State Council', available at http://www.js-n-tax.gov.cn/Page1/StatuteDetail.aspx?StatuteID=8507 (accessed 23 June 2009).

State Statistical Bureau (SSB) (2009), 'Statistical communiqué of PRC's national economy and social development in 2008', available at http://news.xinhuanet. com/newscenter/2009-02/26/content_10903441.htm (accessed 15 March 2009)

Timmer, C.P. (2008), 'Causes of high food prices', ADB Economics Working Paper Series 128, Manila, the Philippines.

United States Department of Agriculture (USDA) (2008), World Agricultural Supply and Demand Estimates, Washington, DC: USDA.

von Braun, J. (2008), 'Rising food prices: what should be done?' IFPRI Policy Brief, International Food Policy Research Institute, Washington, DC, April.

World Bank (2007), *World Development Report 2008: Agriculture for Development*, Washington, DC: The World Bank

World Bank (2009), 'Commodity price data', available at http://go.worldbank. org/5AT3JHWYU0 (accessed 15 May 2009).

Wu, Y.R. (1999), *China's Consumer Revolution*, Cheltenham, UK and Northampton, MA, USA: Edward Elgar Publishing.

Xinhua Net (2008), 'The special export tariff for some chemical fertilisers will be increased to 150%', available at http://news.xinhuanet.com/fortune/2008-08/30/content_9740520.htm (accessed 23 June 2009).

Zhou, Z.Y. (1997), *Effects of Grain Marketing Systems on Grain Production: A Comparative Study of China and India*, New York: The Haworth Press.

Zhou, Z.Y. and L.B. Chen (1995), 'Reforms in China's grain procurement system in 1994: an appraisal', *Reform*, **5**, 55–8.

Zhou, Z.Y. and W.M. Tian (eds) (2005), *Grains in China: Foodgrain, Feedgrain and World Trade*, Aldershot: Ashgate.

9. RMB appreciation or fiscal stimulus, and their policy implications

James Xiaohe Zhang

INTRODUCTION

Despite the accumulated appreciation of the Renminbi (RMB) against the US dollar by more than 22 percent in nominal terms between 2005 and 2010, China's exports keep growing and its trade surplus continues to surge. It is reported that when the RMB broke 7 RMB per US dollar for the first time in 13 years, China's current account surplus hit a historical record of US$296 billion in 2008, accounting for 10 percent of its GDP. This surge has not been disrupted by a continuing appreciation of the RMB in 2010, beating market expectations (BBC, 2010). As a result, China's foreign exchange reserve keeps growing. By June 2010, the reserve had accumulated to over $2.45 trillion.

When the surge of trade surplus and hence the accumulation of foreign exchange reserve both hit a record in history, several domestic issues also emerged. Firstly, despite China's official registered urban unemployment rate having been maintained at a low level somewhere between 4–5 percent, the real figure is much higher because many of the country's more than 200 million rural migrant workers, who have flocked to the cities in recent years, are not registered. More than 20 million migrants who lost their jobs in the current crisis are still out of work. Taking these laid-off migrant workers into account and dividing both the registered unemployed and laid-off migrant workers by an estimated labor supply of 830 million would result in a higher real urban unemployment rate of 6–7 percent. In addition to this, if one also considers the new labor force of 50 million people added annually in the urban areas and the massive underemployment in the rural areas, the actual overall unemployed could be much higher than the official figure has indicated.

Secondly, after the inflation rate hit an 11-year high of 8.7 percent in early 2008, the rate had dropped to negative territory in 2009 until

July 2010 when it rebounded to 3.3 percent. This was accompanied by a slowing down in economic growth in 2008 during a worldwide economic downturn and a relatively tight monetary policy adopted thereafter. To cope with a fall in economic growth and potential emergence of inflation, after the Chinese government adopted a four trillion yuan ($586 billion) stimulus package, the country started to use a tight monetary policy by raising the required reserve ratio by 50 points on the eve of the Chinese New Year in 2010.

Conventionally, when a country has massive trade surplus and foreign exchange reserves, with a flexible exchange rate, an appreciation of the local currency, along with a tight monetary policy, may restore its external balance (Krugman and Obstfeld, 2009). However, as the largest developing country in the world, and with a huge amount of surplus labor and massive underemployment in the rural sector, China is also characterized with a production capacity that is well below its huge economic potential. As indicated by Fan (2008), there are 300 million underemployed rural laborers who earn US$500 per year in the rural areas and 300 million immigrant workers who earn US$1000 per year. Facing such high pressure to create jobs and ease social disparities, policy makers in China may not be able to simply use appreciation alone as a main tool to restore the overall economic balance.

After the RMB became a managed floating currency in 2005, the debates on whether, how and to what extent it should be further appreciated intensify. While some commentators (for example, Goldstein and Lardy, 2006, 2008, 2009; Roubini, 2007) recommend a considerable once-for-all appreciation as an instrument to reduce the growing trade imbalance between China and the rest of the world, others (for example, Corden, 2007, 2009; McKinnon, 2007, McKinnon and Gunther, 2009) advocate alternative policy packages including the use of a fiscal stimulus package to balance the economy.

Despite the fact that many, if not most, of the commentators believe that the undervalued RMB is responsible for the surging trade surplus in China and the massive accumulated trade deficit in the USA, the Chinese authorities are still reluctant to speed up the pace of RMB appreciation. The reasons for this reluctance may include the fear of a possible negative impact to China's economic growth, particularly for employment in its labor-intensive exporting industries and a consequential unrest to the society. Industrial sectors that are most affected by the appreciation are textiles, clothing, shoemaking, toys, motorcycles and agricultural sectors. According to a report released by the Ministry of Labour and Social Security, when RMB appreciates by 5–10 percent, about 3.5 million workers in the non-agricultural sectors lose their jobs. Meanwhile, the employment situation for millions of farmers will also be adversely affected (Chinanews, 2007).

The Chinese official position, nevertheless, is shared not only by most of the economists and business people in China, but also by some Western scholars including Robert Mundell and Joseph Stiglitz, two Nobel laureates in economics. Mundell (2006) maintains that 'a big change of its exchange rate will cut down China's growth rate from 9% now to perhaps half of 9%'. Other adverse economic impacts will include a decrease in corporate profitability, deflation in the agricultural sector, an increase in unemployment and less foreign direct investment. Joseph Stiglitz (2005) also argues that the RMB appreciation will have little effect on the trade balance between the USA and China, because the reduced Chinese imports in the US market could be easily replaced by increased imports from other developing countries.

Based on this background, this chapter has two objectives. Firstly, it attempts to test the Mundell-Stiglitz-McKinnon conjecture that the economic impact of RMB appreciation on China and its major trade partners including the USA, Japan and Australia is virtually negative. Secondly, it attempts to examine the effectiveness of the four trillion yuan ($586 billion) stimulus package implemented by the Chinese government in 2009 as an alternative measure of RMB appreciation to boost the economy, and test the issue raised by McKinnon and Gunther (2009) that expansionary fiscal policy is more preferrable for China to restore its internal as well as external balances.

In order to tackle these issues in a quantitative manner, a multi-country macro-econometric model known as the Fair Model (Fair, 2004, 2009) is used to examine the economic impact and international repercussions of the two distinguished policy recommendations of both Goldstein and Lardy (2006, 2008, 2009) and McKinnon and Gunther (2009). Three fundamental scenarios, namely, a considerable once-for-all appreciation of 20 percent versus a moderate appreciation of 5 percent per year, and a combination of RMB appreciation of 5 percent and an increase in government spending of 20 percent per annum between 2009 and 2012 are investigated, as compared with a base scenario of no change in the RMB rate at all. According to the results of simulations, the considerable once-for-all appreciation would not be appealing to the Chinese. To some extent it would reduce the economic growth to such a level that an economic recession may result, yet it will have little impact on the external trade imbalances between China and the rest of the world.

The rest of the chapter is organized as follows. The next section offers a brief discussion on a stylized theoretical framework of the overall balance in general and on how an expansionary fiscal policy can be used as a substitute of currency appreciation for China in particular. The third section presents the hypothetical perspectives of a the once-for-all 20 percent appreciation, as compared with a moderate appreciation of 5 percent per annum, and a mixed policy package that incorporates RMB appreciation with the fiscal stimulus package. Concluding remarks and the policy implications are summarized in the final section.

A THEORETICAL FRAMEWORK

The theoretical framework for achieving an internal as well as external balance is well documented. While the external balance refers to the balance in the current account, the internal balance refers to the desirable state in the economy where there is a low level of unemployment together with reasonable price stability. One important feature of the interrelations between the current account and the internal economy is the possible conflict between the macroeconomic goals of the two balances. To describe an economy that is out of the overall balance, the Swan diagram (Swan, 1963) can be used as a simple but powerful tool for analysis.

A tailored Swan diagram for the current Chinese economy is displayed in Figure 9.1. While the vertical axis measures the real exchange rate (R), the horizontal axis measures the real domestic expenditures or absorption (D). An increase in R refers to a depreciation and a decrease in R to an appreciation. Besides domestic consumption and investment, D also includes government expenditures which can be manipulated in the pursuit of fiscal policy. To make the diagram more specific to the case of China, the vertical axis is labeled roughly as the real exchange rate of RMB, and the horizontal axis is approximately represented by an annual GDP growth rate that may be needed to achieve the goal of full employment.

While the EE curve shows the various combinations of exchange rates (R) and real domestic expenditures (D) that result in external balance, the YY curve shows the various combination of exchange rates and domestic absorption that result in internal balance of full employment and price stability. The curve EE is upward-sloping because higher domestic demand requires a lower real exchange rate to maintain external balance, as domestic traded goods need to become more competitive to offset increased imports. Conversely, the curve YY is downward-sloping because higher domestic demand requires a higher real exchange rate to maintain internal balance, as spending must be switched from domestic goods to imports to avoid excess demand. External and internal balance can only be simultaneously achieved at point A where the two curves intersect.

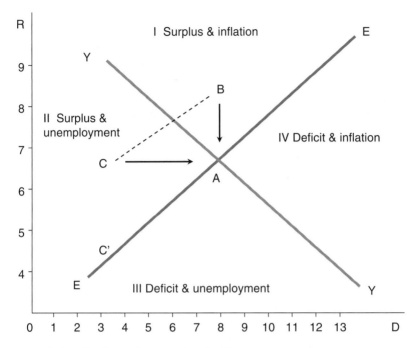

Figure 9.1   The Swan diagram for the Chinese economy

With points above the EE curve referring to external surplus and points below referring to deficits, and with points below the YY curve referring to unemployment and points above referring to inflation, the diagram represents the country with different combinations of domestic demand (D) and the real exchange rate (R) consistent with internal and external balance, respectively, and it can be divided into the following four zones, each reflecting a different combination of missed targets:

Zone I   External surplus and internal inflation;
Zone II   External surplus and internal unemployment;
Zone III   External deficit and internal unemployment; and
Zone IV   External surplus and internal inflation.

The proponents of drastic appreciation policy actually place China in a position such as point B in the figure. If it is the case, then by lowering R only will result in a convergence toward the overall balance point A. This is basically a policy recommendation offered by Roubini (2007), Frankel (2008), and Goldstein and Lardy (2006, 2008, 2009). However, the existence of a large amount of surplus labor (Fan, 2008), combined with excessive saving over investment due to underdevelopment of the financial system (Woo, 2008), and during a process of pursuing a deliberate outward looking trade strategy (Corden, 2007, 2009), will be more likely to place China in an underemployment and trade surplus position of point C in the figure, indicating that China has an external surplus and internal unemployment.

If China is indeed located at point C, it can only use fiscal policy to stimulate the economy until the overall balance point A is reached. If instead China lowers R only, that is, using merely an expenditure switching policy of accelerated appreciation of the RMB, it can achieve an external balance at point C' in the figure, but will be far away from the overall balance point A, indicating a suffering scenario with a large amount of unemployment. As the largest developing country, this could be an economic cost that is too high for China to afford. This is what the Mundell-Stiglitz-McKinnon conjecture is based on.

If the real situation is located somewhere between B and C, anywhere around the dotted line in the figure (for instance, see Frankel, 2008; Krugman and Obstfeld, 2009), a policy package that moves the economy to both internal and external balances is either a rise in absorption by an expansionary fiscally policy, if it is located below the YY curve, or a lowering in absorption by a contractive policy, if it is located above the YY curve, coupled with currency appreciation. As stated in their text, Krugman and Obstfeld (2009, p. 655) maintain that,

> The appreciation works to expenditure switch toward imports and lower inflationary pressures; the absorption increase works directly to lower the export surplus, at the same time preventing the emergence of unemployment that a stand-alone currency appreciation would bring.

Since there is no consensus so far on where about the Chinese economy is located, the question of which policy is more appropriate cannot be justified without empirical investigations. Particularly, because both Goldstein and Lardy's (2008, 2009) recommendation of drastic appreciation and the Mundell-Stiglitz-McKinnon conjecture that a considerable appreciation of RMB will have an adverse impact on China and will have virtually no effect on the trade deficits in the USA are empirical questions that cannot be answered without some quantitative assessment of the interaction and repercussion effects among many countries in the world economy, a simulation exercise based on macro-econometric models is one of the approaches whereby the assessment can be empirically carried out. Given the fact that the empirical study on this area is still very limited, this chapter attempts to fill the gap.

MODEL, SCENARIOS AND RESULTS

The Model

In order to assess the impact of the RMB appreciation and compare it with some alternative policies on the world economy, particularly on China and its main trade partners, a multi-country econometric model (MC) of Ray Fair (2009) is used for the investigation. In the MC model, any changes in one or more exogenous variables in a country will make a difference between the projected dataset and its original dataset which is based on time series regressions of long-term historical statistics (1960–2008) for each variable and for each country. After the model is solved and the results obtained, one could compare the new dataset with the original one and take the divergence between the two datasets as the 'net impact' of the proposed policy or policy package. A group of endogenous macroeconomic variables including GDP growth, inflation, consumption, investment, export, import and current account balance could be then compared and analysed.[1]

The Scenarios

The macroeconomic setting of the effect of appreciation is well documented in economic literature. When a local currency appreciates, the export price level will rise in terms of foreign currencies in the international market and the price of imports in terms of domestic currency will fall in the domestic market. Since the foreign demand for the country's exports falls when the price of its exports increases, the appreciation will lead to a fall in the country's exports, and an increase in its domestic demand for imports simultaneously. The appreciation is thus contractive and deflationary: the level of exports falls, the level of imports rises and the domestic price level decreases. This in turn, through the trade and price links of the MC model, affects production and international trade of all other countries in the rest of the world. Furthermore, so long as the sum of export elasticity and import elasticity is greater than unit, a situation defined as the Marshall-Learner condition in international economics, the current account surplus of the country will be reduced as a result.

The following scenarios were chosen to simulate some of the prescriptions that some economists have recommended (for example, Goldstein, 2004; Tung and Baker, 2004; Goldstein and Lardy, 2006, 2008, 2009), as compared with some alternative measures that the Chinese authority has implemented such as a gradual appreciation of the RMB by 5 percent annually along with the four trillion yuan fiscal stimulus package. The three scenarios that are particularly investigated are:

Scenario 1: The RMB rate is revalued by 20 percent in 2005 and the rate is maintained at 6.62 RMB per US dollar for the rest of the years between 2005 and 2009. This is a drastic once-for-all appreciation and thus is termed a 'drastic appreciation' scenario. Despite its counterfactual nature, it has been advocated by many, if not most, of the commentators.

Scenario 2: This is a mild appreciation of the RMB by 5 percent per year between 2005 and 2009 and then the rate of 6.8 RMB per US dollar is maintained thereafter for the rest of the years between 2009 and 2012. This is a scenario that partially reflects the actual practice that the Chinese authority had implemented until 2010. This scenario is termed 'actual appreciation'.

Scenario 3: This is a mixed scenario which incorporates the 5 percent annual appreciation of Scenario 2 with an expansionary fiscal stimulus policy of spending four trillion yuan ($586 billion) to stimulate China's domestic economy. This is a policy package advocated by McKinnon and Gunther (2009) and Krugman and Obstfeld (2009).

Since the nominal exchange rate of RMB in 2000 had been fixed at 8.27 per US dollar until July 2005, the RMB rate in 2000 is chosen as one of the exogenous variables that were shocked. In the 'drastic appreciation' scenario, it is assumed that the RMB was revalued by 20 percent to the level of 6.62 RMB per US dollar in 2005 and then the rate was maintained at that level for the rest of the years between 2005 and 2009. In the third scenario, it is assumed that the stimulus fiscal expansion plan is materialized with a 20 percent increase in government purchases annually between 2009 and 2012, along with a moderate appreciation of the RMB by 5 percent annually between 2005 and 2009.

The Results

The first scenario of a drastic once-for-all appreciation of 20 percent reflects a perception that accommodates most of the estimations on the degree of undervaluation of the RMB. When the model is solved, the net effect of the RMB appreciation is obtained through comparison of the projected change and the original dataset. By comparing the difference between the two datasets, the impact of the appreciation on the Chinese economy and the rest of the world can be analysed and discussed. To assess the international repercussion of the RMB appreciation, three major trade partners of China, namely, the USA, Japan and Australia, are chosen as the reference countries of the world economy. The percentage change of five major macroeconomic variables, namely, GDP, GDP price index (as a proxy of inflation), export, import and current account balance, are reported in Table 9.1. The result of the 'drastic appreciation' scenario displayed on the left hand side of the table is compared with the result of the 'actual appreciation' scenario displayed on the right hand side of the table.

The adverse impact on production and trade in China of the 'drastic appreciation' scenarios is clearly shown in the table. There are significant drops in four of the five variables, namely GDP, the price level, export and import. The double digit decline in both GDP and trade would have led China into a deep recession, if not an economic crisis, should the drastic appreciation be adopted. Furthermore, the impact on output for the USA, Japan and Australia are all negative because the drastic appreciation would result in declines in both exports and imports for most of the years in these countries. However, with the only exception of Japan, the appreciation does help China and all other countries reduce inflation rate.

While the current account improves in China and deteriorates in Japan and Australia, there is little impact on the trade balance in the USA. While China continues to accumulate its trade surplus, the balance of payment conditions for its major trade partners deteriorate. This again mirrors the actual events in China in the last five years.

Several causes can be used to explain the unexpected change in China's current account balance when the RMB is revalued. Firstly, the Chinese exports are relatively price inelastic, and the price pass-through process is extremely sluggish. This is consistent with the finding of Baak (2008) that a 1 percent depreciation of the RMB raises the Chinese exports to the USA by 1.7 percent, while a 1 percent depreciation of the US dollar raises the US exports to China by around 0.4 percent. Secondly, the Chinese imports are more likely to be dominated by income effect. In the database where the Fair Model is constructed, China's per capita marginal propensity of imports with respect to domestic aggregate demand per capita is as high as 0.81, ranking at the fourth highest in a group of 35 countries (Fair, 2009). This indicates that China's imports are overwhelmingly determined by domestic wealth or income effect and therefore when its GDP falls from its potential level as a result of the drastic appreciation of the RMB, its imports fall at a faster pace. This causes a puzzling phenomenon such that when the RMB appreciates, China's trade surplus surges.[2]

The second scenario attempts to examine the effectiveness of the gradual approach in RMB appreciation experienced by the Chinese economy in the past five years. The results for this actual annual appreciation of 5 percent are summarized on the right hand side of Table 9.1.

As displayed in the table, the 'actual appreciation' scenario seems appropriate for the Chinese economy in the first two years but would become more difficult to manage when the 20 percent appreciation target was

Table 9.1 Results of the drastic appreciation and moderate appreciation

	Scenario 1: drastic revaluation					Scenario 2: actual appreciation				
	GDP	Price index	Export	Import	Current account	GDP	Price index	Export	Import	Current account
China										
2005	-13.57	-5.68	-21.41	-7.22	47.88	-3.52	-1.25	-5.61	-1.83	11.92
2006	-14.63	-9.43	-21.19	-12.85	75.67	-6.91	-3.37	-10.54	-4.96	31.01
2007	-13.86	-11.36	-19.87	-15.60	89.81	-9.50	-5.81	-14.06	-8.35	50.72
2008	-12.68	-12.03	-18.47	-16.33	94.60	-11.51	-8.15	-16.83	-11.46	69.63
2009	-11.54	-11.97	-17.14	-15.95	93.86	-13.05	-10.22	-18.95	-14.08	86.98
USA										
2005	-0.01	0.65	-1.29	-1.05	6.79	-0.06	0.16	0.29	-0.61	1.98
2006	-0.23	0.00	-2.83	-1.84	3.81	-0.08	1.49	0.21	-1.56	2.04
2007	-0.70	-0.93	-3.74	-2.58	2.85	-0.39	1.81	-0.36	-2.29	2.79
2008	-0.87	-1.52	-4.45	-3.07	2.66	-0.54	2.02	-0.81	-3.18	3.92
2009	-0.96	-1.81	-4.90	-3.07	2.43	-0.69	2.30	-1.09	-4.16	4.70

Australia										
2005	-0.37	-0.47	0.96	1.16	15.72	-0.54	-0.48	0.15	1.45	11.67
2006	-0.39	-3.40	0.98	-2.09	48.29	-0.65	-3.73	1.42	-1.38	42.56
2007	0.56	-3.72	1.02	-4.92	27.80	0.51	-4.29	1.89	-4.36	22.44
2008	0.72	-3.51	0.80	-5.43	18.69	0.88	-4.15	1.76	-5.07	14.92
2009	0.63	-3.21	0.58	-5.14	14.46	0.95	-3.73	1.47	-4.93	13.51
Japan										
2005	-0.34	0.65	1.83	-2.07	3.93	-0.51	0.57	0.58	-1.85	7.77
2006	-0.18	1.06	-1.46	-3.65	4.38	-0.22	0.73	-0.68	-2.78	8.74
2007	-0.52	0.70	-3.11	-2.47	-6.46	-0.38	0.31	-1.28	-1.37	-1.59
2008	-0.74	0.40	-4.08	-1.90	-12.90	-0.47	0.07	-1.88	-0.89	-8.65
2009	-0.83	0.16	-4.52	-1.71	-16.66	-0.49	-0.01	-2.40	-1.00	-13.37

Note: The percentage change indicates the difference in values between the variables in the new dataset and their counterpart in the base dataset. Since two of the countries (China and Japan) have trade surplus and the other two (USA and Australia) have trade deficit, a positive figure in the current account indicates an increase in the surplus (deficit) of the corresponding country.

Table 9.2   Results of 5 percent appreciation plus 20 percent increase in government purchases

	GDP	Price index	Exports	Imports	Current account
China					
2005	−0.01	−0.02	−0.06	−0.04	0.12
2006	−0.05	−0.04	−0.15	−0.07	0.04
2007	−0.10	−0.10	−0.21	−0.08	0.08
2008	−0.14	−0.13	−0.24	−0.10	0.09
2009	−0.01	−0.07	−0.05	−0.06	0.16
2010	−0.01	−0.03	−0.05	−0.03	0.08
2011	−0.01	−0.02	−0.05	0.00	0.01
2012	−0.01	−0.01	−0.04	0.01	−0.06
USA					
2005	0.01	0.00	0.02	−0.02	−0.12
2006	0.00	0.02	0.00	−0.02	−0.01
2007	0.01	0.03	−0.01	0.00	−0.26
2008	−0.01	0.04	−0.03	−0.01	−0.19
2009	−0.03	0.03	−0.05	−0.07	0.60
2010	−0.03	0.02	−0.04	−0.10	2.03
2011	−0.02	0.01	−0.03	−0.10	13.53
2012	−0.02	0.01	−0.02	−0.07	−2.86

Note: The percentage change indicates the difference in values between the variables in the new dataset and their counterpart in the base dataset. Since China has trade surplus and the USA has trade deficit, a positive figure in the current account indicates an increase in the surplus (deficit) of the corresponding country.

reached in 2008. As compared with the drastic once-for-all appreciation, the declines in the growth rates of GDP and trade are effectively curbed, while the drops in inflation rate is just about right in the first two years.

As in the 'drastic appreciation' scenario, the impact of the 'actual appreciation' on the USA, Japan and Australia is still negative, although not as bad as that which would emerge in the 'drastic appreciation' scenario.

The third scenario assumes that along with the 5 percent modest annual depreciation between 2005 and 2008, there is an increase of 20 percent in the government purchases between 2009 and 2012 in China. This scenario reflects partially the actual practice that the Chinese authorities have implemented since 2009. The experimental result for this scenario is reported in Table 9.2.

The modest annual appreciation of 5 percent along with an additional expansionary fiscal policy does slow down the economic growth rate and inflation rate in China marginally, yet has no significant impact on the current account balance. In other words, despite having appeared as a by-product, the third mixed policy scenario may help China to stabilize its trade surplus and help the USA cut its trade deficit. As one can see from the table, the significant adverse impact of the drastic RMB appreciation that has been shown in Table 9.1 is almost completely avoided. When the fiscal stimulus policy is implemented in 2009, the trade deficit in the USA starts to reduce. It seems to suggest that the expansionary fiscal policy is a better option not only in boosting the Chinese domestic economy, but also in improving its external balance, including removing some of the trade deficits in the USA, despite quite moderately.

With the current account improving in China and deteriorating in the USA initially, the gap in trade balance would not be narrowed until 2009 when the four trillion yuan stimulus fiscal policy started to work. It is interesting to note that the change in the current account does reflect what has happened in the real world in the past few years: while China's trade surplus continued to grow, the trade deficit in the USA deteriorated before it improved in 2009. In other words, the experimental result does show an increase in current account surplus in China due to an instant impact of improvement in the terms of trade for China and a deterioration in the terms of trade for the USA and hence its current account balance.

CONCLUSION

This chapter examines the economic impact of RMB appreciation on China and its major trade partners. The results of simulation experiments conducted on a simple macro-econometric model (the Fair Model) seem to support the Mundell-Stiglitz-McKinnon conjecture that a drastic once-for-all appreciation of the RMB brings mainly adverse impact not only to China but also to the rest of the world, yet has little impact on the trade imbalance between China and its major trading partners, particularly the USA.

The findings are summarized as follows.

Firstly, a drastic once-for-all appreciation of RMB by more than 20 percent would not be appealing to the Chinese. To some extent it would significantly reduce the competitiveness of China's exports and cut its double digit economic growth rate to a low level that the Chinese policy makers would not like to risk. The drastic appreciation would also have some adverse impacts not only on the growth rate of GDP, but also on the current account deficits in the USA and Australia.

Secondly, despite the fact that a moderate appreciation of 5 percent per annum seems appropriate for the long term health of the Chinese economy, when the accumulated appreciation reaches 20 percent of its 2005 level in 2008, further appreciation may significantly slow the economic growth rate in China. Should this appreciation accelerate, China may encounter a recession or stagflation in the coming years.

Thirdly, as compared with currency appreciation, the expansionary fiscal policy of increasing 20 percent in government spending seems a better alternative not only in maintaining a healthy growth rate in China, but also in improving the trade balance between China and the USA.

However, the projection generated from the experiments may exaggerate some negative consequences of the drastic appreciation,[3] and so a certain degree of caution is called for, this research has rejected a considerable once-for-all appreciation that, as the simulation result has suggested, would do more harm than good to the Chinese economy as well as to the rest of the world. Alternatively, this study advocates some other policy measures, particularly an expansionary fiscal stimulus policy, to restore not only the internal as well as external balance in China, but also the trade balance between China and its major trade partners, particularly the USA.

NOTES

1. The latest version of the MC model includes 39 countries and there are 15 stochastic equations estimated econometrically for each country. Including the 31 stochastic equations in the US model, which is a key component of the MC model, there are 363 stochastic equations and about 4500 variables. Based on its estimation of the coefficients for all stochastic equations, the model allows its users to forecast some proposed policy changes such as appreciation or devaluation of a currency between 2009 and 2012. In its dataset, the exchange rate is defined as local currency per US dollar, so a decrease in the exchange rate is an appreciation against the dollar.
2. The results seem to support the Mundell-Stiglitz-McKinnon conjecture that the RMB appreciation will have little impact on the imbalance in the current account, particularly with respect to the trade imbalance between China and the USA.
3. This is because the simulation results are derived from a model where the Chinese economy is constructed in a rather simple way so some of the results could have been exaggerated. The projection could be greatly improved if the model is modified to introduce more dynamic variables and more appropriate equations particularly in approximating the real exchange rate change into its framework. More research is therefore needed toward these directions.

PART IV

Distortion and economic sustainability

10. From policy-driven opening to institutional opening – a discussion on policy-imposed distortion in China's economic development

Youwen Zhang

INTRODUCTION

China has been successfully opening its economy to the outside world for three decades now. During this time, China has grown from a poor, economically undeveloped country into an emerging influential power in the modern world economy. Furthermore, the country's goals in 'opening up' the economy, and the theme, have changed over the 30 years.

It needs to be recognized that, until now, China's success in economic terms has been pushed forward by the continuous implementation of targeted policies. Although China has eliminated many serious market distortions through its economic reform and opening to the outside world, its mandated special policies have created new distortions that are policy imposed, which have combined with distortions already present to undermine many of the benefits of an open economy. This chapter examines the existing distortions resulting from the opening-up process in China and the impact of such distortions on the economy. Priority is given to the analysis of institutional causes of new distortions and the identification of the key characteristics of an open economic system. It is proposed that the core of building an open economy in China is to eliminate policy-imposed distortions. It is also argued that industry policy, regional policy and scarce factor development policy should replace the existing factor owner differentiation and market preference policies in order to maintain sustainable economic growth and social development in China.

POLICY-IMPOSED DISTORTION AND INSTITUTIONAL DISTORTION

The theory of market distortions in an open economy has demonstrated that the existence of distortion reduces the benefits of an open economy. Therefore, the investigation of whether distortions exist in an open economy has become a major part of analysing the benefits of opening up an economy.

Definition of Policy-imposed and Institutional Distortions

The theory of distortions in an open economy classifies distortions into four types, described by the following:

$$FRT \neq DRT = DRS, \text{ externality distortions exist} \qquad (10.1)$$

$$DRT \neq FRT = DRS, \text{ production distortions exist} \qquad (10.2)$$

$$DRS \neq DRT = FRT, \text{ consumption distortions exist} \qquad (10.3)$$

$$MRS^1_{LK} \neq MRS^2_{LK}, \text{ factor distortions exist} \qquad (10.4)$$

where FRT is the foreign marginal rate of transformation, DRT is the domestic marginal rate of transformation and DRS is the domestic marginal rate of substitution. MRS^1_{LK} and MRS^2_{LK} are the marginal rates of substitution for capital and labor in commodity 1 and commodity 2, respectively.

Regarding the causes of distortions, the four types of distortions may take the form of either endogenous distortions that arise when market imperfection exists in an economy, or policy-imposed distortions that arise under the influence of institutional drivers or policy. Policy-imposed distortions include both autonomous policy-imposed distortions and instrument policy-imposed distortions. Autonomous policy-imposed distortions arise under the influence of a closed economy or certain non-economic objectives, whereas instrument policy-imposed distortions stem from interventionist policies such as taxes or subsidies (Bhagwati, 1971). Policy-imposed distortions are also called 'indirect distortions' or 'secondary distortions' (Williamson, 1987).

Distortion theory is an important contribution made by the economists of developing countries to international economics. This theory has significant policy implications because it can determine whether an open economy has reached optimum conditions and realized the greatest potential benefits by examining the existence and severity of distortions.

The theory postulates that eliminating distortions increases the benefits of an open economy.

An institution can be understood as a basic economic system or an instrument of national economic management. In the latter sense, the institution has policy implications, so we define it as institutional policy. Autonomous policy-imposed distortion can also be defined as an institution-imposed distortion. In a broader sense, institution-imposed distortions originate in a planned economy and the process of transition such an economy must follow.[1] A dislocation in resource allocation stemming from a planned economy is the most fundamental cause of distortion. Planning not only impedes production factor flow at a reasonable price but also causes production, consumption and externality distortions as product and factor prices are dictated by command and control.

Impacts of Distortion on the Benefits of an Open Economy

The distortion theory of modern development economics and international economics has been extensively applied to the study of the impacts of distortion on the benefits of an open economy to demonstrate the unfavorable impacts of distortion on trade welfare. A brief review of studies conducted since the 1990s now follows.

Papageorgiou et al. (1991) conducted a quantitative analysis which revealed that: (i) trade liberalization itself did not lead to any significant change in the production structure or to the reallocation of factors between industries; (ii) the severe factor market distortions limited the effects of improving trade welfare through trade liberalization. Rodrik (1995) compared the degrees of distortion in the labor markets of East Asian and Eastern European countries by measuring the impacts of trade liberalization. Kwon and Paik (1995) calculated the welfare losses caused by distortions in the Korean labor and capital markets using a general equilibrium model, and demonstrated that: (i) eliminating labor market distortions can increase base year GDP by nearly 1 percent; (ii) eliminating capital market distortions can increase base year GDP by approximately 3.2 percent; and (iii) eliminating both labor and capital market distortions can increase national welfare by 5.6 percent. Lindbeck (1997) analysed the economic impacts of distortion in the factor market of Sweden while undergoing its early trade liberalization process. Seddon and Wacziarg (2002) identified that the inter-industry factor reallocation effects of trade liberalization were insignificant in most developing countries. Currie and Harrison (1997) found that state-owned enterprises were far less subject to factor market correction than were private enterprises in the trade liberalization process, implying that distortion in the factor

market of a developing country is to a large extent affected by the institutional arrangement. Krishna et al. (2002) revealed the discrepancy in
the trade benefits of factor market distortion under different institutional
conditions. This study substantiated the existence of a price effect of trade
on the terms of trade, as well as an output effect of trade, by calibrat-
ing the Richardian model, special factor model and factor endowment
model. In a distortion-free economy, positive price and output effects
will increase welfare. In a distortion-plagued economy, the price effect
can improve welfare but the output effect will reduce welfare. A severely
distorted economy will incur actual losses because the favorable price
effects are relatively low. Krishna and Yavas (2004) found that the output
of the sector experiencing distortion may still rise despite cost increases in
the event of labor market distortion arising from the segregation of wage
from ability, and such a distortion will inflict losses on the economy of a
country as trade grows. In the absence of any structural reform, trade liberalization will produce unfavorable effects in a transitional economy or a
developing country.

The research on distortion theory focuses on demonstrating that factor
distortion is the basis and root cause for any adverse impact on the benefits
of an open economy, and therefore requires special attention and research.

ELIMINATION AND FORMATION OF DISTORTIONS UNDER THE OPENING-UP POLICY

The reformist and 'opening-up' policy in China has promoted economic
growth and development. The sources of this growth include the following: (i) reform helps establish a market mechanism and boosts factor
allocation efficiency; (ii) opening promotes factor inflow and increases the
total factor input quantity; (iii) reform releases the idle factors of production and increases the total input factor quantity; (iv) reform boosts factor
utilization efficiency and total factor productivity; and (v) export growth
drives up total demand.

Under distortion theory, the growth benefits of reform and opening up
are attributed to the reduction and elimination of distortions. A planned
economy is replete with distortions. In a planned economy, all factors
are allocated according to a central plan; product and factor prices are
determined by central planners; and foreign trade and factor flows are kept
under strict control. As a result, production and factor distortions abound
and externality distortions thrive in a closed economy. Each stage of reform
and opening up is meant to reduce or eliminate distortions so that factor
allocation is determined by factor prices, product prices are determined by

market forces and domestic prices are amenable to international prices. Reform and opening up of the economy, however, constitute a long process; and during the transition period, distortions still abound under the two systems. More importantly, China has opened up to the outside world under the push of policy incentives. As a result, the Chinese government has created new policy-imposed distortions while eliminating the institutional distortions of the planned economy. Indeed, policy-imposed distortions have become an important characteristic of China's open economy.

The Role of Policy Incentives in Economic Transition and the Elimination of Distortions

Policy incentives are the major driving force behind China's transition from a planned economy into a market economy and from a closed economy into an open economy. Special policies have created new policy-imposed distortions while driving development through various methods.

China's opening-up campaign began with the introduction of special policies, which helped kick off the historical process of opening to the outside world. It is apparently necessary to break down the old institutions by adopting special policies. Special policies can mostly be divided into three main categories, as per the following. The first includes the special economic zone and economic development zone policies. Special economic zones are a product of China's experimentation in opening up to the outside world, while economic development zones are used as a management model when the opening-up campaign has entered the prime stage. The second category is that of trade development policies. Encouraging exports has been one of the major priorities within the opening-up policy. During the early stage of its campaign, China promoted rapid export development, in particular by encouraging the 'three types of processing plus compensation trades'. Meanwhile, the dual-track foreign exchange regime was put in place to encourage exports at a low exchange rate. Moreover, export tax rebates have long been employed by China as a key policy instrument to encourage exports. Finally, the third category includes preferential foreign investment policies, which are designed to attract foreign investment. An enterprise is entitled to any benefits under the preferential policies so long as its capital structure meets the requirements for Sino–foreign joint ventures, cooperative ventures and wholly foreign-owned ventures. To woo foreign investment, the central government, and local governments at all levels, boosted their efforts to attract foreign investment by enacting preferential policies to offer more concessions in terms of tax breaks and land transfer. China has ramped up its foreign investment policy initiatives over the period of economic transition, moving from encouraging exports only towards seeking balance in foreign exchange and finally to opening the domestic market.

The continuing expansion and optimization of such special policies has characterized development over the 30-year period of opening up in China. Special policies have played a fundamental role in China's transition from a closed economy to an open economy. The special economic zone policy has enabled China to carve a bloody path to victory against the traditional institutions and to surmount cognitive yokes and institutional obstacles. It also enabled China to re-establish contact with the world economy in a controlled way to mitigate economic and political risks. As a result, China quickly learned how to adopt the world's advanced management methods and market operation models. The trade incentive policy helped China swiftly eliminate foreign exchange shortages, create massive employment and turn external markets into a powerful driver of growth. The foreign investment incentive policy also helped China rapidly overcome capital shortages and combine foreign investment with foreign trade to create a major source of China's export products. In particular, the policy promoted the formation of a competitive market environment at home.

By conducting an analysis under the distortion theory framework, we find that special policies not only tore apart the planned economy and its severe distortions but also created policy-imposed distortions. Special economic zones and economic development zones are the products of a region differentiation policy, and special economic zones have been established mainly for exploratory and experimental purposes, meant to generate first-mover effects by taking the lead in reform and opening to the outside world. The primary purpose of economic development zones is to encapsulate a space for concentrated development by promoting concentrated land use and developing industry clusters. Under the development policy framework, special economic zones and economic development zones also form part of an industry and region differentiation strategy. This strategy is designed to concentrate factors in specific regions, especially those with international geographical advantages, in order to drive higher production efficiency. Therefore, the policy is also of vital significance to economic development. While reducing externality distortions, region differentiation special policies have played an increasing role in shaping the price mechanism of special economic zones and realigning domestic prices with international market prices. Externality distortions are reduced in economic development zones where product and factor prices are determined by market forces.

The export encouragement policy is a market differentiation policy aimed at encouraging exports. The need to encourage exports arose from China's foreign exchange shortages at the time. The policy was designed to concentrate economic resources in the export industry in order to expand export capacity rapidly and to acquire foreign exchange earning power and import capability. Taking the national economy as a whole, policy costs can be compensated for by the benefits of importation. The export incentive policy was designed to channel factors via fiscal subsidy into the export industry; realize cheap resource and labor advantages on the international markets; optimize resource allocation; alleviate foreign exchange scarcity; and reduce foreign exchange distortion under strict control.

The foreign investment policy is a factor differentiation policy. Offering preferential treatment or concessions for foreign investment helped attract foreign investment and at home mobilize idle factors into the production process. Capital shortage reduced the value of massive natural resources and idle labor to zero. The significance of introducing foreign investment is to form new production and create new national income through eliminating the distortion of the idle production factor.

The classical distortion theory that developed in the 1970s focused on analysing trade distortions without examining international capital flows. Actually, this analysis can be conducted under a unified distortion theory. Optimizing global capital allocation eliminates capital price distortions and enhances benefits, which can then be distributed globally. More importantly, policy-imposed distortion created by a capital recipient country for the capital factor has become an important form of distortion in an open economy.

The Formation of Distortions in Incentive Opening-up Policies and the Loss of Benefits Due to Distortions

China's remarkable development on all fronts has evidenced the success of its 30-year-old opening-up policy. However, it is also clear that certain potential benefits have been lost during this time. This is because the country's policy of reform has created new policy-imposed distortions and limited the benefits to be derived from an open economy, while still eliminating the old institutional distortions and creating remarkable achievements in terms of development.

1. Factor distortions under the preferential foreign investment policy

The preferential foreign investment policy has been an important preferential policy in opening China's economy to the outside world. This policy not only caused massive foreign capital inflow but also created an unfavorable environment for domestic capital utilization. Handing China's potential for rapid growth over to foreign investors after a dramatic change in capital scarcity puts domestic investors in an unfavorable position and leaves domestic capital idle, thereby resulting in a great deal of unusual phenomena. On the one hand, China enacted preferential policies to allow foreign investors to share excess returns on investment; yet, on the other hand, the country chose either to leave enormous foreign exchange resources idle or to buy low-yield United States (US) Treasury bonds. The preferential policies boosted the ongoing inflows of foreign capital but a tremendous amount of capital in the domestic banking system could not be put into effective use. The preferential foreign investment policy is a typical capital factor distortion policy: when different policies (for example, different income tax rates) are enacted for either foreign investment or domestic investment, the economy is naturally predisposed to use foreign investment instead over its domestic counterpart.

A pronounced phenomenon in factor price distortion is land price distortion. In China, local governments compete with each other over foreign investment projects by offering various concessions. As a result, the price of land transferred by private agreement is way below the market price of land reached through auction. Thus, severe distortions exist in land prices. The average auction prices per are of land (1 are = 100 square meters) were RMB 62 500 and RMB 68 500 in 2004 and 2005, respectively, whereas the average prices of land sold by other methods (mainly government transfer by private agreement) were RMB 20 900 and RMB 15 000 per are, respectively, which were 33.44 percent and 21.9 percent lower than market prices. Land price distortion arose from the low prices of land transferred by private agreement. Such a distortion has eroded national wealth and affected national welfare. In 2005, as a further example, if market prices had been used to replace private transfer prices, the unit price of land would have increased to RMB 53 500 per are and the total price would have reached RMB 306.02 billion, which was 55.6 percent higher than the actual total transfer price and accounted for 2.24 percent of GDP (RMB 13 651.5 billion). In 2006, the difference between the private transfer price and the market price was RMB 69 400 per are of land. The private transfer price was only 16 percent of the market price and the total land price difference accounted for 3.65 percent of GDP.[2]

2.   Resource factor price distortion and resource product export

Excessive exportation of resource-intensive products is one of the characteristics of China's brute force approach to economic development and is attributable to resource price distortion. In China, resource prices have long been set by the central government at a level lower than international prices. Price distortion has directly reduced the potential benefits under open economic conditions. Low resource prices have led resource-consuming industries to expand and enabled foreign investors to garner low-cost production and high-margin exports. Additional resource costs are in fact hidden in exports.

When prices are distorted, the individual costs of an enterprise are higher than social costs and the advantages of low-cost exports of an enterprise include the hidden costs paid by society. The nominal export benefits are therefore not truly beneficial. International Energy Agency (IEA) statistics show that China's industrial electricity price is 5.1 cents/kWh, which is 62.5 percent of the price level in developed countries such as Japan and Italy; 83.3 percent of the price level in developing countries such as Argentina and Korea; and 76.9 percent of the price level in the resource-oriented countries such as Canada and Australia. China's urban water price is only one third of the international water price. Some scholars estimate that domestic enterprises have unreasonably saved at least 20–40 percent of production costs because the factors of production are underpriced (Li, 2007a). The actual export costs of Chinese enterprises are therefore underestimated and the export benefits are overestimated.

Unreasonably low resource prices set by the government have not only distorted resource factor prices but also encouraged rent-seeking activities. Charging miners an artificially low royalty for natural resources has created conditions for them to reap windfall profits and has opened the floodgates for rent seeking. China offers foreign investment enterprises the right to mine natural resources and charges them a low royalty for doing so. Meanwhile, there is a market price for natural resources mining rights and some enterprises have acquired mining rights by paying the market price. Actually, local governments control local resources and as a result, local governments seek rents from the central government and seek greater control over their local resources.

3. Labor factor price distortion and export disadvantage

Cheap labor is a key advantage for China in participating in the global economy. Labor-intensive product export and processing trade has become a distinctive feature of foreign trade in China. At the preliminary stages of development, this was the only viable approach for China to participate in the international division of labor due to its shortage of capital, technology and international market channels. However, the excessive labor supply along coastal regions has long subdued the labor price at a low level. This has not only impacted laborer interests but also resulted in an unfavorable situation in which China has been excessively dependent on labor-intensive industries in the international division of labor.

In China, total payroll as a percentage of GDP has been in decline since the 1970s. For example, the share of payroll declined in 12 of the 16 years from 1989 to 2005 and took a nosedive in the late 1990s to reach a level 5 percent lower than the 1980s figure. From 1989 until 2005, payroll accounted for 12.56 percent of GDP on average. In 2005, payroll totaled

RMB 1978.99 billion, accounting for only 10.81 percent of GDP. In Western developed countries, however, payroll usually accounts for 50–60 percent of GDP (Chen, 2007).

Compared with developed countries, China lags far behind in terms of labor productivity in secondary industries. For example, China's labor productivity in secondary industries is only 1/16, 1/18 and 1/15 that of the United Kingdom (UK), the USA and Japan, respectively. Meanwhile, China's wage level is merely 1/27, 1/21 and 1/22 that of the UK, the USA and Japan, respectively. Compared with emerging market economies, China's labor productivity is 1/7 and its wage level 1/13 that of Korea. Looking at developing countries, China's labor productivity is 1/3 and three times that of Malaysia and India, respectively, while its wage level is 1/4 and two times the wage level in Malaysia and India, respectively. The 'White Paper on International Economy and Trade' of Japan shows that average labor costs account for 4 percent of product costs in Asian countries and regions (3.5 percent in China) (Jun, 2006).

Labor price distortions have not only reduced foreign trade benefits but have also frustrated the objective of allowing all members of society to share the benefits of development. In recent years, laborer wages have risen slightly nationwide but dropped in some areas because governments at all levels are still heavily dependent on maintaining cheap labor as a comparative advantage in the process of development. As a result, local governments have chosen to set low wage rates. Institutionally, improving the treatment of laborers is the correct tactic to adopt to eliminate labor price distortions.

When a country's labor prices are distorted, it cannot realize a reasonable international division of labor by opening up trade. As a result, the country may experience an inadequate or excessive division of labor. One result of opening to the outside world is to bring in scarce factors and market mechanisms to keep product and factor prices at a reasonable level and to allocate resources in a more equitable way. Unfair resource allocation will reduce the welfare and living standards of citizens as a result of income decreases in those sectors that have an excessive labor supply and employment decline in other sectors. Migrant peasants will accept low-paid jobs in cities and force urban residents out of work. In coastal regions, landless peasants become an idle labor force. In this case, welfare losses cannot be more pronounced. In China, the phenomenun of unreasonable labor allocation is partly due to uneven development between regions.

The massive migration of labor from the underdeveloped mid-western and rural areas into coastal regions results in excessive labor supply in coastal regions. This structural imbalance of labor in coastal regions is related to excessive low-end labor supply. As the simple processing trades only require low-skilled laborers, urban technical workers cannot find suitable jobs. Urban workers who decline low-end job offers end up joining the unemployment line. This is a manifestation of the structural issues in the employment market. The massive migration of rural labor is due to financial market distortion, making it impossible to provide adequate agricultural investment and boost agricultural productivity and income. Labor market distortions also distort comparative advantages. As a result, China has long been relying on cheap labor and developing its labor-intensive industries. This will affect China's industry structural readjustment in the medium and long term.

4. Erosion of trade benefits under the export incentive policy

The primary focus of the opening-up policy is to encourage exports. Under the export tax rebate and low exchange rate policy, China has realized rapid export growth but has also lost certain potential benefits of growth.

The powerful export tax rebate policy is one of the key drivers of China's fast export growth. Under this policy, it is more profitable to sell products on the international market than on the domestic market. As a result, the policy has sparked export-driven economic growth.

RMB undervaluation leads to exchange rate distortion and externality distortion. In recent years, Chinese enterprises have garnered rapid labor productivity gains, which in turn should raise laborer benefits or compensations. RMB undervaluation is a key factor driving productivity increase. In the past 20 years, China's manufacturing industry has realized an annual increase of 6 percent in total factor productivity, compared with average increases of 3–4 percent in developed countries and 1–2 percent in developing countries. A report released by the International Labor Organization shows that China's per capita output grew 63.4 percent from 2000 to 2005, more than doubling that of India (26.9 percent). China registered a labor productivity growth rate of 9.5 percent in 2006, ranking number 1 globally and leaving India (6.9 percent), the USA (1.4 percent) and the European Union (EU) (4.1 percent) far behind (Li, 2007b). This has become an internal driving force for RMB appreciation.

However, RMB appreciation is not an effective policy for China to adopt to eliminate externality distortions. If exchange rate distortions arise from exchange rate policies or government control over exchange rates, distortion theory dictates that we should adjust exchange rates and eliminate distortions. However, China's exchange rate distortions are rooted in factor price distortions. In particular, low labor, land and natural resource prices have caused exports to soar and foreign direct investment (FDI) inflows to surge. Low prices encourage enterprises to use an enormous quantity of such factors and thus reduce demand for advanced equipment and technology importation, making it impossible to slash the high trade surplus by importing technology and equipment. Therefore, adjusting exchange rates does not conform to the principle of direct policy relevance within distortion theory. It is not the optimal policy for China at the present time and is at best a suboptimal policy.

5.   The negative externality of production fails to fully compensate for losses

An important source of productivity distortion is the excess of individual business costs over social costs. Negative externality is the major cause of benefit losses. Inadequate compensation for the negative externality of export-oriented and foreign-funded enterprises has directly reduced the benefits of an open economy.

Environmental pollution is both a typical example of negative externality and a typical case of social costs exceeding business costs. In the event of businesses failing to pay requisite compensation fees for environmental pollution, business costs are lower than social costs and as a result businesses acquire competitive advantages at a low price on the international market. However, the costs paid by the state and society are not included in these business costs, and so the comparative advantages are exaggerated. The benefits of developing foreign trade or utilizing foreign investment under this approach are therefore simply untrue.

In recent years, China has paid hefty environmental costs in exchange for economic growth. In 2004, China realized an industrial GDP of RMB 15987.8 billion and incurred a virtual treatment cost of RMB 287.44 billion, accounting for 1.8 percent of GDP. Under the environmental pollution treatment cost accounting method, China needs to expend RMB 1080 billion (excluding sunk investments or costs) to treat the pollutants emitted into the environment in 2004 using current treatment technologies, accounting for 6.8 percent of GDP. Under the pollution loss accounting method, China's environmental pollution and degradation costs totaled RMB 511.82 billion in 2004, accounting for 3.05 percent of GDP. The actual and virtual treatment costs totaled RMB 387.98 billion, of which actual treatment costs accounted for 26 percent. Evidently, China has incurred but not disbursed an enormous amount of environmental pollution treatment costs.[3] It is worth noting that by treating the pollutants emitted each year, China needs to spend 6.8 percent of GDP. This price is more than one half of its GDP growth, even in the fast-growing coastal regions.

ELIMINATE POLICY-IMPOSED DISTORTIONS AND BUILD AN OPEN ECONOMIC SYSTEM

As mentioned earlier, China's current distortions are due partly to the incompleteness of its economic transition and partly to policy incentives driven by the economic reform and opening up. Therefore, distortions are comprised of both policy-imposed distortions and institutional distortions. The primary way to eliminate the existing distortions is to build an open economic system.

Policy Competition in the Regional Development-oriented Market Economic System

The distortions in China's open economy are related to the 'regional development oriented' market economic system (Zhang and Chen, 1998) in which local governments have sweeping economic power and irrepressible libido for growth. Offering policy incentives becomes a key means to development and attracting foreign investment is a key path to development. This system or institution has been the weapon used by China to realize fast development in the past 30 years, but also a major source of policy-imposed distortion.

The strength of China's economic system lies in the powerful economic functions and development incentives of local governments. This is one of the key factors underpinning the long-term, sustained rapid growth in China. It is also worth noting that excessive economic functionality of local government has produced some unfavorable results as well. In an export-oriented economy, local governments are engaged in a vicious circle of policy competition by offering more policy incentives than their competitors to woo foreign investment. Excess competition leads to excess concessions and the erosion of national interest, and places Chinese local governments and businesses in a passive and weak position at the negotiation table with multinational firms. Empirical studies indicate that China's opening-up strategy has been the correct strategy but that the benefits of an open economy have been lost primarily as a result of institutional flaws.

The foreign investment-oriented development policy of local government is the root cause of policy-imposed distortion. Wooing foreign investment to realize local economic development is the first and foremost mission of governments at all levels. To realize this objective, local governments must leverage their advantages by offering policy concessions and providing a superior investment environment with low land and labor prices to attract foreign investors. China boasts an enormous economic scale and each locality has strong demand for development. This avid demand for foreign investment has inevitably pitted one local government against another in policy competition. As a result, the social costs of enterprise production have increased and the factor prices have been distorted. Therefore, these distortions are not endogenous market distortions but policy-imposed distortions, or more accurately institutionally imposed distortions.

The implementation of special policy has been a path selected by China to reform and open up its economy to the outside world. After this campaign of opening up swept across the nation, special policy was used not only to differentiate foreign investment from domestic capital, but also by local governments to attract foreign investment and drive economic development. At this time, rent creation and allocation (of rent from foreign trade funded by foreign investment) became an important means by which the opening-up policy was realized. The power of local government to enact preferential policy constitutes a phenomenon of rent creation and rent seeking under China's special conditions.

Rent seeking is a significant cause of distortion because it affects resource allocation by way of directly unproductive profit seeking (DUP). Krueger (1974) conducted her well-known research on the existence of rent and defined the limits of rent-seeking behavior by quantifying rents based on the value of import quota calculated. To acquire such rents, people will commit various political and economic resources, thereby resulting in economic waste and even political corruption. People may also conduct rent-seeking activity to seek franchise and monopoly rights (Buchanan et al., 1980). Such activity is non-productive because obtaining a prerogative is tantamount to gaining a profit (Bhagwati and Srinivasan, 1980; Bhagwati, 1982; Bhagwati et al., 1984).

Rent-seeking activity will unavoidably lead to the reduction of social welfare and of the benefits of an open economy. Special policies enacted by local governments will inevitably result in the policy-led flow of resources but such resource allocation is not optimal. In the midst of fierce competition for foreign investment, the special power of local government for rent creation and distribution leads directly to excessive concession and deregulation and results in the loss of the benefits to be derived from an open economy.

It is worth noting that an important difference between Chinese and Western market economies is the dualistic nature of rent seeking in the Chinese economy at the transition stage, such that it is both non-productive and productive. For domestic and foreign-funded enterprises, seeking rents from local government is seeking non-productive profits. Non-productive profits can be realized only through the production process. Meanwhile, the production and trade process will be expanded by realizing such profits. This dualistic nature of local governments' rent-seeking behavior is testament to the sources of benefits and the welfare losses caused by decentralization. The benefits arise from production expansion as demonstrated by an outward shift of the production possibility frontier, whereas welfare losses stem from the resource allocation distortion in the business rent-seeking and government rent-allocation process. As regards the at once productive and non-productive nature of rent in China's economic system, it is wrong to simply call for the elimination of rent-seeking activities. Instead, non-productive rent should be eliminated and productive rent retained. When the power of the executive branch in terms of allocation is reduced to a minimum during the transition process, non-productive rents will be almost eliminated yet productive rents will remain. In this case, productive rents are acquired not through administrative channels but by factor use optimization (Zhang, 1994).

The Changing Features of Distortion During the Transition from a Closed Economy to an Open Economy

The shifts in the nature of distortions during the transition from a closed economy to an open economy are characterized by the negation of the negation. Policy-imposed distortions broke down the old institutions and moved the economy from closed to open and from planned to market oriented. The role of the market in resource allocation yet needs to be strengthened if it is impossible for policy-led resource allocation to reach Pareto optimality; resource allocation will be more effective only if policy ceases to play a role. It is fair to say that policy-imposed distortion has carried out its historical mission and no longer serves its purpose.

Over the past three decades, China's economic development has been characterized by 'factor-driven' growth (Wang, 2005). Significant factor investment was an indispensable feature of China's economic development during the preliminary stages, and this was especially true 30 years ago when China commenced economic development under conditions of abject poverty. China started the growth engine with the processing trades and wooed foreign investment via compensation deals. In this regard, it appears that China can only restart its growth by relying on resources and cheap labor. However, a country cannot pursue long-term development by relying solely on primary factors.[4] After breaking through the development objectives at the preliminary stage, advancing to a higher-level development stage and experiencing greater factor scarcity, China clung steadfastly to the 'factor-driven' policy and institutional arrangement aimed at reducing factor prices, thereby creating more distortions which caused significant welfare losses. However, increasing labor costs and growing land, natural resource and environmental resource scarcity make it impossible for local governments to realize growth by cutting factor prices.

Eliminating factor price distortion is one of the main priorities in eliminating distortions. The industry structure in China, especially of the foreign-funded sector, is determined by factor prices. Eliminating factor price distortion therefore requires restructuring the industry. The development mode of wooing foreign investment with low labor, land and natural resource prices should be replaced by a development approach in which costs are better reflected in prices. China's industrial structure can then be upgraded to a new level.

Human capital growth and innovation-driven growth will be the characteristics of this new phase of development. Eliminating low primary factor price distortion requires the elimination of the policies that begot distortions in the first place, and replacing them with new policies that encourage the formation and utilization of new factors. This will expedite economic transition. Under the distortion theory framework, this is also an optimal policy for eliminating distortions. The 'tax cum subsidy' principle posits that taxing factor 1 is equivalent to subsidizing factor 2. On the one hand, China should impose strict control over the excess use of land and natural resources and raise laborer wages. On the other hand, this factor price policy shall encourage the use of factors such as technology in favor of innovation.

The Basic Characteristics and Policy Options of an Open Economic System

The basic characteristics of an open economic system are as follows: (i) economic openness is dictated by stable laws and regulations; (ii) there is neither frequently changing policy arrangements nor inter-regional policy competition, and the regional policy differences have been gradually eliminated; (iii) the policies for domestic and foreign-funded enterprises and national and international markets are consistent with each other, there is neither protection for domestic markets nor policies that favor external markets, and the policy differences are mainly reflected in industrial policies and regional development policies; and (iv) the unified and standardized market system constitutes an institutional impetus for opening to the outside world, and the government administrative institution complies with World Trade Organization (WTO) requirements, including commitments tied to opening up and transparency.

The core of building an open economic system is to eliminate policy-imposed distortions and meet the requirements for the allocation of resources based on market demand and supply. Openness has become an essential characteristic rather than policy orientation, and has enabled open and optimal allocation of resources. An open economy does not discriminate against special policy. The shift from factor differentiation policy to development differentiation policy and the substitution of industrial policy and regional policy for foreign investment and foreign trade policy are the policy characteristics of an open economic system.

Assessing the historical role of special policy does not necessitate the complete refutation of the role of policy in economic development, but requires replacing development policy with factor policy. Factor policy is the soul of special policy. A policy motivates factor inflow and concentration and encourages scarce factor owners. Refuting special policy equates to refuting its role as a factor policy rather than denying its role as a development policy or a development objective-oriented policy.

The fundamental characteristic of development policy is to determine policy differentiation based on development objectives (including policies favoring scarce factor development) instead of opting for factor owner differentiation policy and factor differentiation policy. Different factor owners will receive the same incentives so long as they meet development objectives. Industrial policy and regional policy are the most basic development policies. Industrial policies lean towards key development industries such as strategic industry and high-tech industry, whereas regional policies tend to cover specific regions such as key industrial parks and underprivileged regions. Under such a policy regime, the policies are differentiated not based on the nature of factor ownership but pursuant to the specific development needs.

Classical policy-imposed distortion theory rejects policy-dictated factor allocation because it breeds distortions. It is worth noting that the theory presumes that the market is perfect and free of distortion, and capable of effectively allocating resources. Therefore, any policy-imposed market intervention behavior creates distortions and causes the loss of benefits. Meanwhile, development theory has proved that the market does not always possess such ability because the long-term development of an industry or region does not ensure profits in the short term. Therefore, development can only be a strategic option for government and cannot always be an autonomous option for the market. It is therefore inevitable for a development policy to have such a characteristic: the policy regulates resource allocation with a force beyond the reach of the market to realize the development objective. In the short term, it is likely to create distortions and benefit losses. In the long term, however, such losses can be more than compensated for by development achievements. Policy thus plays an important role in the economic development process. By expediting the formation of the new mechanism, the policy stewards resource allocation and speeds up economic development. At the preliminary development stage, especially when the market has not fully taken up the responsibility for resource allocation, it is necessary for the policy to mobilize and guide resource allocation. Policy may cause distortion but this is not the pretext for rejecting any policy. Under development strategy, industrial policy and regional policy create special development conditions for an industry or region and realize the development strategy by way of policy-imposed factor distortion. This is a positive effect of policy-imposed distortion in the special development period. Kwon and Paik (1995) examined the outcomes of capital market distortion and concluded that distortion will create faster capital formation and higher capital stock concentration. Under Korea's industrial policy structure, financial incentives will generate greater distortion effects than fiscal incentives will do.

This principle of industrial policy is also reflected in foreign trade policy. Industrial policy may be used to guide foreign trade and replace any preferential market policy. The export tax rebate policy may be changed to set different tax rebate rates for different industries rather than encouraging exports without discrimination. Such change can encourage technology application and eliminate distortion for the lack of reasonable compensation for the technology factor. It can also promote the export of products with high technological content and inhibit the export of products with high energy and resource consumption. Moreover, it can reduce the negative externality of exportation.

CONCLUSION

This chapter sheds new light on the twin themes of deepening reform and opening to the outside world in China based on an analysis conducted under the distortion theory framework. The objective of opening the Chinese economy to the outside world at the current stage is to increase the benefits of an open economy by deepening domestic reform rather than strengthening the opening-up policy. The incentive-driven opening up should be put to an end, and the implementation of well-balanced opening-up policy and the standardization of the opening-up institution ought now to become the key priorities. China will be able to create a better investment environment by standardizing policy, institutional and administrative management. In addition, China should shift its focus from relying on preferential policy to relying on institutional standardization, from relying on incentive measures to relying on environmental investment, and from relying on concessions to attract foreign investment to relying on industry cluster and development opportunities, with a view to realizing the transition from a closed economic system to an open one. In conclusion, the strategic focus on increasing the benefits of an open economy should be widened by optimizing the opening-up policy to promote openness by deepening reform, thereby realizing the transformation from a policy-oriented opening up to an institutionally based opening up of China's economy.

NOTES

1. In the book *Dual Institutional Distortions and Foreign Trade Benefits* (in Chinese) by Youwen Zhang, the author introduced the concept of 'institutional distortion' and the four types of institutional distortion during China's transition period (Zhang, 1995, p. 224).
2. Calculated based on the Communiqués on Land and Resources of China. The total and unit land transfer prices in 2003 are derived from the data in *China Financial and Economic News* 29 March (2005).
3. Refer to *China Green National Accounting Study Report 2004* compiled by the State Administration of Environmental Protection and the National Bureau of Statistics.
4. In *Competitive Advantages of Nations*, Michael E. Porter (1990) pointed out that the cheap labor advantage of a developing country will disappear sooner or later and cannot therefore become the development advantage to be counted on by a developing country in the long term.

REFERENCES

Bhagwati, J.N. (1971), 'The general theory of distortions and welfare', in J.N. Bhagwati, R.W. Jones, R.A. Mundell and J. Vanek (eds), *Trade Balance of Payments and Growth*, Amsterdam: North-Holland, pp. 80–84.
Bhagwati, J.N. (1982), 'Directly unproductive profit-seeking (DUP) activities', *Journal of Political Economy*, **90**(5), 7–8.
Bhagwati, J.N. and T.N. Srinivasan (1980), 'Revenue seeking: a generalization of the theory of tariffs', *Journal of Political Economy*, **88**(6), 58–9.
Bhagwati, J.N., R.A. Brecher and T.N. Srinivasan (1984), 'DUP activities and economic theory', *European Economic Review*, **24**, 291–307.
Buchanan, J., G. Tullock and R. Tollison (eds) (1980), *Towards a General Theory of the Rent-seeking Society*, Texas: Texas A&M University Press, pp. 109–10.
Chen, X. (2007), 'An analysis of the changes in China's labor price and economic growth path', *Economic Issues*, **4**, 2–3.
China Financial and Economic News (2005), 'An analysis of the rent distribution between land owners and land users on the property market in China', 29 March, available at http://biz.cn.yahoo.com/050329/127/8rto.html (accessed on 30 September 2009).
China Green National Accounting study Report 2004, compiled by the State Administration of Environmental Protection and the National Burean of Statistics, available at http://news.xinhuanet.com/fortune/2006–09/3007/content_5062167.htm (accessed 23 September 2010).

Currie, J. and A.E. Harrison (1997), 'Sharing the costs: the impact of trade reform on capital and labor in Morocco', *Journal of Labor Economics*, **15**(3), 44–71.

Jun, C. (2006), 'Gauging China's labor price advantages and trends from an international perspective', *China Economic and Trade Herald*, **8**, 1–3.

Krishna, K. and C. Yavas (2004), 'When trade hurts: consumption indivisibilities and labor market distortions', *Journal of International Economics*, **67**(2), September, 413–27.

Krishna, K., A. Mukhopadhyay and C. Yavas (2002), 'Trade with labor market distortions and heterogeneous labor: why trade can hurt', NBER Working Paper No. 9086, 7–9 July.

Krueger, A.O. (1974), 'The political economy of the rent-seeking society', *American Economic Review*, **64**(3), June, 46–9.

Kwon, J.K. and H. Paik (1995), 'Factor price distortions, resource allocation, and growth: a computable general equilibrium analysis', *Review of Economics and Statistics*, **77**, 664–76.

Li, W. (2007a), 'The present economic trade imbalance and its treatment path', *Foreign Economic and Trade Practice*, **8**, 12–14.

Li, W. (2007b), 'Addressing economic imbalance: enhancing production factor price reform', *China Economic Times*, 14 June, 4–6.

Lindbeck, A. (1997), 'Stabilization policy in open economies with endogenous politicians', in *The Political Business Cycles*, New York: North-Holland, pp. 473–91.

Porter, M.E. (1990), *The Competitive Advantages of Nations*, New York: Free Press, pp. 69–130.

Papageorgiou, D., A.M. Choksi and M. Michaely (1991), *Foreign Economic Liberalization: Transformations in Socialist and Market Economies*, Oxford: Basil Blackwell, pp. 37–56.

Rodrik, D. (1995), 'Trade and industrial policy reform', in H. Chenery and T.N. Srinivasan (eds), *Handbook of Development Economics,* New York: North-Holland, pp. 2925–82.

Seddon, D. and R. Wacziarg (2002), 'Review of Easterly's: the elusive quest for growth', *Journal of Economic Literature*, **40**(3), 907–18.

Wang, D. (2005), 'Who distorted the labor and capital price ratio relationship?', *Economic Herald*, 13 July, C01.

Williamson, J. (1987), *The Open Economy and the World Economy*, New York: Basic Books, pp. 121–44.

Zhang, Y. (1994), 'Rent-seeking in the transition to an open market system', *Academic Quarterly*, **2**, 75–6.

Zhang, Y. (1995), *Dual Institutional Distortions and Foreign Trade Benefits,* Shanghai: Sdxjoint Publishing.

Zhang, Y. and L. Chen (1998), 'An international comparison of market economic systems', *Orient Press*, 109–10.

11. Urban sustainability: the case of the transportation system in big cities[1]

Jianling Li, Siamak Ardekani and Stephen Mattingly

INTRODUCTION

Transportation occupies a critical position in the economy and urban life of China. Since the beginning of the new century, the Chinese automobile industry has grown rapidly. In recent years, China has become the largest car market and the second largest automobile maker in the world (Hogg, 2009; RIA Novosti, 2009). The growth in automobile production, income and vehicle ownership, along with the increasing intensity of Chinese engagement in global economic activities, has resulted in a significant increase in travel demand, which in turn has put great pressure on China's transportation infrastructure, especially in the urban areas. Traffic congestion and air pollution have affected production efficiency in the economy and the quality of life in Chinese cities. Meanwhile, there is a lack of resources for coping with these problems. Hence, how to develop and maintain a financially, socially and environmentally sustainable transportation infrastructure has become a challenge facing transportation professionals in China. Previous experience has demonstrated that the success of building and maintaining a sustainable transportation system depends largely on the adopted transportation financing and operating/management (O&M) policies. In order to facilitate policy making, transportation professionals need tools that can assess policy impacts.

The main objective of this chapter is to introduce a planning tool that can assess the impacts of transportation financing and operating policies, and has the potential to assist transportation planners and policy makers when making decisions in China. In the following section, we discuss the current challenges faced by transportation policy makers and planners in China, analyse the current transportation management and financing practices, and offer some thoughts about new policy directions for sustainable transportation in China. In the third section, we present the planning tool and explain its theoretical base and techniques for developing the tool. In the fourth section, we introduce several pricing policy options that may be useful for developing a sustainable transportation system in China and assess the potential policy impacts based on the price elasticity of travelers in Dallas and Houston in Texas, USA. We conclude the chapter with a summary of the findings and potential implications for China.

TRANSPORTATION ISSUES FACING CHINA

China's transportation issues are similar to, but more challenging than, issues in the USA and many other countries. These issues can be observed from the growth in economic and travel demand, as well as the current status of transportation management and financing practices in China.

Traffic Congestion and Economic Growth

In the past several years, travel demand has increased rapidly in China. For example, nationwide passenger travel increased 50.7 percent while passenger-kilometers increased about 76.1 percent between 2000 and 2007 in China, according to the National Bureau of Statistics of China (NBSC, 2008). During the same period, demand for public transit in cities grew about 62.6 percent.[2] China's growth in travel demand was much faster than the growth in the USA during this time period.[3]

Traffic congestion is a well-known problem in many Chinese cities and has caused significant economic loss. For example, in Beijing, before the government imposed a traffic restriction measure, a driver usually took about an hour to travel 15 kilometers from his home to the central business district (CBD) during the commuting period; a typical work day congestion period could last about eight hours according to a recent news article in *China Today* (Liu, 2009). In Shanghai, the economic loss caused by congestion was 10 percent of its GDP in 2003 (Feng, 2006).

The traffic problem in China is even more challenging for the near future due to growing income and private vehicle ownership. According to the National Bureau of Statistics of China (NBSC, 2008), the gross national income increased from about ¥9.8 trillion in 2000 to more than ¥25 trillion in 2007. The annual per capita disposable income of urban households increased from ¥6280 in 2000 to ¥13 786 in 2007,[4] about an 119 percent increase. Meanwhile, private vehicle ownership in 2007 was about 28.8 million, about 3.6 times more than the number (about 6.3 million) in 2000. The rapid growth in private automobile ownership will likely last at least another ten years because the automobile is a vital part of the economy in China (Dai, 2004). The following news article excerpt is a snapshot of a strong demand for automobiles in China during the period when the global economy is slowing down:

> According to statistics released by the China Association of Automobile Manufacturers (CAAM), in the first quarter of 2009, 2.6788 million automobiles were sold in China, placing it first worldwide, an increase of 3.88 percent over the same period last year. In Beijing, a total of 250,000 automobiles were sold, marking a 17.4 percent hike, much higher than the national average. (Liu, 2009)

The growth in private vehicles will add a huge pressure on the already overcrowded transportation infrastructure. On the other hand, population densities in many Chinese cities are high, and there is a limit in land and financial resources to build additional transportation infrastructure to accommodate the increasing travel demand and traffic problems. According to the 2007 statistics, the overall population density of city districts is about 2104 persons per square kilometer; the average municipal paved roads is 6.6 kilometers per 10000 people; and the per capita area of paved roads is 11.4 square meters (NBSC, 2008). Many large cities have built multiple layers of roads vertically. There is simply a lack of space to build more roads, and the cost of building transportation infrastructure will also be enormous.

Urban Policies, Planning and Management Practices

Chinese governments have worked very hard to solve traffic congestion problems through supply- and control-oriented approaches. For example, China has strict land use control policies, and the government largely owns the land. In urban planning, China long ago adopted a high density, mixed land use policy for new development and urban revitalization. These land use control policies and planning practices are crucial for sprawl control and maintaining a useful landscape for public transportation; however, urbanization in China has grown rapidly. According to the World Bank (2007), the urbanization rate in 2003 was 1.4 percent, which is equivalent to an increase of about 20 million new urban residents a year. Moreover, the World Bank report indicates that in recent years, the amount of revenues obtained by municipal governments from converting rural land to urban land has become a major driving force for urban expansion in many Chinese cities. The speed and forces driving this urbanization have led to some issues. One example is that the planning and construction of effective public transport systems lag behind urban expansion.

For traffic management, many cities have implemented various Intelligent Transportation Systems (ITS) strategies in recent years; these include actuated and adaptive intersection signal controls and electronic information systems to improve the flow of vehicular and pedestrian traffic. In addition, some cities have implemented other ad hoc control measures for transportation demand management. For example, Beijing started a rotating one-day-a-week restriction on car use based on license plate numbers in October 2008 and recently decided to continue the measure for at least another year. In Guangzhou, there have been measures such as prohibiting certain types of vehicles entering the CBD during peak hour periods, as well as setting an annual quota for new vehicle registrations.

These current practices are supply- and control-based in nature. While overall these supply- and control-oriented approaches have played a large role in solving traffic congestion problems, they are limited in terms of efficiency and effectiveness. For control measures to be effective, they require the public to be fully cooperative and comply with the rules set by the governments. In reality, this is a difficult task since there are too many people and too many cars. In addition, the back door phenomenon is well known in China and will stay for at least some time. The so-called back door phenomenon gives special treatment to people who have '*guanxi*' (connection) and allows for traffic violations to go unpunished. '*Guanxi*' also permits people to obtain vehicle licenses exceeding the quota. Potentially, strong enforcement could overcome these obstacles and ease the problems to a certain extent. However, the cost of enforcement could be expensive for the same reasons stated above.

Urban Transportation Service Provision and Finance

The supply-based approach is also reflected in urban transport infrastructure development and service provision in China. In the last decade, municipal governments have responded to the rapid growth in vehicle ownership and travel demand mainly by building and improving urban streets and expressway networks, expanding metro systems, and allowing private entities to provide bus and taxi services. For example, the overall expenditure on roads has accounted for about 3.5 percent of the GDP since 1998. Total investment in transport fixed assets in 2006 was US$103.4 billion. Investment in highway construction constituted about 87 percent of the total investment, and about half of these were for roads other than the national trunk highways. At the end of 2007, 22 metro or light rail lines had been built in ten cities, and another 36 lines were under construction. Together, the 22 metro or light rail lines accounted for a total of 621 route-km (World Bank, 2007).

Despite the impressive investment and speedy construction of transportation infrastructure, the supply-based approach has its limit and cannot be sustained in the long run. Most of the transport supply is provided by state-owned enterprises or joint ventures, with financing from multiple sources, including municipal and provincial governments, domestic loans and bonds, toll and other user fees, and limited foreign and private investments. According to available data, domestic debts dominate the total transportation investment (World Bank, 2007). With the exception of expressways and other revenue-generating projects, which are expected to be covered by tolls and other revenues for their debts and O&M costs, the costs for other projects need to be absorbed.

The current transportation policies in China mostly favor automobiles. With a low fuel tax and relatively cheap fuel prices, the use of automobiles is fundamentally 'under-priced'. In addition, user fees, such as vehicle purchase fee, transportation management fee and so on, are not linked to the time, location and frequency of vehicle usage. Urban roads and bridges are largely 'free' for automobile users. The current system does not affect travel decisions and has led to an overuse of urban transportation infrastructure and the expansion of urban space.

The under-priced automobile usage further hinders the effectiveness of other urban transportation modes. As stated in the World Bank report (2007), 'pedestrians and cyclists have suffered from longer trips and lower safety levels' due to the urban space expansion enabled by automobiles, and the 'speed and reliability of road-based public transport has been undermined by road traffic congestion' caused by excessive automobile use.

While most bus operators have been able to replace buses with loans from local banks, there is a lack of adequate depot facilities for storing buses. There is also a funding shortage for enhancing the quality of transit service, such as investments in information technology for routine business, operation and maintenance, high quality interchange terminals and passenger information systems (World Bank, 2007). All of these factors have imposed a great financial burden on local governments for keeping up with the demand.

Towards Sustainable Transportation

The above discussions on transportation needs and the status of planning and financing practices uncover the urgent and complex challenges faced by Chinese governments and transportation professionals. In order to effectively manage traffic and sustain financial resources for building and maintaining an adequate transportation infrastructure to meet the growing transportation demand, Chinese governments would need to strengthen travel demand management in addition to the current supply- and control-based policies and practices. Specifically, China may consider congestion pricing for automobile use in cities.

Congestion pricing is a market- or demand-based strategy. Under congestion pricing, users are charged higher prices when demand for roadways is high and vice versa. It assumes travel decisions are made rationally according to economic principles. Therefore, the higher the charge, the more people would be deterred from driving. They may change the time of travel, routes of travel or mode of travel; some may even forego their trips altogether. Congestion pricing is considered an efficient approach to reduce peak hour traffic congestion and to maximize the efficient use of society's economic resources, including both the capital invested in roads and the time motorists spend on commuting. With the availability of electronic toll collection technologies, congestion pricing has been successfully implemented in Singapore, London and other European cities.

Congestion pricing could be in the form of charging all automobile users the same price, giving high-occupancy vehicles (HOVs) preferential treatment, a combination of both or other forms. How may different pricing schemes affect travel demand, transportation system performance, vehicle emissions, and toll revenues? In the following section, we introduce a planning tool that has the potential to enable planners to search for answers to these questions in China.

PRICING POLICY EVALUATION MODEL

The toll pricing evaluation tool was initially developed in a project sponsored by the Texas Department of Transportation, USA in 2002 and later refined in 2005 (see Li et al., 2002, 2005). It is a tool specifically designed for pricing policy impact assessment of managed lanes (MLs), referring to 'highway facilities or a set of lanes where operational strategies are proactively implemented and managed in response to changing conditions' (FHWA, 2005). Examples of MLs are high-occupancy toll (HOT) lanes, express lanes, or value pricing. MLs are often adjacent to 'free' highway lanes known as general purpose (GP) lanes. The concept of MLs is based on economic theories of demand, supply and utility maximization. MLs provide an alternative travel option for those who wish to pay for faster and more reliable travel, and can ease traffic congestion and vehicle emissions on GP lanes as some travelers opt to use MLs. It is also expected that MLs will generate revenue for transportation improvements. In recent years, MLs have emerged as a promising option that combines the advantages of government intervention, market-based strategies and application

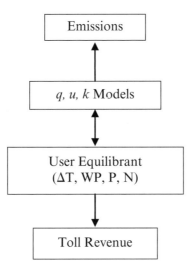

Figure 11.1   Conceptual framework

of ITS technologies for dealing with congestion and financing problems in the USA.

Conceptual Framework

The conceptual framework of the pricing policy evaluation tool is illustrated in Figure 11.1. The tool is developed on the basis of the price elasticity concept, traffic flow theories and vehicle emissions modeling. At the core of the framework is the user equilibrant, which models the relationship among travelers' price elasticity, travel time saving between MLs and GP lanes (DT), as well as users' willingness to pay (WP) for time saving (aka time value). Traffic models are in operation as they continue to receive demand inputs from the price-demand curve, and produce time saving information as an output to be fed back to the user equilibrant. Once user equilibrium is reached, toll rates, average speed, traffic volume and emissions are produced as outputs of a model run. Toll revenue will be calculated according to the toll rates and vehicle distribution between the GP and managed lanes. Emissions will also be computed as depicted in Figure 11.1.

The relationship among the elements in the user equilibrant is displayed in Figure 11.2. As shown, the price-demand curve is determined by the price elasticity of users. In other words, as price (P) goes up, the number of users (N) decreases. The number of users on the toll road/MLs affects traffic conditions on the toll road/MLs. When time saving increases, more users are

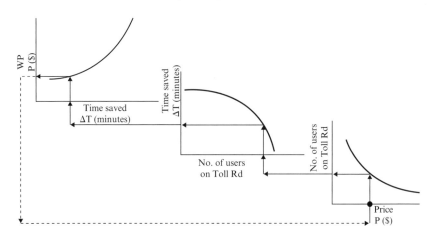

Figure 11.2   User equilibrant

willing to pay (WP) for using the toll road/MLs. As demand for toll road/
MLs increases, time saving decreases, which reduces the users' WP for using
the toll road/MLs. The cycle will continue until user equilibrium is reached.

Price Elasticity

In our study, the price elasticity of demand for transportation is defined
as the percent change in using a specific transportation service in response
to a percent change in price or/and other factors (Small and Winston,
1999). A binary logistic model is used to predict the probability of a trave-
ler's decision on choosing one transportation service over other options.
Regression models are specified as equations (11.1) and (11.2):

$$\text{Probability of event } (P) = \left(\frac{1}{(1 + e^{-Z})} \right) \tag{11.1}$$

$$\text{Ln} \left(\frac{P}{(1 - P)} \right) = B_0 + B_1 X_1 + B_2 X_2 + \ldots + B_n X_n \tag{11.2}$$

where:

Z = *utility of event P* (in this case choosing ML)
$\text{Ln} (P/(1 - P))$ = the logit or log odds
P = probability of choosing the ML
B = model coefficients
X = independent variables
n = number of independent variables

The dependent variables in this model are the lane choice (ML or GP). The independent variables consist of socio-demographic variables, freeway performance and pricing policy (Goodin et al., 2008).

The q, u, k Model

The Greenshields' Model is utilized to characterize the relationship between speed, flow and concentration. Equation (11.3) is utilized to calibrate the Greenshields' Model by estimating the values of the model parameters, k_j and u_f (see Ardekani et al., 2007). The Greenshields' Model also yields equation (11.4) to estimate the flow as a function of speed and concentration.

$$u = u_f(1 - k/k_j) \qquad (11.3)$$

$$q = u_f k (1 - k/k_j) \qquad (11.4)$$

where:

u = speed (mph)
u_f = free flow speed (mph)
q = flow (vehicles per hour (vph))
k = concentration (vehicles per mile (vpm))
k_j = jam concentration (vehicles per mile (vpm))

The theoretical maximum flow per lane (saturation flow per lane) implied by equation (11.4) is determined to be $q_{max} = u_f k_j/4$. In conditions where demand, d, exceeds capacity, the speeds are expected to vacillate between $u = 0.5u_f$ (at $d = q_{max}$) and $u = 0$ (at $d = 2q_{max}$). In such cases, the model linearly interpolates the speed between $0.5u_f$ and zero for demands between q_{max} and $2q_{max}$. For demands higher than $2q_{max}$, speed is considered to be zero (jam condition). The q-k-u relationships are illustrated in Figure 11.3, in which the speed-concentration curve the speed-flow curve, and the flow-concentration curve are depicted in the first, second and the fourth quadrants, respectively.

Vehicle Emission Modeling

Emissions estimates are largely based on a series of regression models that predict the emissions amounts as a function of the average speeds of various vehicles (Yerramalla, 2007). The generic model for estimating carbon monoxide (CO), volatile organic compound (VOC), nitrogen oxide (NOx), carbon dioxide (CO_2) and sulphur dioxide (SO_2) emissions is shown in equation (11.5).

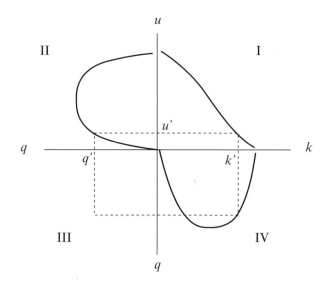

Source: Li and Govind (2003).

Figure 11.3   The q-u-k *curves*

$$E = \alpha + \beta * (1/v) + \lambda * v^2 \qquad (11.5)$$

where:

E = emission (grams/mile)
v = average speed (mph)

α, β and λ are parameters, which vary by types of emissions and vehicles, and are calibrated based on data and simulation runs of the EPA MOBILE 6.2 (USEPA, 2003).

Model Inputs and Outputs

Several inputs are required in order to use the model for pricing policy impact analysis for a specific ML facility. First, the model requires information for the facility being investigated. The facility information includes the number of lanes, maximum speed (mph), maximum density (pcplm), density at maximum flow (pcplm) and saturation flow per lane (pcphpl) for both managed and GP lanes, as well as corridor length (miles).

Second, information about user composition for the investigated facility is needed. This comprises information about total corridor demand, percentage of various vehicle types and their corresponding passenger car equivalents (PCE). Vehicle types included in the model are SOV, HOV2, HOV3+, para-transit, vanpool, bus, motorcycle, light freight vehicles, heavy freight vehicles with single trailer and heavy freight vehicles with double trailer. Definitions of vehicle types are specified in the help menu embedded in the model.

The last input required for using the model is the price sensitivity parameters of the various user groups. The parameters are the percentage of users willing to pay at a price increment of $0.10/mile for a time savings of 0.50 minute per mile, 1 minute per mile and 2 minutes per mile, respectively.

The model outputs include estimates of peak-hour volumes and average speeds on MLs and GP lanes, estimate of corridor toll revenue, as well as estimates of CO, VOC, NOx, CO_2 and SO_2 emissions (kilograms/mile).[5]

POLICY IMPACT ASSESSMENT

Using the pricing evaluation model, we estimated potential impacts of several pricing options for managing travel demand in large cities in China. The pricing scenarios, roadway facility and price elasticities are based on experience in Texas, USA. Detailed model assumptions are provided in the Appendix. We assess the impacts of pricing policies from three dimensions. First, we examine how the pricing level may affect system performance, air quality and toll revenue. In addition, we analyse how pricing preferential treatment, namely charging user groups with different prices, may affect system performance, air quality and toll revenue. Further, we explore the question of how to achieve one or more objectives with different pricing policies. The results are presented below.

Impacts of Pricing Level

To analyse how the pricing level may affect travelers' decisions and the resulting impacts, we ran models with a price scenario that charges single occupancy vehicles (SOV) full price, two-passenger vehicles (HOV2) half price, and lets vehicles with three or more passengers (HOV3+) travel for free at four pricing levels: $0.10/mile, $0.25/mile, $0.40/mile and $0.50/mile. Table 11.1 shows the model estimates for each scenario. The results indicate that given the price elasticity and other assumptions provided as

Table 11.1   Impacts of pricing level

	$0.10/mile	$0.25/mile	$0.40/mile	$0.50/mile
Speed (mph)				
ML	55	55	60	65
GP lane	51	52	47	38
Vehicle emissions				
CO (10 kg/mile)	5.08	5.08	4.92	4.64
VOC (kg/mile)	0.93	0.93	0.94	0.97
SO_2 (kg/mile)	0.08	0.08	0.08	0.08
NO_x (kg/mile)	5.03	5.03	4.94	4.75
CO_2 (1000 kg/mile)	2.08	2.08	2.12	2.32
Corridor revenue				
($/peak hr)	1580	3910	4642	3792

the inputs to the model, toll rates between $0.10/mile and $0.25/mile do not significantly distinguish the average travel speed on MLs from that on the GP lanes. A toll at the $0.50/mile level will result in considerably better service on the MLs.

Table 11.1 also shows that within the price range of $0.10/mile and $0.50/mile, there is no significant variation in the impact of VOC and SO_2 emissions. However, pricing at the level of $0.40/mile would decrease CO and NOx emissions but slightly increase CO_2 emission. The impacts of the toll at the $0.50/mile level on CO_2, CO and NOx would be noticeable. Specifically, the differences in emission impacts between the pricing level of $0.40/mile and $0.50/mile range from an increment of 187 kg/mile in CO_2 emission, to a decline of 2.86 kg/mile in CO emission and 0.2 kg/mile in NOx emission.

Given the assumptions of price elasticity, demand and distribution of user groups, and the configuration of facility, the impacts of pricing level on corridor revenue is non-linear as seen in Table 11.1. As expected, pricing at the level of $0.10/mile yields the least revenue; however, pricing at the $0.50/mile level does not result in the highest revenue. The optimal pricing level occurs at $0.40/mile, which would generate about $4642 in toll revenue per peak hour.

To summarize, too low a pricing level would not have significant impacts on system performance and vehicle emissions. Because of an insignificant difference in travel speed between MLs and GP lanes, pricing policies at a low level may not provide an incentive for using MLs. On the other hand, too high a pricing level would not necessarily yield the best results for vehicle emissions and toll revenues.

Impacts of Pricing Preferential Treatments

Conventional wisdom suggests that traffic congestion occurs when too many vehicles are on the same highway facility at the same time. In order to ease traffic congestion, the spatial and temporal distribution of vehicles needs to be dispersed. Transportation planners have long advocated a variety of transportation demand management (TDM) strategies to reduce traffic congestion. Examples of TDM include HOV lane, HOV parking priority, guarantee ride home, flexible and compressed work hours, and free or subsidized transit pass. A ML can provide incentives for carpooling, vanpooling or public transit and reduce SOVs by reducing the price for HOV or letting these user groups use MLs for free. How may pricing user groups differently affect system performance, vehicle emissions and toll revenues? In this section, we investigate this question by analysing the impacts of a pricing level with different combinations of pricing treatments for different user groups. Specifically, we examine the impacts of the following six pricing policy scenarios:

1. Charging all for using managed lanes (All Pay);
2. Charging SOVs only (SOV full, HOV free);
3. Charging SOVs full toll and all HOVs half of the full toll (SOV Full, HOV ½);
4. Charging SOVs full toll and HOV2 half of the full toll, and letting HOV3+ use managed lanes for free (SOV Full, HOV2 ½, HOV3+ Free);
5. Charging SOVs and HOV2 full toll and HOV3+ half of the full toll (SOV & HOV2 Full, HOV3+ 1/2); and
6. Charging SOVs and HOV2 full toll and HOV3+ half of the full toll (SOV & HOV2 Full, HOV3+ Free).

We choose to focus on policy scenarios at the pricing level of $0.50/mile, since pricing at the levels of $0.10/mile and $0.25/mile would not provide much incentive for using MLs, nor do they have significant impacts on vehicle emissions as seen from the analysis in the above section. As seen from Table 11.2, giving HOVs pricing preferential treatment in general would have noticeable impacts. For example, giving all HOVs free access to MLs would attract more HOVs to use MLs, therefore reducing the speed on MLs and increasing the speed on GP lanes. On the contrary, charging all user groups the same price would reduce the demand for MLs. As a result of fewer vehicles on MLs, the travel speed on MLs would be higher while travel speed on GP lanes would be lower. Giving HOVs

Table 11.2   Impacts of pricing preferential treatments

	All Pay	SOV Full, HOV Free	SOV Full, HOV ½	SOV Full, HOV2 ½, HOV3+ Free	SOV & HOV2 Full, HOV3+ ½	SOV & HOV2 Full, HOV3+ Free
Speed (mph)						
ML	72	61	68	65	70	68
GP lane	33	45	36	38	34	36
Vehicle emissions						
CO (10 kg/mile)	4.49	4.91	4.55	4.64	4.57	4.56
VOC (kg/mile)	1.00	0.93	0.96	0.97	1.01	0.96
SO_2 (kg/mile)	0.08	0.08	0.08	0.08	0.08	0.08
NO_x (kg/mile)	4.66	4.94	4.72	4.75	4.68	4.73
CO_2 (1000 kg/ mile)	2.52	2.13	2.33	2.32	2.50	2.33
Toll revenue ($/peak hr)	3550	3215	4160	3791	3826	3458

different preferential pricing treatments would have different levels of speed impacts on MLs and GP lanes.

The effects of preferential pricing treatments on vehicle emissions are relatively mild. However, these relatively small emission differences occur during several peak periods every day, and their cumulative effects may be substantial. As seen from Table 11.2, SO_2 and VOC emissions are stable across all pricing policy scenarios. Giving all HOVs free access to MLs would decrease CO_2 emissions, but would increase CO and NOx emissions as compared to other pricing policy scenarios. The emissions impacts vary little among other pricing policy scenarios.

The results in Table 11.2 also indicate that the impact of preferential treatment on toll revenue is perceptible. Among all scenarios, having HOVs pay half of the full price would generate the highest toll revenue. The difference in toll revenue between option 4 (SOV full, HOV2 ½, HOV3+ free) and option 5 (SOV & HOV2 full, HOV3+ ½) is small. However, giving all HOVs free access to MLs would generate the least toll revenue.

Overall, giving HOVs preferential treatments would result in a difference in system performance, vehicle emissions and toll revenue, though the level of impacts may vary among different pricing scenarios. The results show that giving all HOVs free access to the MLs would attract more HOV use of MLs, reduce traffic congestion on GP lanes and reduce CO_2 emission. However, these benefits are achieved at the expense of a reduction in toll revenues.

Optimal Solutions

The above analyses have focused on the impacts of pricing level and preferential treatments of user groups. These are important for transportation planning. However, it is not enough to know the potential impacts of pricing policies. In practice, transportation planners and policy makers may also face such questions as: what pricing policy options may enable the achievement of the same or similar objectives, and what would be an optimal policy option that can lead to the same or similar policy outcomes as other policy options? The answers to these questions are imperative because some policy options may be more acceptable for the public than others. Winning the public's support is crucial for policy implementation. In this section, we explore the question of what pricing options are available for maintaining a speed of 60 mph on the MLs, a service level that may make MLs attractive to travelers during peak-hour periods.

The model estimations indicate that there are six pricing options for maintaining the service level at 60 mph on MLs (Table 11.3). Due to the same speed, the emissions impacts of the six policy options are the same. However, the impact on toll revenue varies across the policy options.

As seen in Figure 11.4, the pricing policy of having all travelers pay a toll of $0.37/mile for using MLs (Scenario 1) would yield the most toll revenue, followed by the option of giving HOV3+ users a half price preferential treatment (Scenario 5). Alternatively, a pricing policy of charging SOVs a higher toll of $0.45/mile while giving all HOVs free access to MLs (Scenario 2) would generate the least amount of toll revenue. If the public accepts the same toll for all user groups, Scenario 1 is obviously the optimal choice. However, if promoting HOV use is the top policy objective, the optimal solution would be Scenario 2 to maintain the service level on MLs. Depending on the public's attitudes towards tolls and the degree of public acceptance of HOV preferential treatment, an optimal option could be determined among the rest of the scenarios.

CONCLUSION

This chapter analyses issues facing transportation professionals and policy makers and the current practices in response to these issues in China. In

Table 11.3 Pricing options for maintaining a service level on managed lanes

Policy scenario	Toll amount ($/mile)			Peak hour volume (vph)		Peak hour average speed (mph)		Peak hour emissions (kilograms/mile)				
	SOV	HOV2	HOV3+	ML	GL	ML	GL	CO	VOC	NOx	CO_2	SO_2
1	$0.37	SOV	SOV	3258	7742	60	47	49.24	0.94	4.94	2124	0.083
2	$0.45	Free	Free	3231	7769	60	47	49.23	0.94	4.94	2124	0.083
3	$0.38	0.5xSOV	0.5xSOV	3251	7749	60	47	49.23	0.94	4.94	2124	0.083
4	$0.40	0.5xSOV	Free	3233	7767	60	47	49.24	0.94	4.94	2124	0.083
5	$0.37	SOV	0.5xSOV	3247	7753	60	47	49.23	0.94	4.94	2124	0.083
6	$0.39	SOV	Free	3233	7767	60	47	49.23	0.94	4.94	2124	0.083

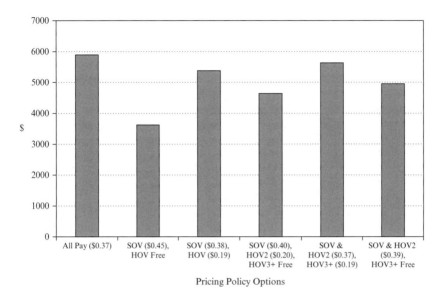

Figure 11.4   Corridor revenues ($/peak hour)

addition, the chapter introduces a policy assessment tool that has the potential to assist transportation planners and policy makers in their search for sustainable transportation planning and development solutions in China. It also shows several pricing policies that may be of use in dealing with the challenges facing China and the estimated impacts of those policies based on elasticity of travelers in the Dallas and Houston areas, USA.

The analyses indicate that China needs sustainable transportation development in order to resolve the incompatibility of traffic congestion and the rapid growth in demand for automobiles, ecological sustainability and economic development, as well as the need for transportation infrastructure and sustainable resources. While the current supply- and control-based strategies have played a large role in controlling traffic congestion and meeting the increasing travel demand, these strategies are limited in terms of efficiency and effectiveness. Demand- and market-based traffic management strategies such as congestion pricing can offer potential to supplement the current supply- and control-based strategies to address the complicated issues faced by the central and municipal governments in China, and help sustain transportation development in China.

Congestion pricing could be in the form of charging all automobile users the same price, or giving HOVs preferential treatment. As shown in the chapter, the potential impacts of congestion pricing options vary from one form to another. These results imply that pricing options will need to be determined with clear objectives in mind.

Congestion pricing would be more effective when it is implemented with improvement in public transit. This is especially so since international experience suggests that buses will continue to be the backbone of public transit and can offer advantages in cost, flexibility and broad coverage relative to other transit modes. The effectiveness of congestion pricing can also be enhanced by implementation of parking pricing, as well as coordination with planning and development of parking regulations. While limited to roadway pricing only, the tool in this chapter is useful for sketch planning in evaluating the possible impacts of pricing policies on system performance, air quality and toll revenue. It is simple, easy to use and portable for any given demand level and location. The tool, with some modifications, can be used to evaluate some demand-based pricing options in cities and to facilitate decision making in China. The theoretical basis and conceptual framework introduced in this chapter provide a foundation for such modifications to develop a more comprehensive pricing evaluation tool that is capable of assessing the multi-modal impacts of holistic policy options such as road pricing in conjunction with transit improvement and parking management.

Besides transit and parking planning and management, certain changes are necessary in order for congestion pricing to be effective. One example is to reduce or eliminate the private use of automobiles covered by public funds. As stated before, congestion pricing is based on the promise of utility maximization. In this case, automobile use is determined by toll cost, all else being equal. However, it is well known that in China a significant number of automobiles for private use are not privately owned, which presents a challenge for linking automobile usage with cost and limits the effect of congestion pricing on traffic management. The private use of public vehicles also has financial and social consequences. It affects financial sustainability because when public funds rather than the automobile user cover tolls, the reality will be that funds are transferred from one public account to another and no new revenue source is generated for development and maintenance of transportation infrastructure. If tolls are set too high in order to generate sufficient non-public toll revenue, it will affect the cost for other users and economic activities and affect economic and social sustainability.

The results of impact assessment presented in this chapter also shed light on some broader issues in transportation finance and management in China. The findings show that the financing objective (toll revenue) may be in conflict with the traffic management objective, and that overall sustainability requires some tradeoff among objectives from different perspectives, as well as differences between private and public sectors. These are important insights to be considered in developing future sustainable transportation policies in China.

NOTES

1. Part of this chapter is based on a research project sponsored by the Texas Department of Transportation (TxDOT) and performed at the University of Texas at Arlington (UTA) and the Texas Transportation Institute (TTI) of the Texas A&M University System. The authors wish to thank TxDOT for its financial support and UTA/TTI for their research facilities. The authors would also like to thank many researchers who contributed to the TxDOT project. The contents of this chapter reflect the views of the authors, who are responsible for the facts and the accuracy of the data presented herein. The contents do not necessarily reflect the official views or polices of the Federal Highway Administration or the Texas Department of Transportation.
2. Travel demand is measured by person-times carried by buses, trolleys, subways, light rail and streetcars, excluding trips made by taxis and private vehicles.
3. According to the US Department of Transportation (2008), the growth in passenger miles of travel for all modes between 2000 and 2006 was 12.2 percent.
4. All income figures are in current RMB.
5. For more details about the model and model usage, see User Guide to Toll Pricing Model v3.1: TPM-3.1 by Ardekani et al. (2007).

REFERENCES

Ardekani, S., F. Kashefi, K. Abdelghany and A. Hassan (2007), *User Guide to Toll Pricing Model v3.1: TPM-3.1*, Draft, University of Texas at Arlington.

Dai, D-C. (2004), 'Issues and strategy: understanding of China', available at http://www.adb.org/Documents/Events/2004/Infrastructure_Development/Second-Workshop/Dai-china.pdf (accessed 24 December 2009).

Federal Highway Administration (FHWA) (2005), *Managed Lanes: A Primer*, FHWA-HOP-05-031, available at http://www.ops.fhwa.dot.gov/publications/managelanes_primer/managed_lanes_primer.pdf (accessed 5 November, 2008).

Feng, L. (2006), 'Transportation related socio-economic issues in China', *World Transport Policy & Practice*, **12**(4), 35–40.

Goodin, G., M. Burris, C. Dusza, D. Ungemah, J. Li and S. Mattingly (2008), *The Role of Preferential Treatment for Carpools in Managed Lanes*, Report No. FHWA/TX-09/0-5286-2, Research report prepared for the Texas Department of Transportation (TxDOT).

Hogg, C. (2009), 'China's car industry overtakes US', BBC News, 2 October, available at http://newsvote.bbc.co.uk/mpapps/pagetools/print/news.bbc.co.uk/2/hi/business/7879372.stm?ad=1 (accessed 27 September 2009).

Li, J. and S. Govind (2003), 'An optimization model for assessing pricing strategies of managed lanes', Paper No. 03-0082, in *Proceedings of the 82nd Annual Meeting of the Transportation Research Board*, CD-ROM, Washington, DC.

Li, J., S. Govind, J. Williams, S. Ardekani and R. Cole (2002), *Assessing Pricing Strategies and Users' Attitude Towards Managed Lanes*, Report No. FHWA/

TX-01/4009-1, Report prepared for the Texas Department of Transportation (TxDOT).

Li, J., S. Ardekani, S. Govind, S. Mattingly, J. Williams and R. Cole (2005), *Developing a Comprehensive Pricing Evaluation Model for Managed Lanes*, Report No. FHWA/TX-01/4818-1, Research report prepared for the Texas Department of Transportation (TxDOT).

Liu, R. (2009), 'Intractable traffic jams', *China Today*, 19 June.

National Bureau of Statistics of China (NBSC) (2008), *China Statistical Yearbook 2008*, Beijing: China Statistics Press.

Russian News & Information Agency (RIA) Novosti (2009), 'World – China becomes world's largest car market', En.rian.ru, 2 June available at http://en.rian.ru/world/20090206/120007709.html (accessed 27 September 2009).

Small, K.A. and C. Winston (1999), 'The demand for transportation: models and applications', in José A. Gómez-Ibáñez, William B. Tye and Clifford Winston (eds), *Essay in Transportation Economics and Policy: A Handbook in Honor of John R. Meyer*, Washington, DC: Brookings Institution Press, pp. 11–55.

US Department of Transportation (USDOT) (2008), *National Transportation Statistics*, Washington DC: US Department of Transportation.

US Environmental Protection Agency (EPA) (2003), *Users Guide to MOBILE 6.2*, Washington, DC: US Environmental Protection Agency.

World Bank (2007), 'An overview of China's transport sector – 2007', Easte Working Paper No. 15, Washington, DC, 20433, December.

Yerramalla, A. (2007), 'Vehicular emissions models using MOBILE6.2 and field data', Master of Science Thesis, Department of Civil and Environmental Engineering, University of Texas at Arlington. Arlington, Texas.

APPENDIX

Model Assumptions

Policy scenarios are analysed within the context of I-30 managed lane facility, a newly developed highway segment connecting the cities of Fort Worth and Dallas in the DFW area. Figures 11.A1 and 11.A2 display the configuration of the managed lane facility being investigated and the user compositions of the facility, respectively.

Price sensitivity parameters used for this impact analysis are shown in Table 11.A1. These parameters of various user groups were derived from the price elasticity estimates based on the stated preference (SP) survey data collected in the DFW and Houston areas. The SP surveys were conducted under the research projects TxDOT4818 (Li et al., 2005) and TxDOT5286 (Goodin et al., 2008) sponsored by TxDOT in 2004 and 2006.

Facility Information

General purpose lane information			Managed lane information		
Number of lanes : 4			Number of lanes : 2		
Maximum speed:	80	mph	Maximum speed:	80	mph
Maximum density:	110	pcplm	Maximum density:	110	pcplm
Density at maximum flow:	55	pcplm	Density at maximum flow:	55	pcplm
Saturation flow per lane:	2200	pcphpl	Saturation flow per lane:	2200	pcphpl
Corridor length:	5	milles	Corridor length:	5	milles

Figure 11.A1   Facility configuration

User Information

Corridor demand	11000 vph		
Vehicle type:	% in Mix	PEC	Toll Policy (%)
SOV	76.4	1.0	100
HOV2	10.0	1.0	100
HOV 3+	5.0	1.0	0
Para-transit	0.5	1.5	0
Van-Pool	1.5	1.2	0
Bus	0.2	1.2	0
Motorcycle	0	1.2	100
Light freight	0.8	1.5	100
Heavy freight (single trailer)	5.2	2.0	100
Heavy freight (double trailer)	0.4	3.0	100

Figure 11.A2   User composition

Table 11.A1   Price sensitivity parameters

Price ($/mile)	0.50 (mins/mile) (%)	1.00 (mins/mile) (%)	2.00 (mins/mile) (%)
SOV			
0.10	49.9	65.3	87.1
0.20	31.2	46.2	75.6
0.30	17.1	28.2	58.5
0.40	8.6	15.2	39.2
0.50	4.1	7.5	22.7
HOV2			
0.10	34.6	47.1	71.7
0.20	20.6	30.4	55.3
0.30	11.3	17.6	37.8
0.40	5.9	9.5	22.9
0.50	3.0	4.9	12.7
HOV3+			
0.10	42.5	53.2	73.1
0.20	23.4	32.1	52.9
0.30	11.3	16.4	31.8
0.40	5.0	7.5	16.2
0.50	2.1	3.3	7.4

12. Has capital been utilized efficiently in China?

Yanrui Wu

INTRODUCTION

Although less developed economies are often hampered by the shortage of funds during the course of their economic development, China seems to be an exception. Within three decades, China has accumulated the largest foreign reserve in the world, and undertaken many ambitious capital-intensive projects such as the Three Gorges Dam (with a cost of about US$200 billion), the Hangzhou Bay Bridge (about 36 kilometres across the ocean), the extravagant Beijing Olympic Games and the massive fiscal stimulus package of four trillion yuan (around US$586 billion) announced in November 2008. The appearance of many new highways and buildings across the nation gives the impression that the country is flooded with money. This is also reflected in China's statistics as the country has for years been the largest recipient of foreign direct investment and maintained one of the highest saving ratios in the world. As a result, it has been questioned whether money has been used efficiently in China. An investigation of China's investment efficiency is timely as the country's policy makers are charting the course of economic development in the coming decades.

There are numerous empirical studies of capacity utilization in developing economies such as Korea (Lee and Kwon, 1994), India (Gajanan and Malhotra, 2007) and Bangladesh (Salim, 2008). Some authors have also addressed the efficiency or utilization of the single production factor. Examples include Wu (1998) on labour utilization, Voulgaris et al. (2002) on asset utilization and Green and McIntosh (2007) on the underutilization of skills. China's capital utilization issues have so far only been marginally covered in three studies (Boyreau-Debray and Wei, 2004; Bai et al., 2006; Dollar and Wei, 2007). Boyreau-Debray and Wei (2004) examined China's capital market segmentation and hence potential distortions in capital allocation. Bai et al. (2006) investigated the return to capital and its impact on the allocation of capital across the regions as well as among the sectors. Dollar and Wei (2007) employed firm-level data to estimate the return to capital and analyse the potential gains from efficient capital allocation. The objective of this chapter is to make a contribution to the literature. In this chapter, a novel approach is for the first time proposed to evaluate the performance of capital in China. It is found that there may be considerable gain by improving capital utilization among China's regional economies. The empirical findings also show that China's economic policies should focus on narrowing the gap between the regions in terms of capital efficiency. The next section presents some stylized facts about China's investment in the last decades. This is followed by discussion about the measurement of capital performance. Subsequently the estimation results and their interpretation are presented. The chapter then explores the determinants of regional variation in capital efficiency. Finally, the chapter is concluded with some summary remarks.

INVESTING FOR GROWTH

To promote economic growth, China has invested substantially for several decades. Figure 12.1 demonstrates that, with an average rate of growth of 21.6 per cent during the period 1981–2009, China's gross investment has undergone several waves of rapid growth. The first wave of growth took place immediately after the adoption of the economic reform programme in the early 1980s. Liberalization policies boosted rural growth and income and hence led to the boom of township and village enterprises (TVEs) due to the investment of rural surplus funds. In the meantime, foreign direct investment (FDI) increased rapidly, though from a low basis (Figure 12.1).

The second wave of investment was triggered by the 'southern tour' of the former leader Deng Xiaoping in 1992. During his tour of southern China, Mr Deng encouraged more economic openness. Subsequently more radical reform policies were implemented in China. The consequence is that both domestic and foreign investment surged during 1992–93 as shown in Figure 12.1. The most recent wave of investment boom came with China's accession to the World Trade Organization (WTO) in November 2001. Since then, both domestic and FDI have maintained strong growth. In addition, this round of the investment boom was also boosted by the launch of China's 'western development programme' in 1999, the host of the 2008 Olympic Games in Beijing and implementation of the fiscal stimulus package of US$586 in the aftermath of the sub-prime crisis.

Due to continued growth in investment, gross capital formation (GKF)

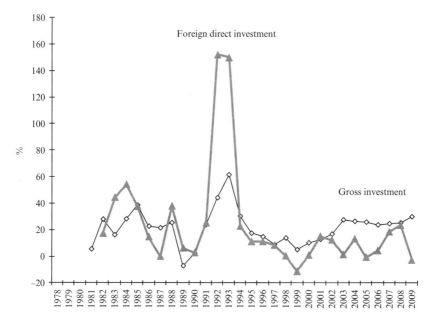

Source: NBSC (2004, 2008, 2009).

Figure 12.1   Growth rates of gross investment in fixed assets and FDI

as a proportion of China's GDP has maintained a robustly high level since 1978 when economic reform was initiated. The overall average during the period of 1978–2008 is 37.5 per cent according to Figure 12.2. During the same period, China's real GDP per capita rose from just under US$200 to about US$3300. At the similar income level, gross capital formation as a share of GDP amounted to 35.8 per cent in Japan (1961–70), 29.0 per cent in South Korea (1969–83), 21.4 per cent in Brazil (1962–79) and 29.5 per cent in Thailand (1970–92). Thus, China has invested much more than other economies at a similar stage of development. Accordingly, investment is also high among China's regional economies though there is considerable variation (Table 12.1). In general, the investment ratio is high among regions which are less export-oriented and hence confronted with net imports. These regions are mainly located in western China which has also enjoyed an investment boom due to the implementation of the western development programme since 1999.

In the meantime, though extremely volatile, incremental investment as a share of incremental GDP during 1978–2008 averaged about 36.5 per cent according to Figure 12.2. Thus the contribution of investment to

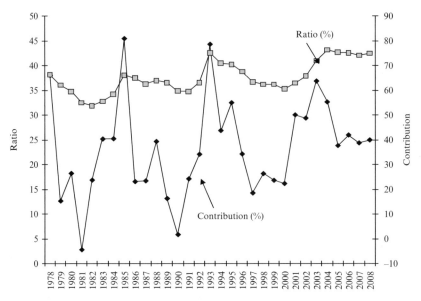

Source: NBSC (2009).

Figure 12.2   Gross capital formation over GDP (%), 1978–2008

economic growth is no doubt substantial. However, how efficient has the country's money been utilized? Can the Chinese regions make better use of their funds? These questions are to be explored in the empirical analysis of the chapter.

CAPITAL UTLIZATION MEASUREMENT

There are many approaches towards the measurement of performance. This chapter adopts an approach which originated from the literature of efficiency measurement.[1] To introduce this model, it is assumed that a vector of inputs $x = (x_1, \cdots, x_N) \in R_+^N$ are employed to produce a single output, y. Then a standard stochastic frontier production function can be expressed as

$$\ln y = \ln f(x; \beta) + v - u \qquad (12.1)$$

where β is a vector of parameters to be estimated, v is the standard white noise with zero mean and constant variance, σ_v^2, and u is assumed to capture the inefficiency effect in the production process. The latter is

Table 12.1   Regional investment and exports over income, 2007

Regions	Investment/ gross regional product (%)	Export/ gross regional product (%)
Coastal	*49.3*	*44.6*
Guangdong	38.4	92.6
Zhejiang	45.6	55.9
Fujian	45.7	40.8
Shanghai	46.5	87.0
Hainan	47.1	10.3
Hebei	48.0	12.0
Jiangsu	50.2	61.8
Shandong	51.7	23.0
Beijing	53.1	25.5
Tianjin	57.2	57.8
Liaoning	58.6	24.6
Central	*52.3*	*7.8*
Heilongjiang	40.0	10.8
Hunan	43.2	5.5
Hubei	46.7	6.7
Anhui	47.2	8.8
Jiangxi	51.8	7.6
Henan	54.9	4.6
Shanxi	58.5	12.8
Jilin	76.1	5.9
Western	*64.6*	*7.7*
Gansu	49.0	4.7
Guangxi	49.9	6.3
Guizhou	50.1	5.7
Sichuan	52.5	3.8
Qinghai	63.7	2.9
Chongqing	63.8	7.8
Yunnan	64.6	6.9
Shaanxi	65.0	7.6
Xinjiang	66.4	23.4
Ningxia	74.9	12.3
Inner Mongolia	80.2	4.8
Tibet	94.7	6.5

Note: Author's own calculation.

assumed to be non-negative, and independent of v. Given equation (12.1), the technical efficiency score (TE) can be defined as the ratio of the actual or observed output over the potential or best practice output, that is,

$$TE = e^{-u} \qquad (12.2)$$

which can be estimated using its conditional expectation value, that is, $E(e^{-u}|v - u)$.[2] In practice, several environmental factors (z) are also incorporated into the inefficiency term to reflect the impact of these factors on efficiency performance. Thus equation (12.1) becomes

$$\ln y = \ln f(x; \beta) + v - u(z; \delta) \qquad (12.3)$$

The widely cited studies in this strand of literature include Kumbhakar et al. (1991), Reifschnieder and Stevenson (1991), Huang and Liu (1994) and Battese and Coelli (1995). In this chapter, it is assumed that two inputs (x's), capital (X_k) and labour (X_l) are employed to produce one output Y, and that efficiency performance is subjected to the influence of several region-specific environmental factors (z's), that is, production technology (Z_T), infrastructure development (Z_I), economic reforms (Z_R), economic openness (Z_O) and FDI (Z_F). A time trend (t) is also included. Thus, equation (12.3) becomes

$$\ln Y = \ln f(X_k, X_l; \beta) + v - u(z; \delta) \qquad (12.4)$$

In the meantime, capital efficiency (CE) can be defined as the ratio of the optimal amount (X_k^o) required over the actual use of capital (X_k), given technology, outputs and other inputs. Symbolically,

$$CE = \min \{\theta: (X_k^o, X_l) = (\theta X_k, X_l) \text{ can produce } Y\} \leq 1 \qquad (12.5)$$

The property of duality in production economics implies that, if capital is utilized efficiently, the production process is also technically efficient. Thus, let u in equation (12.4) be zero, the following equation can be derived

$$\ln Y = \ln f(X_k^o, X_l; \beta) + v \qquad (12.6)$$

Equations (12.4) and (12.6) can then be combined to obtain

$$\ln f(X_k^o, X_l; \beta) - \ln f(X_k, X_l; \beta) + u = 0 \qquad (12.7)$$

One can then substitute $CE = X_k^o/X_k$ or $X_k^o = CE \cdot X_k$ into equation (12.7) and solve the transformed equation to obtain a solution for CE, namely, the capital efficiency indicator. In logarithmic form, the empirical model can be specified as follows

$$\ln Y = \beta_0 + \beta_1 t + \beta_2 t^2 + \beta_3 \ln X_k + \beta_4 \ln X_l + \beta_5 (\ln X_k)^2 + \beta_6 (\ln X_l)^2$$

$$+ \beta_7 \ln X_k \ln X_l + \beta_8 t \ln X_k + \beta_9 t \ln X_l + v - u \qquad (12.8)$$

where $u = \delta_0 + \delta_1 t + \delta_2 Z_T + \delta_3 Z_I + \delta_4 Z_R + \delta_5 Z_O + \delta_6 Z_F + \varepsilon$ and ε is assumed to be independently distributed and obtained by truncation of a normal distribution with zero mean and constant variance of σ^2. Therefore, u is non-negative truncation of the normal distribution with mean $\delta_0 + \delta_1 t + \delta_2 Z_T + \delta_3 Z_I + \delta_4 Z_R + \delta_5 Z_O + \delta_6 Z_F$, and variance of σ^2. Combining equations (12.7) and (12.8) gives the following relationship

$$a(\ln CE)^2 + b \ln CE + c = 0 \qquad (12.9)$$

where $a = \beta_5$, $b = \beta_3 + 2\beta_5 \ln X_k + \beta_7 \ln X_l + \beta_8 t$ and $c = u$. To solve the unknown $\ln CE$ in equation (12.9), apply the quadratic root formulae to obtain[3]

$$\ln CE = (-b + \sqrt{b^2 - 4ac})/(2a) \qquad (12.10)$$

and the capital efficiency indicator

$$CE = e^{\ln CE} \qquad (12.11)$$

ESTIMATION RESULTS AND INTERPRETATION

The empirical estimation is based on panel data of China's 31 administrative regions over the period 1993–2006. The variables are described as follows:

- The dependent variable, Y, is measured using gross regional product (GRP).
- The capital input variable, X_k, represents capital stock.[4]
- The labour input variable, X_l, is measured using the number of employed persons.[5]
- The production technology variable (Z_T) is represented by capital-labour ratio, that is, capital-labour intensity. It may capture the impact of production technology on technical efficiency.

- Variation in infrastructure development is assumed to affect technical efficiency. The infrastructure variable (Z_I) is defined as the geometric mean of the length of highway per square kilometre of land and length of railway per square kilometre of land. The reason for considering the density of both railways and highways is to avoid the bias due to the dominance of one of the facilities in some regions.

- The degree of economic reform variable (Z_R) is introduced to assess the effect of economic liberalization among the regions. It is defined as the ratio of non-state sector employment over total employment.[6]

- The economic openness variable (Z_O) is defined simply as the ratio of the value of exports over the value of GRP.[7]

- To reflect the participation of FDI (Z_F) in regional economies, the ratio of foreign capital stock over regional total capital stock is included.[8]

- All value-based variables are expressed in real terms (or constant prices).

The regression results of equation (12.8) are presented in Table 12.2. In the table, most t-values are significantly high. In addition, λ is close to one (it is rounded up to one in the table), implying that inefficiency accounts for a large share of the combined error term. A log-likelihood ratio test rejects the null hypothesis that the coefficients (δ_i, i =1, . . .6) of the environmental variables are equal to zero simultaneously.[9] Therefore, the estimation results are generally satisfactory, and hence employed to estimate the scores of capital efficiency following the technique presented in equations (12.9) to (12.11).

The regional mean scores of capital efficiency are presented in Table 12.3. As expected, efficiency performance varies substantially across the regions. In general, the coastal regions have been more efficient (with a mean score of 71 per cent) than the central and western regions (with mean efficiency scores of 59 and 43 per cent, respectively). The overall weighted mean rate of capital efficiency for China is about 66 per cent.[10] Thus there is considerable scope for improvement in capital efficiency. In addition, the regional efficiency difference shown seems to be consistent with findings by other authors. For example, Qin and Song (2007) found that the coastal regions are generally more efficient than the western regions in terms of 'capital productivity' and Boyreau-Debray and Wei (2004) argued that capital has been diverted to the less productive western regions. In recent years, more funds have probably been allocated to the western regions due to the implementation of the western development programme. The findings in this study point out that drastic policy

Table 12.2   Estimation results

Name	Coefficient	t-value
β_0	−1.5634	−4.17
β_1	0.1863	7.78
β_2	0.0015	4.11
β_3	−0.2640	−2.30
β_4	1.1937	8.70
β_5	0.0494	5.18
β_6	−0.0854	−5.29
β_7	0.0608	3.47
β_8	−0.0129	−4.71
β_9	−0.0130	−4.98
δ_0	0.0730	0.54
δ_1	0.0099	1.91
δ_2	−0.0077	−0.84
δ_3	−0.9631	−3.18
δ_4	0.5753	3.24
δ_5	−0.4702	−4.16
δ_6	−0.5601	−2.37
σ^2	0.0202	12.17
λ	1.0000	2853.72
LL	264.68	

Note: $\lambda = \sigma^2/(\sigma_v^2 + \sigma^2)$ and other coefficients are defined in equation (12.8). LL is short for the log-likelihood value. The results in this table are derived using FRONTIER 4.1 (Coelli, 1996).

Source: Author's own estimates.

changes may be needed in order to improve investment efficiency in the western regions.

To further investigate regional variation in capital efficiency, several factors are considered. They include production technology, infrastructure development, economic reforms, economic openness and FDI. These factors are selected due to either the availability of data or a prior knowledge. The results of the regression of the capital efficiency (*CE*) scores against the selected explanatory variables together with a time trend are demonstrated in Table 12.4. The Lagrange multiplier (LM) test values show that the fixed and random effect models are preferred to the traditional model with a constant intercept. However, the Hausman tests imply that the random effect models should be rejected. Thus the fixed effect regression results are presented in Table 12.4.

Table 12.3 Mean scores of capital efficiency

Regions	Capital efficiency (*CE*)
Coastal	*0.714*
Shanghai	0.937
Tianjin	0.927
Guangdong	0.899
Liaoning	0.799
Beijing	0.746
Fujian	0.738
Zhejiang	0.674
Hebei	0.603
Jiangsu	0.593
Shandong	0.572
Hainan	0.363
Central	*0.593*
Heilongjiang	0.720
Jilin	0.699
Hunan	0.599
Anhui	0.561
Shanxi	0.560
Hubei	0.554
Jiangxi	0.532
Henan	0.517
Western	*0.426*
Inner Mongolia	0.667
Sichuan	0.560
Guangxi	0.557
Shaanxi	0.470
Xinjiang	0.423
Gansu	0.419
Yunnan	0.418
Chongqing	0.405
Ningxia	0.381
Tibet	0.300
Guizhou	0.292
Qinghai	0.219

Source: Author's own estimates.

*Table 12.4   Determinants of capital utilization variation
            (fixed effect regression)*

Names	Coefficients (*t*-values) (Model 1)	Coefficients (*t*-values) (Model 2)
Time trend	−0.0128 (−13.622)*	−0.0124 (−12.997)*
Infrastructure (Z_I)	1.1688 (6.825)*	1.1547 (6.770)*
Reform (Z_R)	0.3107 (3.711)*	0.2865 (3.408)*
Openness (Z_O)	−0.1363 (−3.045)*	−0.3100 (−3.407)*
Openness-squared ($Z_O \cdot Z_O$)		0.2043 (2.189)**
Capital-labour ratio (Z_T)	−0.0043 (−1.243)	−0.0049 (−1.433)
Foreign capital (Z_F)	0.5557 (4.138)*	0.6125 (4.499)*
Sample size	434	434
Log-likelihood	796.22	798.83
LM test	1752.79*	1734.09*
Hausman test	29.42*	31.93*
R^2	0.96	0.96
$\bar{R}^2$	0.95	0.95

Note: * and ** indicate significance at the level of 1 percent and 5 percent, respectively.

DETERMINANTS OF CAPITAL UTILIZATION

The estimation results in Table 12.4 show that capital utilization is affected positively by the level of infrastructure development, degree of economic reforms and the participation of FDI. It is not difficult to understand the positive role of infrastructure development shown in Table 12.4. Better infrastructure can reduce the cost and time of transactions in businesses and hence contributes to higher returns to capital. Furthermore, the economic reform variable essentially captures the role of the private sector. There is ample evidence to show that the private sector or firms are more efficient than the public sector or state-owned enterprises (SOEs). Some authors have even argued that it is the private firms' ability to generate internal finance and raise funds from informal channels and to maintain high efficiency that underlies China's sustained growth in the past decades (Cull et al., 2007; Ayyagari et al., 2008; Guariglia et al., 2008). Finally, the finding about FDI's relationship with capital efficiency complements others such as Hu and Jefferson (2002), Liu (2002) and Wu (2008). These authors argued that FDI has positive spillover effects on productivity, particularly in the long run.

The negative coefficient of the time trend in the model is statistically significant implying that capital utilization tends to fall over time. Surprisingly, the degree of openness is negatively related to capital utilization. To explore this matter further, a squared openness term is included in the regression (Model 2) and the estimated coefficient is significantly positive. Thus there may be a learning process in improving capital utilization as far as openness is concerned. In addition, this unexpected relationship may also be driven by a few outliers. Tables 12.1 and 12.3 demonstrate that a few regions have achieved above-average efficiency while their openness indicators have relatively low values. These regions include Liaoning, Beijing, Hebei, Heilongjiang, Jilin and Inner Mongolia. Finally, the technology (capital-labour ratio) variable has a negative but insignificant coefficient. Thus, investment in more capital-intensive economies may not necessarily be more efficient in the Chinese case and vice versa. Guangdong is probably a good example. It is the most export-oriented regional economy in China (see the numbers in Table 12.1) and has achieved relatively high efficiency in investment. However, in 2006, Guangdong's capital-labour ratio was 1.943 which is well below the national mean of 3.357, not to mention the figures of 19.178 for Shanghai, 11.016 for Tianjin and 9.950 for Beijing in the same year.[11]

Furthermore, to examine the potential variation between the coastal, central and western regions, two dummy variables are introduced into the regression. Once again, the LM test values show that the fixed and random effect models are preferred to the tradition models. However, due to the inclusion of the two dummy variables, the Hausman statistics and the coefficients of the two dummy variables in the fixed effect model cannot be computed using LIMDEP. Thus, the random effect regression results must be treated with caution though they are reported here (Table 12.5). In general, the results of Models 3 and 4 are consistent with the findings in Table 12.4. The estimated coefficients of the two dummy variables representing the central and western regions are negative implying low capital utilization relative to the coastal region. This is in conformity with the mean scores illustrated in Table 12.3. Especially, the estimated coefficient of the western region dummy variable is statistically significant. It can be concluded that capital utilization is relatively low in the western region.

In Table 12.4 the regressions of the capital efficiency (*CE*) variable against a set of region-specific factors may lead to biased results due to the fact that the *CE* values are bound between zero and one by definition. To provide an assessment, a Tobit model is considered. For a fixed effect model, LIMDEP imposes a lower limit on the dependent variable and in this case, a value of zero for the *CE* scores (as *CE* is non-negative

Table 12.5   Determinants of capital utilization variation (random effect regression)

Names	Coefficients (*t*-values) (Model 3)	Coefficients (*t*-values) (Model 4)
Time trend	−0.0123 (−13.428)*	−0.0119 (−12.813)*
Infrastructure (Z_I)	1.1335 (6.846)*	1.1265 (6.834)*
Reform (Z_R)	0.2146 (2.878)*	0.1893 (2.514)**
Openness (Z_O)	−0.1238 (−2.939)*	−0.2835 (−3.151)*
Openness-squared ($Z_O \cdot Z_O$)		0.1853 (2.006)**
Capital-labour ratio (Z_T)	−0.0014 (−0.442)	−0.0018 (−0.577)
Foreign capital (Z_F)	0.5934 (4.647)*	0.6375 (4.942)*
Dummy (central)	−0.0583 (−1.153)	−0.0684 (−1.353)
Dummy (western)	−0.1823 (−3.898)*	−0.1928 (−4.115)*
Intercept	0.4819 (7.468)*	0.5191 (7.763)*
Sample size	434	434
LM test	1640.34*	1599.31*
R^2	0.49	0.48

Note: * and ** indicate significance at the level of 1 per cent and 5 per cent, respectively.

conceptually).[12] The estimation results of Models 5 and 6 are presented in Table 12.6, and are generally consistent with those reported in Table 12.4 (in fact the estimated coefficients are almost identical). Therefore, we may conclude that regional variation in investment efficiency may be due to the impact of infrastructure development, economic reforms and the presence of offshore investors among the regions. The effects of economic openness and production technology are, however, not clear-cut.

CONCLUSION

This chapter adopts a novel approach to evaluate capital utilization in China's regional economies. It is found that there is considerable scope for improvement in the performance of capital in China. In particular, Chinese regions have achieved very different levels of efficiency with the coastal regions being well ahead of the western areas. This finding calls for rethinking about China's western development programme which has led to the diversion of funds towards the western regions. The latter should adopt policies focusing on the improvement of capital utilization.

This study also shows that several factors are responsible for the regional

Table 12.6   Tobit regression results (fixed effect regression)

Names	Coefficients (*t*-values) (Model 5)	Coefficients (*t*-values) (Model 6)
Time trend	−0.0128 (−14.243)*	−0.0124 (−13.606)*
Infrastructure (Z_I)	1.1688 (7.136)*	1.1547 (7.087)*
Reform (Z_R)	0.3107 (3.880)*	0.2865 (3.568)*
Openness (Z_O)	−0.1363 (−3.183)*	−0.3100 (−3.566)*
Openness-squared ($Z_O \cdot Z_O$)		0.2043 (2.292)**
Capital-labour ratio (Z_T)	−0.0043 (−1.300)	−0.0049 (−1.501)
Foreign capital (Z_F)	0.5557 (4.327)*	0.6125 (4.709)*
Sample size	434	434
Log-likelihood	796.22	798.83

Note: * and ** indicate significance at the level of 1 per cent and 5 per cent, respectively.

disparity in capital performance. In general, infrastructure development, economic reform and participation of foreign investment have positively affected the performance of capital. Thus, improvement in these areas has the potential to narrow the efficiency gap between the regions, especially between the coastal and western areas. In the meantime, it is found that economic openness and production technology are not explicitly related to capital performance among the regions.

NOTES

1. For comprehensive surveys about efficiency measurement, see Kumbhakar and Lovell (2000), Coelli et al. (2005) and Greene (2008), to cite a few. There is also a large pool of empirical studies such as Kumbhakar and Bhattacharyya (1992), Kleit and Terrell (2001) and Christopoulos (2007).
2. For pioneering work in this field, see Jondrow et al. (1982), Aigner et al. (1977) and Meeusen and van den Broeck (1977).
3. A similar framework was first developed for the analysis of environmental efficiency by Reinhard et al. (1999).
4. Regional capital stock data are drawn from Wu (2008).
5. It is noticed that the actual hours worked are preferred to the number of employed persons but the former is hardly available in the Chinese statistic sources.
6. It is argued that this indicator of economic reform or marketization may be biased due to its ignorance of many other factors. The author is aware of other measures of marketization for the regions such as the one developed by the National Centre for Economic Research, Beijing (Wang, 2004). These measures are, however, not available in the form of panel data.
7. There are many different ways measuring economic openness. For a brief survey, see Harrison (1996) and Edwards (1998).

8. The stock of foreign capital is estimated following the perpetual inventory method by assuming a rate of depreciation of 4 per cent.
9. The calculated test statistic is about 164 which is far greater than the critical c^2 value given the degree of freedom of 5.
10. The weights are regional shares of capital stock in 2006.
11. These numbers are derived according to the author's own estimates.
12. Due to the failure of the Hausman test in Models 3 and 4, random effect Tobit models are not considered.

REFERENCES

Aigner, D.J., C.A.K. Lovell and P.J. Schmidt (1977), 'Formulation and estimation of stochastic frontier models', *Journal of Econometrics*, **6**(1), 21–37.
Ayyagari, M., A. Demirgüç-Kunt and V. Maksimovic (2008), 'Formal versus informal finance: evidence from China', *Policy Research Working Paper No. 4465*, The World Bank.
Bai, C.-E., C.-T. Hsieh and Y. Qian (2006), 'The return to capital in china', *NBER Working Paper 12755*, National Bureau of Economic Research.
Battese, G.E. and T. Coelli (1995), 'A model for technical inefficiency effects in a stochastic frontier production function for panel data', *Empirical Economics*, **20**, 325–32.
Boyreau-Debray, G. and S.-J. Wei (2004), 'Can China grow faster? A diagnosis of the fragmentation of its domestic capital market', *IMF Working Paper WP/04/76*, International Monetary Fund.
Christopoulos, D. K. (2007), 'Explaining country's efficiency performance', *Economic Modelling*, **24**, 224–35.
Coelli, T. (1996), 'A Guide to FRONTIER 4.1: a computer program for stochastic frontier production function and cost function estimation', *CEPA Working Paper 96/7*, Department of Econometrics, University of New England, Armidale, Australia.
Coelli, T., D.S.P. Rao, C.J. O'Donnell and G.E. Battese (2005), *An Introduction to Efficiency and Productivity Analysis*, 2nd edn, New York: Springer.
Cull, R., L.C. Xu and T. Zhu (2007), 'Formal finance and trade credit during China's transition', *Policy Research Working Paper No. 4204*, The World Bank.
Dollar, D. and S.-J. Wei (2007), 'Das (wasted) kapital: firm ownership and investment efficiency in China', *NBER Working Paper 13103*, National Bureau of Economic Research.
Edwards, S. (1998), 'Openness, productivity, growth: what do we really know', *Economic Journal*, **108**, 383–98.
Gajanan, S. and D. Malhotra (2007), 'Measures of capacity utilization and its determinants: a study of Indian manufacturing', *Applied Economics*, **39**(6), 765–76.
Goodin, G., M. Burris, C. Dusza, D. Ungemah, J. Li and S. Mattingly (2008), *The Role of Preferential Treatment for Carpools in managed hanes*, Report No. FHWA/TX-09/0-5286-2, Research report prepared for the Taxes Department of Transportation (T×DOT).
Green, F. and S. McIntosh (2007), 'Is there a genuine under-utilization of skills amongst the over-qualified?', *Applied Economics*, **39**(4), 427–39.

Greene, W. (2008), 'The econometric approach to efficiency analysis', in *The Measurement of Efficiency*, H. Fried, K. Lovell and S. Schmidt (eds), New York: Oxford University Press, chapter 2.

Guariglia, A., X. Liu and L. Song (2008), 'How does internal finance affect the growth of Chinese firms?', paper presented at the conference 'Microeconomic Drivers of Growth in China', Oxford University, 29–30 September.

Harrison, A. (1996), 'Openness and growth: a time–series, cross-country analysis for developing countries', *Journal of Development Economics*, **48**, 419–47.

Hu, A.G.Z. and H. Jefferson (2002), 'FDI impact and spillover: evidence from China's electronic and textile industries', *World Economy*, **25**(8), 1063–76.

Huang, C.J. and J.T. Liu (1994), 'Estimation of a non-neutral stochastic frontier production function', *Journal of Productivity Analysis*, **5**, 171–80.

Jondrow, J., C. Lovell, I. Materov and P. Schmidt (1982), 'On the estimation of technical inefficiency in the stochastic frontier production function model', *Journal of Econometrics*, **19**(2/3), 233–8.

Kleit, A. and D. Terrell (2001), 'Measuring potential efficiency gains from deregulation of electricity generation: a Bayesian approach', *Review of Economics and Statistics*, **83**, 523–30.

Kumbhakar, S.C. and A. Bhattacharyya (1992), 'Price distortions and resource use efficiency in Indian agriculture: a restricted profit function approach', *Review of Economics and Statistics*, **74**, 231–39.

Kumbhakar, S.C. and C.A.K. Lovell (2000), *Stochastic Frontier Analysis*, Cambridge: Cambridge University Press.

Kumbhakar, S.C., S. Ghosh and J. McGuckin (1991), 'A generalised production frontier approach for estimating determinants of inefficiency in US dairy farms', *Journal of Business and Economic Statistics*, **9**(3), 279–86.

Lee, Y.J. and J.K. Kwon (1994), 'Interpretation and measurement of capacity utilization: the case of Korean manufacturing', *Applied Economics*, **26**(10), 981–90.

Li, J., S. Arde Ram, S. Govind, S. Mattingly, J. Williams and R. Cole (2005), *Developing a comprehensive Pricing Evaluation model for managed hanes*, Report No. FHWA/TX-01/4818-1, Research report prepared for the Taxes Department of Transportation (T×DOT).

Liu, Z. (2002), 'Foreign direct investment and technology spillover: evidence from China', *Journal of Comparative Economics*, **30**(3), 579–602.

Meeusen W. and J. van den Broeck (1977), 'Efficiency estimation from Cobb–Douglas production functions with composed error', *International Economic Review*, **18**(2), 435–44.

National Bureau of Statistics of China (NBSC) (2004), *China Statistical Yearbook 2004*, Beijing: China Statistics Press.

National Bureau of Statistics of China (NBSC) (2008), *China Statistical Abstract 2008*, Beijing: China Statistics Press.

National Bureau of Statistics of China (NBSC) (2009), *China Statistical Yearbook 2009*, Beijing: China Statistics Press.

Qin, D. and H. Song (2007), 'Sources of investment inefficiency: the case of fixed-asset investment in China', *Working Paper No. 584*, Department of Economics, Queen Mary University of London.

Reifschnieder, D. and R. Stevenson (1991), 'Systematic departures from the frontier: a framework for the analysis of firm inefficiency', *International Economic Review*, **32**, 715–23.

Reinhard, S., C.A.K. Lovell and G. Thijssen (1999), 'Econometric estimation of

technical and environmental efficiency: an application to Dutch dairy farms',
American Journal of Agricultural Economics, **81**(1), 44–60.

Salim, R. A. (2008), 'Differentials at firm level productive capacity realization in
Bangladesh food manufacturing: an empirical analysis', *Applied Economics*,
40(24), 3111–26.

Voulgaris, F., D. Asteriou and G. Agiomirgianakis (2002), 'Capital structure,
asset utilization, profitability and growth in the Greek manufacturing sector',
Applied Economics, **34**(11), 1379–88.

Wang, X. (2004), 'Marketisation in China', in R. Garnaut and L. Song (eds)
China: Is Rapid Growth Sustainable?, Canberra: Asia Pacific Press, pp. 11–136.

Wu, Y. (1998), 'Redundancy and firm characteristics in Chinese state-owned
enterprises', *Asia Pacific Journal of Economics and Business*, **2**(1), 33–44.

Wu, Y. (2008), *Productivity, Efficiency and Economic Growth in China*, London
and New York: Palgrave Macmillan.

Index